D1195809

BASEBALL
AN INFORMAL HISTORY

Douglass Wallop

BASE

New York

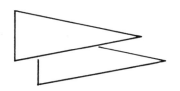

BALL

AN INFORMAL HISTORY

W · W · Norton & Company · Inc ·

Contents

Part One THE BEGINNING

1 A Question of Paternity   15
2 The Mists of Memory   31
3 "The Black Shadow of Treachery"   49
4 "Ve Lick der Stuffings out of Every Team
      in Baseball"   61
5 Order out of Chaos   79

Part Two THE GOLDEN DAYS

6 The Blue Sky and the Green Grass   99
7 The National Folk Drama   123
8 Golden Bats, Golden Arms   139
9 Scandal   159

Part Three THE RISE AND FALL OF THE
      NEW YORK YANKEES

10 The Babe   183
11 The Gas House Gang   199
12 On the Outskirts of Town   215

13 The New York Game   229
14 The White Ceiling and the Beige Rug   239

APPENDIX   249
BIBLIOGRAPHY   252
INDEX   254

Acknowledgments

In the preparation of this book I am particularly indebted to Bill Veeck for his counsel and his library; to Jack Redding, Ken Smith, and Lee Allen, all of the Baseball Museum at Cooperstown, New York; to James T. Gallagher, of the Baseball Commissioner's Office, who, although he does not embrace *all* the sentiments expressed in this book, gave aid in checking its facts; to Eric Swenson, of W. W. Norton & Company, for his help and guidance; and to various members of the staff at that remarkable arm of government, the Library of Congress in Washington.

THE

BEGINNING

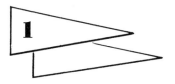

A Question of
Paternity

ON TUESDAY, JUNE 15, 1869, IN BROOKLYN, NEW YORK, A CELE-brated game of baseball was played between the redoubtable Cincinnati Red Stockings and the old New York Mutuals. The Red Stockings were on a transcontinental barnstorming tour to win ball games for the greater glory of Cincinnati, and so far they were undefeated. For more than a month they had been traveling from city to city, taking on all comers, and on Monday they had arrived in New York on the wings of a fourteen-game winning streak. The Mutuals were the pride of the East and, in the opinion of their partisans, the best team in the country.

Brooklyn in the years to come would establish a solid reputation for its obsessive attitude toward baseball. In 1869 it was a city of some 300,000 souls and from all accounts a large

number were already obsessed. One historian, writing in 1907
from an eyewitness report, states flatly that "excitement was
at fever heat." The local fans had little doubt that the Cin-
cinnatis would be mauled. As important as they would become
to baseball history and for all their gaudy record, to New
Yorkers the Red Stockings were merely a little-known band
of rustics who had dared invade the metropolis and would
now receive their comeuppance at the hands of the invincible
Mutuals. Brooklyn animosities were showing, and on the
morning of the game, as well as the night before, the Red
Stockings were jeered and hooted everywhere they went.

Such a harsh display of civic confidence might have placed
lesser athletes under a severe psychological handicap, but the
Red Stockings were athletes of self-esteem "in whose vocabulary there was no such word as fail." Their leader was the
peerless Harry Wright, who was not only skilled on the diamond but was also a young man of estimable character. Unlike, for example, such of his managerial descendants as John
McGraw or Leo Durocher, he reacted with forbearance when
he found his men giving less than their best. No matter what
the offense, whether bobble, whiff, or hangover, his words of
censure were said to be invariably the same: "You need a
little ginger."

Brooklyn even then was known as the City of Churches,
and on the day of the game their spires were outlined against
cloudy skies. In spite of the threat of rain, the crowds began
to gather in early morning, coming from all parts of Brooklyn
and even—by ferry boat—from Manhattan, headed for the
old Union Grounds in Ridgewood, where the game was scheduled to begin at two o'clock. Long before game time the
streets around the park were thronged with people on foot
and in horse-drawn conveyances, all contributing to a mon-
strous traffic jam. Even though the park was finally closed to
further admissions, the crowds already inside overflowed the
stands, spilling out onto the field, and it took the Brooklyn
police fully an hour of pushing and shoving to make room for

the players, so that the game was very late in starting. Those who couldn't get into the park jostled for a view at knotholes in the fence, while others took to the rooftops overlooking the field.

The players were dressed, then as now, in flannel knickerbockers clasped firmly below the knee with elastic. The stockings of the Cincinnati team were of bright scarlet. Their flannel tunics were laced at the throat with a crisscross drawstring and their collars flared up about the neck. Their caps had a squared-off effect, with the shape and contour of those worn by locomotive engineers, the sort of cap that has been revived by the California Angels of today. Beneath the relatively short bills of the caps, the faces were adorned, after the fashion of the day, with luxuriant mustaches and long sideburns. Some of the players even sported full beards, most notably Harry Wright himself and Asa Brainard, the Cincinnati pitcher, a wily right-hander who "rarely pitched the ball where the batter expected it" and whose pitching motion has been described as follows: "He would cross his legs, planting his left toe on the ground behind his right foot, then take one step forward."

His catcher was Doug Allison, and it was said that a "pluckier catcher was not to be found. As a batsman he was first class and his red-hot daisy cutters to left field were hard to stop." Like other catchers of that era, Allison took a stand some ten or twelve feet behind the batter and usually received the pitch on the first bounce. He wore no protective equipment because as yet there was none.

There was a lone umpire, a Mr. Charles Walker of New York, and while players of both teams would later agree that he had done a creditable job, it seems probable that in return for his modest fee he had a tense afternoon with the partisan spectators. In baseball's early days reviling and abusing the umpire was accepted as a large part of the fun, a sport to which the spectators were entitled with the price of admission and one in which they indulged themselves freely, particularly the drunks and gamblers among them. The people of the

United States in that period had a drinking problem which they seemed to enjoy carrying out to the ball park, where it was shared by many of the players, and it is reasonable to suppose that among those present that day there were many who bore witness through reddened eyes and dulled senses and that some of the players may have performed under the same handicaps.

Professional gambling was as prevalent as alcoholism—before the turn of the century the two would combine with owner avarice very nearly to kill baseball while it was still in its infancy—and the professional gamblers were not above betting against the home team nor were they above offering bribes, which all too often were accepted. The Mutuals were the betting favorites that day, at odds varying from 5–4 to 4–3. Among those present was John Morrissey, a noted gambler, an ex-pugilist, and later a U.S. Congressman from New York. Before placing his bets, he sought the advice of one Harry Millar, a Cincinnati sportswriter touring with the Red Stockings. Noting the roughness of the crowd and the frequent jeers and catcalls, he asked if the Red Stockings might not be rattled, even intimidated. Millar replied that the Red Stockings were not to be shaken in their firm resolve, whereupon Morrissey "pursed his lips thoughtfully" and got a hefty bet down against the home team. Ironically, a man to whom Morrissey was introduced during the game was Henry Chadwick, originator of the baseball box score and a newspaperman who would devote much of his life to a crusade to rid the game of the gambling element. That day, seated beneath an awning near the first-base line, he acted as official scorer.

For those Brooklyn fans who had *not* bet against the home team, it was an afternoon of frustration, a state in which Brooklynites would all too frequently find themselves in the years to come. In an era of marathon scoring, the aptly named Brainard, cunningly mixing his pitches, tugging now and then at his beard, stood the Mutuals on their collective ear, and although the Red Stockings hardly rattled the fences they scored often enough to send Mr. Morrissey and his fellow apostates home winners.

And when it was done, when the final Mutual batsman had gone down before Brainard's crafty delivery, the fans tumbled steadily or unsteadily from the stands and down from the rooftops and straggled away, repairing, as the gas lights began to come on, to their favorite saloons, there to have surcease after the long afternoon's excitement and misfortune, there to tote up their losses, there perhaps to mutter over and over the 1869 version of "youse bums, ya," hardly aware of the importance to baseball history of the team they had watched that day—the day Harry Wright's old Cincinnati Red Stockings, a team of professionals, beat the New York Mutuals, a collection of talented amateurs, by a score of 4–2.

The Red Stockings of 1869 were the first professional baseball team in the United States, hand-picked athletes who plied their skills that year from April until mid-November, roaming the land from coast to coast and completely changing what until then had been the amateur complexion of baseball. Not only did they chalk up a fabulous winning streak—sixty-five games without defeat—but they did something of far greater importance to the history of baseball and indirectly the history of the United States. By demonstrating that baseball could be a paying venture, they opened the way for a billion-dollar industry.

In April 1969 professional baseball in America became one hundred years old. For better or worse, it has been part of the national scene for a full century. Those who say for better have always been more numerous—or, at any rate, more articulate—than those who might suggest that the national pastime has been something less than beneficial. Whatever its worth, it has nearly always been with us. Since that summer of 1869 wars have been fought, won, stalemated, and passed into history. Nineteen presidents have been inaugurated. The internal-combustion engine has been invented along with the phonograph, the incandescent light bulb, the electric refrigerator, the telephone, radio, television, the vacuum cleaner, the airplane and, most recently, a system of rocketry capable of projecting a space capsule to the moon, whose powder-fine soil and pitted surface may or may not make baseball feasible there.

For the nation and the world it has been a century of transcendent change. Yet baseball, save for minor adaptations, is virtually the same game it was on that day back in June 1869. Even the uniforms look the same.

A game slow to change, baseball indeed may be said to have resisted change at every turn. It hardly seems unfair to say that what changes it *has* seen fit to adopt have been primarily for the benefit of the owners, not the public. For example, it took the club owners almost sixty years after that day in 1869 to hit upon the very obvious idea of sewing numbers on the backs of the players' uniforms, a means of player-identification that any fan might rightfully have deemed a mighty long time in coming. Night baseball, although a convenience to the fan, is also for the financial benefit of the owner.

For reasons that must be obscure even to keen legal minds, baseball has always been judged in the courts to be a sport or entertainment rather than a business under the jurisdiction of the anti-trust laws. Yet that it is a business, and a highly profitable one, cannot be doubted. For the long barnstorming tour they took in 1869, Harry Wright and the Cincinnati Red Stockings showed a net profit of $1.39. Thereafter, so greatly did the profit picture improve that at the end of professional baseball's one hundredth season a Minneapolis businessman, Robert Short, paid the staggering sum of $9 million for the privilege of owning the franchise of the Washington Senators, a last-place team in 1968 and a club with a consistently mediocre record over the years. Baseball, it is true, may not have been so lucrative as, say, the steel industry or the automotive industry, but neither has anyone deigned to say that the latter are sports rather than businesses.

Yet the significant thing, remarkable in itself and baseball's hidden asset, is the fact that the average fan could not care less. For only yesterday the fan was a kid of nine or ten bolting his breakfast on Saturday morning and hurtling from the house with a glove buttoned over his belt and a bat over his shoulder, rushing to the nearest vacant lot, perhaps the nearest alley, where the other guys were gathering, a place where it would always be spring. For him, baseball would always have the sound and look and smell of that morning and of other mornings just like it. Only by an accident of chance would he find himself, in the years to come, up in the grandstand, looking on. But for a quirk of fate, he himself would be down on that field; it would be his likeness on the television screen and his name in the newspaper high on the list of .300 hitters. He was a fan, but a fan only incidentally. He was, first and always, himself a baseball player.

With the possible exception of the movies, what other American industry has had so very much going for it? Where else has the consumer been so deeply in love with the product?

Baseball has had benefits that are almost immeasurable in their impact and all totally free to the club owner. It has had national identification never enjoyed by other industries. Although bread is said to be the staff of life, no one suggests that it is patriotic or admirably American to patronize the bakery industry. Yet men high in political life, men responsible for governing the United States of America, have time and again stated publicly their firm belief that baseball is not only thoroughly American but that, in microcosm, it *is* America.

Baseball Magazine, in its second issue, published in May 1908, had the following cover: Its name was emblazoned in large black letters, and directly above it, in flowing red script, was the inscription—perhaps the admonition, or even threat: "For Red-Blooded Americans."

Whether the magazine was the first to use the phrase, or

even whether it was the first to apply it to baseball, is of little interest, but the intent, and perhaps even the national sentiment, was clear. The United States at the time was chauvinistic in the extreme—and if the sentiment for embracing baseball within the larger national chauvinism was perplexing, no one at the time seemed noticeably perplexed.

Jacques Barzun, professor of philosophy at Columbia University and frequent commentator on U.S. mores, has written: "Whoever wants to know the heart and mind of America had better learn baseball."

It seems not unreasonable to invert the statement and to say that whoever wants to understand baseball might well study the heart and mind of America.

To understand the tone and temper of America of 1869, it may be well to recall that it was still a very young country, less than a hundred years old. The Civil War had ended a mere four years earlier. The frontier was very real. Although, with the war ended, the country was again warming to the task, it had not nearly completed the extermination of the Indians and of pocketing those it did not exterminate. Andrew Johnson had been impeached and his ouster had barely been averted. He had left office and Ulysses S. Grant was the newly inaugurated President. In the South the job of reconstruction was being botched so heinously as to insure a century of intraracial and interracial misery. It was hardly a mannered country. Except perhaps for San Francisco and a few other pockets of culture, and for the thin band along the Atlantic coast of British-influenced aristocracy, the populace more often than not was rowdy, uncouth, even vulgar, and although Mother and Home would receive ever-increasing play as American bulwarks, the fact is that a large percentage of the population took its meals at boarding houses. Above all, it was a youthful country, brash, cocky, with the confidence of youth and with youth's weaknesses and rawness. It took to baseball with the same zest that sent its young and its old tracking endless wastes into the West, building railroads, slavering after gold, gouging the land's natural resources. It was a populace with a bursting libido and it took to baseball with the same untrammeled vigor that it bestowed, often heedlessly, upon the continent. Small wonder that the hapless umpire was regarded with approximately the same affection as the Red Indian and the bison. Umpire baiting was, of course, a far safer pursuit than hunting Indians and buffalo, and there is evidence to suggest that of the three, umpire baiting would, in time, as baseball began to clean itself up, be considered by far the most reprehensible.

If, as some have said, the U.S.A. and baseball were made for each other, if their destinies were meant to be intertwined, then the Civil War was merely an interruption in the headlong rush to destiny. It might even be said that the war gave destiny a helpful shove, bringing together as it did men from all over the country and enabling those who already knew the game (New Yorkers, in the main) to introduce it to those who had never heard of it. More than once the dullness of camp life was enlivened by an exhibition ball game and, according to baseball historian Lee Allen, the benefit to the game's future was substantial:

"A game played on Christmas Day, 1862, between clubs selected from the 165th New York Volunteer Infantry, Duryea's Zouaves, was witnessed by about 40,000 soldiers. That game, played in South Carolina, was the talk of the military world for months thereafter and when the war was over, men who had witnessed the game for the first time—Confederate prisoners of war among them—introduced the sport in their home localities."

Baseball, in underdeveloped forms, had been played in the United States many years before the Civil War, and its exact origin has been the subject of controversy—controversy often dull and of little concern to the fan, who traditionally has displayed only tepid interest in baseball's executive or his-

torical squabbles, apparently considering them merely irritat-
ing distractions from the only thing that truly matters—the
game.

One approach to the game's genesis—the best known—is
the Abner Doubleday theory, now discredited. Abner Doubleday was an upstate New Yorker and a career army man who
served as a general in the Civil War, and in fact was a Union
officer at Fort Sumter when it was fired upon by irate South
Carolinians.

In the minds of certain turn-of-the-century nabobs, all this
seemed to make him eminently qualified to be dubbed the
Father of Baseball. According to this theory, a sort of Adam
and Eve theory, baseball sprang almost full-grown from the
fertile brain of Doubleday the young man on a day in 1839
in a cow pasture in or near the present site of Cooperstown,
New York. For many years the legend persisted, until further
research indicated that, among other things, at the time Doubleday was supposed to have been in the cow pasture laying
out the diamond he was in fact attending classes at West
Point, which he entered as a cadet in 1838.

It is all too clear that the diamond moguls in question felt
they were acting in the best interests of baseball as well as
of the nation—and the two have generally been considered
inextricable. Strong among them was a group which felt that
baseball should become known as uniquely American. If it
was indeed to be deemed the national pastime—and by the
1890's it was already being called the national pastime, the
national game—then it should be dissociated from any hint
of foreign antecedents.

Calling baseball the "froth and foam and chalice of life,"
the *Reach Baseball Guide* for 1887 goes on to note that "when
the Pilgrim Fathers landed in America they brought with them
the English national game of cricket." This, the *Guide* continues,
"was too slow a sport for the blood of young America," and
young America set it aside for a game of its very own.

All this colored investigative thinking when, in 1907, a commission was appointed to cast about and establish a Theory of Origin. It is hard to avoid the suspicion that certain members of the group may have been unable to extricate the best interests of baseball and the nation from the best interests of themselves.

The commission was formed by A. G. Spalding, a good pitcher in the game's early days and later the owner of the Chicago White Stockings and founder and head of the sporting-goods company that still bears his name. According to some accounts, the investigation grew out of an argument between Spalding, who insisted that baseball was uniquely American, and Henry Chadwick, the "Father of the Box Score," who insisted that its origins could be traced to England.

It is worth noting that the membership of the commission was roughly divided between sporting-goods magnates and retired National League presidents. Of the former, in addition to Spalding, there was Alfred J. Reach, another good ball player in 1870's and senior member of A. J. Reach & Co., which not only manufactured bats and balls but published the *Reach Guide*. There was also Harry Wright's brother George, a star member of the 1869 Red Stockings and, in 1907, head of the Wright and Ditson sporting-goods company. The former National League presidents were Morgan G. Bulkeley, A. G. Mills, and Nicholas E. Young. There was also the president of the AAU (Amateur Athletic Union) and, doubtless to lend an air of impartiality, a U.S. Senator from Maryland.

The commission was not long in receiving the testimony of one Abner Graves, a boyhood crony of Abner Doubleday, who had long since died and hence had not the power either to uphold or deny. Graves, then living in Colorado, said he had been right there with Doubleday and had seen him drawing in the ground with a pointed stick. On the basis of what Graves had to say, the commission quickly decided that the originator of baseball could certainly have been no other than Abner Doubleday. Doubtless with relief and gratitude, the members of the commission, in their mind's eye, could even *see* the young, perspiring, disheveled Abner staking out the diamond, right there in the cow pasture, which lay just outside the town limits of Cooperstown. Although they could not be certain of the weather, it seemed likely that the day had been sunny.

Its job well done, the commission announced its findings in 1908 in the official baseball guide. Not only had it put to rest any hint of foreign influence, but there was an added advantage, an unlooked-for plus. What could be more fitting than for the Father of Baseball to have been a military man —and a general at that?

In view of the commission's methods, it hardly comes as a surprise to read this evaluation of its accomplishment by no less an authority than the Encyclopedia Britannica: "Many of the old-time players refused to entertain the thought that a foreign nation had anything to do with inventing a great U.S. institution like baseball, and especially A. G. Spalding, who had made a fortune out of sporting goods. Hence the Spalding commission, composed not of skilled investigators but of baseball men assisted by a United States senator, appointed ostensibly to investigate the origins of the game but really to prove its exclusively U.S. origin."

Since most of the old-time baseball men were dead by 1908, and since nobody seemed to care very much anyway, the report aroused no controversy and in fact was accepted as history. For years the Doubleday theory persisted, dying finally under the impact of painstaking research compiled most notably by Robert W. Henderson, of the New York Public Library, who established that the game's origin was English and its development quite gradual, chalking up a clear-cut victory for the evolutionists.

Although baseball executives reluctantly yielded to the scholars, they have been stuck, if stuck is the word, with all the rather elaborate trappings and establishment which resulted from long years of Doubleday canonization. The National Baseball Museum and National Baseball Library are at Cooperstown, as is the Baseball Hall of Fame. The cow pasture today is surrounded by the village and is now a well-kept baseball diamond—superimposed upon the original field where Abner Doubleday apparently did not invent baseball. There is a fair-sized grandstand and, to compound the fiction, it is here, at Doubleday Field, entered through a turnstile from Main Street in Cooperstown, that each year two major-league teams play the so-called Hall of Fame game, an exhibition game that features ceremonies at which baseball stars of the faroff and recent past are admitted into the Baseball Hall of Fame, sometimes posthumously.

Among baseball men there seems to be no particular remorse, no sense of wallowing along through baseball history in the backwash of a hoax. As one observer states, "Hell, it had to be *somewhere,* and it might just as well be Cooperstown as somewhere else. We can't pick up the damn museum and *move* it."

Had baseball's shrine been somewhere else, the village of Cooperstown would have been left wholly as the historical precinct of James Fenimore Cooper, the linsey-woolsey-leathern American novelist who was Cooperstown-born and -bred, author of *The Last of the Mohicans* and *Leatherstocking Tales,* among others, and a favorite target of Mark Twain. Cooperstown stands on the southwest bank of Lake Otsego, a body of water known in Cooper's novels as "Glimmerglass." At present, Cooperstown's historical tone is divided about equally between Cooperiana and baseball. Had the baseball museum been somewhere else, Cooperstown today undoubtedly would not have a baseball field squarely on its main street. Nor, one may surmise, would it include among its eateries the Shortstop Restaurant, which now stands on Main Street not far from the intersection of Main and Leatherstocking.

In Cooperstown the baseball shrine stands and doubtless will remain. Yet to say offhand that it might as well be in

Cooperstown as anywhere is to display utter disregard for the
wholly legitimate claim of Hoboken, New Jersey. Had the
commission on the theory of origin been more exacting in its
research, had it leapt less eagerly to the easy solution offered
by Abner Graves, the shrine might today be in Hoboken—
even though there is no evidence to indicate that Hoboken
ever craved it.

One of the lesser-known members of the Hall of Fame is a
certain Alexander Cartwright, who never played a game of
major-league baseball in his life. What he did do, however,
was to perform such signal services to the game as to make
himself far more eligible for the title Father of Baseball than
Abner Doubleday.

Cartwright was a member of the Knickerbocker Club, a
group of Manhattan young bloods who in the early 1840's
sometimes took their pleasure in Hoboken, a pleasant ferry-
boat ride across the Hudson and a favorite resort for New
Yorkers. Members of the Knickerbocker Club, apparently as
early as 1840, were amusing themselves with a game very
much resembling baseball. Gradually the game they played
was given refinements and innovations, and the prime innovator
and closest student of the game's possibilities clearly seemed
to be Cartwright. No military man, Cartwright was a surveyor
by profession and perhaps for that reason was admirably qualified for the task of laying out the geometry of the diamond.

One of the services Cartwright performed was to establish
the distance between bases at precisely ninety feet, a distance
which has never changed in all the years since. Whether he
acted by special divination or whether it was merely a fortui-
tous guess is difficult to say, but it is interesting to note that a
man who "circles the bases" is traveling exactly 360 feet—the
number of degrees in a circle—and it is difficult to believe that
Cartwright was oblivious of the correlation. In any case, today,
over a hundred years later, the distance between bases is still
and has always been a perfect distance for baseball's purposes,

a distance which wrings the utmost in drama from any number of the game's variety of dramatic situations. When, for example, a base runner sets out from first base to steal second, it is almost invariably a nip-and-tuck affair, so admirably is the distance between bases correlated to the limits of human speed and the power of the throwing arm. Had the distance been, say, ninety-two feet, stealing second would have been so difficult as to be seldom achieved. Had it been eighty-eight, stealing second might have been too easy. Few baseball players in history—Ty Cobb and Maury Wills chief among them—have had the speed and base-stealing technique to give the runner the upper hand, and even they made no mockery of it. For most of the rest, the attempt to steal second is a drama whose outcome is usually in doubt. Stealing third, of course, is a different matter and is seldom attempted, since it requires a much shorter throw by the catcher than does the long throw to second base and is hence a more hazardous venture.

The ninety-foot span is also important in considering the attempt of a batter to reach first safely. At ninety feet, a batter is easily retired on routine bounders, yet he is often rewarded by being able to beat out a ball hit to deep shortstop, for example, or one not handled cleanly by the infield. Ninety feet leaves the issue in doubt, and Cartwright is to be congratulated for his precision, whether or not it was guesswork.

Cartwright's contribution to the game does not end with geometry. It was he who established that there should be nine men to a side; he set the foul lines, and even ordained that the batter was entitled to try to reach first base if the catcher failed to hold a third strike. As yet, however, there was no stipulation that a game was to last nine innings. The winning team was the first to score twenty-one runs—or "aces," as they were then called.

On June 19, 1846, a Sunday, members of the Knickerbocker Club and of a rival Manhattan group known simply as the New York Club took a ferry ride across the Hudson, looking for a place to play ball. The setting is recaptured in a volume compiled by the old-time baseball historian, Seymour Church.

"A walk of about a mile and a half from the ferry up the Jersey shore of the Hudson river, along a road that skirted the river bank on one side and was hugged by trees and thickets on the other, brought one suddenly to an opening in the 'forest primeval.' This open spot was a level grass-covered plain, some 200 yards across and as deep—surrounded on three sides by the typical eastern undergrowth and woods, and on the east by the Hudson. It was a perfect greensward for almost the year round."

They had stumbled upon the Elysian Fields near Hoboken, and here they played the first baseball game in history. The game was umpired by Alexander Cartwright, who fined a member of the New York Club six cents for swearing. Even though they had the umpire and the rule maker on their side, it was not the Knickerbockers' day. They got bombed 23-1. The game ended after four innings, and they all got back on the ferry and went home.

Whatever a numerologist might make of it, it is hard to overlook Cartwright's—and baseball's—absorption with the number three and multiples thereof. Three strikes. Three outs. Three bases. Nine players. Ultimately nine innings. Three men in the outfield. Six in the infield, and, of course, ninety feet between bases. Whether elements of mysticism went into his conception of the game is impossible to say. Cartwright was a young man, only twenty-five, when he umpired that first game in Hoboken. Baseball magnates, so far as one knows, have made nothing of this aspect of triplicity. Although they have not hesitated to identify their game with *patria*, they have so far resisted, at least in public, any temptation to say that it has the solid backing of the Trinity.

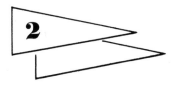

The Mists of

Memory

AN ARCHAIC DESCRIPTION OF HOW BASEBALL WAS TO BE PLAYED
was included in a pamphlet entitled *A Manual of Cricket and
Base Ball,* published in Boston in 1858.

Baseball, it begins, "besides an ordinary field requires only
a ball and a bat or stick resembling a common rolling pin but
not quite so heavy, and of the same size all the way down. The
ball is the common one used in the games played with ball
except cricket and football.

"The game is played by first fixing four spots called bases
at nearly equal distances and marked by a stone or small
plug. . . . In the center is another place called the seat where
the 'feeder' or thrower stands to give or throw the ball to the
one who has the bat."

Noting that the game requires at least ten or twelve players

and that "20 or 30 are not too many," the pamphlet gets on
to the action: "The 'in' side begin by standing at a spot called
the 'house,' one of them taking the bat while the feeder, who
is one of the 'out' party, stands at his seat and throws the
ball. . . . When the ball is thus given, the batsman's object is
to hit it far and low over the field and his side put out at once
[sic]. . . .

"Each player after striking the ball runs to the first base, A,
then to B, C and D, according to the distance he has knocked
the ball.

"After passing D, he calls 'Tally!' and scores one."

An out was recorded in any one of the following ways: if
the batter struck out; if he hit a ball caught either on the fly
or first bounce; or if he himself was struck by the ball, either
thrown or batted, while he was off base.

The anonymous pamphleteer gives this additional bit of
guidance: "In playing stated games of baseball, a certain number of tallies should be played for, say 50, the making of which
by either side shall constitute the game."

The pamphlet notes that baseball was then "the favorite
game throughout New England." If some of the rules indicate
that the game was not yet fully developed, it was still baseball
and there is evidence, Doubleday aside, that it had been a
favorite game in New England for quite some time, and before
that a favorite game in England as well.

It is perhaps just as well that A. G. Spalding went to his rest
before his work was challenged. Spalding was a proud, rugged
man, and to have given him the lie in the form of something
called *A Little Pretty Pocket-Book* would have been a case of
extreme cruelty. Yet *A Little Pretty Pocket-Book* did much to
undermine the Spalding commission's work. Others who contributed, even if unwittingly, were Jane Austen and Oliver
Wendell Holmes, along with the unknown author or authors
of another early volume, *The Boy's Own Book*, published in
London in 1828.

In her novel *Northanger Abbey*, written in the 1790's, Jane Austen says of her heroine: "It was not very wonderful that Catherine, who had by nature nothing heroic about her, should prefer cricket, baseball, riding on horseback and running round the country at the age of fourteen, to books." Oliver Wendell Holmes was a member of the class of 1829 at Harvard, where, he later recalled, he played a great deal of baseball during his days as an undergraduate.

But the real Spalding-breaker was *A Little Pretty Pocket-Book*, published in England in 1744, which left no doubt that even in that early day, and in a foreign land at that, B stood for Baseball. Illustrated with crude woodcuts, according to historian William E. Brandt, "It pictures and describes in doggerel quatrains 26 children's sports—one for each letter of the alphabet. And 'B' is represented by 'Baseball.' "

The text notes that the batter hits the ball and runs the bases. The illustration shows pitcher, catcher, batter, and basemen. The bases are marked by posts.

The Boy's Own Book, published in 1828, is even more explicit, and the game it describes bears a much closer resemblance to modern American baseball than does rugby to its acknowledged offspring, U.S. football.

Hence, once one succeeds in ignoring Spalding and Doubleday, the origin and evolution of baseball become clear. Baseball was played first in England. In the west of England it was called "rounders," in London it was called "feeder," and in the southern counties it was called baseball. By whatever name, it was a game in which a ball was pitched and batted. There were bases and there were fielders. It was a game brought over to the colonies from England. It was played in early America and it was basically the game played today.

In any review of baseball history, one comes inevitably upon versions of the game known as "town ball" and "old-cat"— one old-cat, two old-cat, etc. The evidence shows that "town ball" was merely another name, a New England name, for rounders (baseball) and hence new—and American—in name only. "Old-cat," the Spalding commission deposed, was truly indigenous to America. In fact, it was the only base game the commission would concede had existed before Doubleday's "invention," and the only foundation upon which Doubleday could build.

It would appear, however, that old-cat was merely the name for a pickup game resorted to when there were not enough players to permit a full-scale game. It was the same as the makeshift game called "one-knocker" or "two-knocker" in more modern sandlot parlance. In one-knocker, there is a single batsman and a single base. So long as the batsman hits the ball far enough to make it to first and back home, he remains at bat. Two-knocker involves two batsmen, again using only one base. A batsman, however, need not make it to first base and back home on his own power. If he arrives safely at first, he may remain there until driven home by the second batsman.

There are, of course, obvious and basic differences between the early game and the modern. The bases, for example, were often holes or posts, or sometimes the "plugs" referred to in *A Manual of Cricket and Base Ball*. The distances between the bases were usually considerably less than the ninety feet established by Cartwright. The distance from pitcher to batter also fluctuated, as it continued to do even after the game became professional. And, as noted, a ball caught on the first bounce was an out just as surely as if it had been caught on the fly.

But the most significant difference lay in the old rule that a batter could be put out by hitting him with the ball while he was on the base paths, a rule that would be as bizarre in today's big-league baseball as one that would have required, say, Ty Cobb, Leo Durocher, Willie Mays, or Yogi Berra to carol "Tally one!" as they crossed home plate.

The chaos in the early days must have been considerable. A reasonably agile runner surely had little trouble dodging a thrown ball, particularly such a small one, and once the ball had missed him and gone on into the outfield or some obscure corner of the premises, the runner was free to make merry on the base paths.

Another disadvantage was that the game had to be played with a relatively soft ball, for if a fielder had hurled a version of today's hard ball at the base runner and happened to hit him in a vital area, the runner's retirement might have been permanent.

(There is, of course, a vestigial rule still in effect today: a runner struck by a batted ball is automatically out. If this qualifies as an anachronism, it nevertheless makes sense, since a runner might kick or otherwise deflect a batted ball so as to give an advantage to the batsman, and whether he had done so accidentally or intentionally might be a matter of fierce contention.)

In any case, the old rule permitting the runner to be pelted with the ball was the early game's principal weakness. Its elimination from the rulebook was Alexander Cartwright's— and America's—major contribution to the fundamentals of baseball. Not until it was eliminated was it possible to use a hard ball, which for a variety of reasons (it was more difficult to handle in the field and more difficult to hit, yet it traveled greater distances when it *was* hit) gave the game much greater zest. Not until then did baseball go adult—or, if one prefers, did it become a game played by grown men as well as boys.

Just as there were great composers before Beethoven, so indeed were there formidable baseball teams before the Cincinnati Red Stockings of 1869, but they were all amateur. After Cartwright codified the rules, baseball clubs flourished all through the land, in the larger cities as well as in towns and hamlets. The old Knickerbocker Club was one of the very best, along with the New York Gothams, the Mutuals, the Philadelphia Olympics, and the Forest Cities Club of Rockford, Illinois, a team for which A. G. Spalding once pitched with considerable success. By 1858 interest was so widespread as to permit the formation of the National Association of Baseball Players, an amateur group, and in 1865, after the Civil War, a baseball convention was held in New York with ninety-one clubs represented.

Spirit was keen, civic pride was high, and the rivalries were intense, but all was on a refined amateur basis, for during these years baseball was the special province of so-called gentlemen's clubs, which were determined to see to it that the game was played only by young men of breeding. The designation "baseball club" has persisted until the present day, even though for many years there have been no clubs as such; there is instead a team of players hired by a corporation that has bought a franchise in a given city.

In the full flower of its days of elegance, baseball, one may believe, was a game played in the garden-party, white-flannels atmosphere of lawn tennis. The clubs fought fiercely to keep it that way, just as fiercely as yacht clubs today might fight to preserve certain aspects of yacht racing. As an indication of the club approach to the game, *A Manual of Cricket and Base Ball* contains these rather prissy guidelines:

In choosing sides for a game, the club president (or, in his absence, the director) shall designate two choosers, or captains, and "each player, as he is chosen, shall take a stand beside the player preceding him in order that no confusion may ensue. If a sufficient number of members of the Club be not present at the time appointed for playing, persons not members may be chosen to make up the match," the *Manual* states, and then adds sternly: "But in all cases, members shall have preference at the time of choosing."

Even the umpire, so beleaguered in later years, enjoyed in those days a dignity of office which has never been equaled. His job was considered an honor and he dressed accordingly, wearing a Prince Albert coat and high silk hat and carrying a cane. His vantage point was between home plate and first base and he was even given a stool on which to rest one foot as he viewed the proceedings. The official scorer's table was off to the right of the catcher, the *Manual* notes, and "inasmuch as refreshments, both liquid and solid, were served, the scorer fared sumptuously." So, presumably, did the umpire.

Baseball in this era, then, was an antiseptic game for amateurs and for twenty-three years it would remain so, firmly in the grip of dilettantes on the one hand and, perhaps curiously, professional gamblers on the other. According to Lee Allen, "The idlers thought the game should be played only by gentlemen in their leisure. They feared that if skill were the only requisite, undesirable people would soon be playing the game. . . . The influences baseball had to be freed from were the influences of aristocratic New York, influences originally British."

From this and other historical notes on the game's early years, one gets the strong, and again curious, impression of a sport bursting to go pro but restrained from doing so by an unwholesome group of Anglophilic aristocrats who gripped the game with long, slender fingers, jealously protecting their right to keep baseball for their very own. Aiding them in their fight to retain custody was a group of strange bedfellows, a band of professional gamblers—easterners who also wanted to keep the game amateur. One also gets an impression of a continent rife with scum and vulgarity the moment one traveled west of, say, Hoboken—of vast hordes of the unwashed, waiting to grab the game the instant the dilettantes relaxed their grip. Significantly, this same attitude would be reflected a few years later when eastern cities tried to deny league representation to certain noneastern cities, particularly Cincinnati, St. Louis, and Louisville, all of which were accused of being river towns (a geographical fact), and hence assumed to be vulgar and brawling.

The exact role of the professional gamblers is a matter for some reflection. If one accepts the premise that gamblers were eager to keep the game in amateur hands, it is difficult not to reach the conclusion that they must have considered the aristocrats easier to manipulate than professionals would be, a conclusion that would reflect most unfavorably upon the character of the dilettantes who were claiming the game for their own.

If this was indeed the case, their fears were unfounded, for all too many players in the professional game's early years would prove themselves most cooperative, and once the pro game was established any gambler with a desire to fix games could not possibly have yearned for the good old days of amateurism.

In attempting to establish why baseball went professional when it did, it is difficult to overlook economics. The history of the entertainment industry would seem to support the view that an enterprise goes professional when there is a large enough paying audience to support it. Today, although polo, for example, is still very much an amateur sport and one considered the pastime of "gentlemen," it seems certain that if the general public displayed an interest in paying to see polo matches, some thoughtful promoter would very shortly be forming a professional polo league.

In the case of baseball, a more immediate reason was sheer rivalry—the eagerness of cities to win baseball games from other cities. The game became pro because of the amateurs' increasingly fierce will to win.

Although the 1869 Red Stockings were baseball's first professional team, there were cases as early as 1866 and 1867 of particularly accomplished players occasionally being paid for their services. The practice was spasmodic, but even so it aroused the rage of the amateur bigwigs who saw it as a sign of baseball's doom.

In addition to outright pay, according to one historian there was a poorly camouflaged financial arrangement which calls to mind the economic opportunities made available to certain present-day college athletes. "Some of the 'stars' of the amateur teams around the country in the late 1860's enjoyed clerkships that came to them on account of their ability to play the game rather than in recognition of their business grey-matter." The full story of the Red Stockings is told in *Baseball in Cincinnati* by Harry Ellard. The Red Stockings themselves had included four paid players among their ranks in 1868, which made them in effect a semi-pro organization. Even with four semi-pros on the field, however, the team's 1868 performance fell far short of Cincinnati hopes, and at a club meeting after the 1868 season ended it was decided that the amateur element must go. In the interest of excellence, it was even agreed that the recruiters might proselytize in other sections of the country, stripping other teams of established stars if possible—a clear indication of the will to win, since until then Cincinnati, along with other cities, took great civic pride in fielding teams composed solely of local talent.

As playing captain and manager, the recruiters settled on Harry Wright, who was a member of the 1868 team and already something of an idol. When he was married in September of that year, the club had given him a handsome gold watch wrapped neatly in a $100 government bond.

In the parlance of the sports page, a "brother act" is said to exist when two or more brothers of requisite ability play for the same ball club. Over the years baseball has known a number of brother acts, prominent among them being Dizzy and Paul Dean, Paul and Lloyd Waner, Morton and Walker Cooper, and Wes and Rick Ferrell. (No fewer than three DiMaggio brothers played in the major leagues simultaneously, but each played for a different club and whether this can properly be called a brother act is dubious.)

The Cincinnati Red Stockings of 1869 could be said to have featured professional baseball's very first brother act, for there was not only Harry Wright but his brother George, who played shortstop marvelously well and received the team's top salary, $1,400, for the April–November season, $200 more than Harry himself was paid. George Wright had been filched from a team in New Jersey, where he had won a reputation as "the model ballplayer in the United States."

Salaries ranged from George Wright's $1,400 down to the $600 paid Richard Hurley, the team's lone substitute.

In addition to the battery mates Asa Brainard and Doug Allison, other members of the team were Charlie Gould, 1b; Charlie Sweasy, 2b; Fred Waterman, 3b; Carl McVey, rf; and Andrew Leonard, lf.

In thumbnail sketches of the team, George Wright was described thus: "Take him all in all, George was the very beau ideal of a shortstop."

Charlie Gould—"Always working with a will and always to be found at his post." First-sacker Gould, as things worked out, was the only Cincinnati boy on the team.

Charlie Sweasy—"Never flinched" when a ball came to him.

Fred Waterman—"Known as 'Innocent Fred' because of his bland and innocent expression."

The most worshipful accolade is reserved for Harry Wright, who was described as follows: "The efficient captain was always quiet and self-sustained in his demeanor but he gave his orders with decision and these were always obeyed implicitly. In correcting any mistake of his men, he never did it in an offensive or arbitrary manner. His favorite expression— 'you need a little ginger'—acted as effectively as stronger language to infuse an extra amount of vim and action in his players. He was considered the best captain in the world."

Harry, who was obviously a man among men, went on later to a distinguished managerial career at Boston. After his death it was written that he was "a man to whom the whole baseball fraternity owes a debt of gratitude, especially those who are earning their bread from the game. During the years when questionable policy was being participated in, he ever kept himself and his players untainted. He was the first real baseball man professionally, in all its requirements and lofty ideas. He was the . . . tutor and moral adviser of his players. He raised the moral tone of professional ball and put it on the high road."

(Clearly there were those who felt the title of Father of Baseball might best have been bestowed upon Harry Wright. In addition to Doubleday and Alexander Cartwright, other candidates advanced, with varying degrees of enthusiasm, have been A. G. Spalding and Cap Anson, of the Chicago White Stockings. Yet another is Henry Chadwick, for his gambling crusade. In a 1909 editorial, *Baseball Magazine* said, flatly: "Henry Chadwick is the Father of Baseball." With so much confusion over its paternity, it is perhaps understandable that baseball should have behaved so badly during its adolescence.)

In spite of the many accolades that would be granted Harry Wright, it seems reasonable to assume that as the 1869 season approached he was thinking not so much of being a baseball pioneer as he was of winning ball games and of seeing to it that a buck was turned often enough to enable the club to meet the payroll. Once the team was assembled and a couple of practice games played against pickup nines, the Red Stockings begin their eastern swing. En route to the momentous game in Brooklyn they polished off Great Western, 45 to 9, and the catchily named Kekiongas of Fort Wayne, Indiana, by the catchy score of 86 to 8, and then registered successive victories at Mansfield, Ohio; Cleveland; Buffalo; Rochester; Syracuse; Albany; Lansingburg, New York; Albany again; Boston; and New Haven before arriving in Brooklyn for their 4–2 victory over the Mutuals, a game that has been called the "best-played game of ball on record, both nines playing in a style throughout rarely seen."

When news of the great victory reached Cincinnati, there were scenes of wild excitement. Salutes were fired and red lights burned, and the effect upon the populace was said to be so salubrious that "many were willing to lend their friends . . . any sum without question."

At their hotel that night, the Red Stockings received the following telegram:

On behalf of the citizens of Cincinnati we send you greeting.
The streets are full of people who give cheer after cheer for
their club. Go on with the noble work. Our expectations have
been met.

All the citizens of Cincinnati

After three quick victories in Philadelphia, the team went
on to Washington for two more victorious games, one of which
was witnessed by President Grant, who later honored the
Cincinnati players with a meeting at which he "treated them
cordially, complimented them on their playing," and smoked
cigars throughout the interview. The festivities in Washington
also included a sightseeing tour and a number of social engage-
ments. In the course of making the rounds, we are told, the
Red Stockings often sang the following song:

> We are a band of baseball players
>   From Cincinnati city.
> We come to toss the ball around
>   And sing to you our ditty
> And if you listen to the song
>   We are about to sing
> We'll tell you all about baseball
>   And make the welkin ring
> The ladies want to know
>   Who are those gallant men
> In Stockings Red, they'd like to know . . .

At this juncture, the players, still in song and verse, introduced themselves one by one. A Washington newspaper stated
that the team "drew the most aristocratic assemblage at its
games that ever put in an appearance at a baseball match."
What the Washington journalists thought of the team as song-
smiths is unknown.

From Washington the team returned to Cincinnati, which
understandably was rapturous but hard put to find a token of
its esteem of suitable magnitude. The next day there was a

welcome-home game against a pickup team, and when it was over a wagon was driven onto the field. On the wagon was a baseball bat, the gift of a grateful city. The bat was twenty-seven feet long, nineteen inches around at the fat end, and nine and a half inches around at the handle.

Later the ladies of Cincinnati gave the team a handsome silk banner, presenting it to Harry Wright, who made a highly predictable acceptance speech: "We shall always carry this banner with us," he said, "and though it may not on every occasion float over a victorious ball field, yet it shall ever wave over us as victors over all temptations."

Undeterred, the Red Stockings swept on, toppling every-thing before them in the East and Midwest and later in the summer journeying all the way to San Francisco. It is not difficult to picture them, with their beards and sideburns, riding the trains that puffed between the principal cities and then the horse-drawn omnibuses or trolleys out to whatever passed as the local ball park. We can imagine the youthful Harry, with his luxuriant beard, keeping his men on the straight-and-narrow as best he could, doing his utmost to keep "Innocent Fred" Waterman innocent, keeping the team ever untainted, steering his men away from the fleshpots and the influence of gamblers, bedding them down in respectable boarding houses where, in the evening after the game was done and won, they might lounge on the veranda, rehash the game, spit tobacco juice over the railing, and watch the girls go by.

Day after day they won, like the professional strong man of an old-time circus touring the provinces, taking on all comers and throwing down the rubes who dared challenge. In those days, civic pride was very strong, particularly in the provinces, and one may imagine how deeply the locals were stirred to know that Harry and his men were coming, and with what boastful threats the locals prepared, weeks in advance, to do battle—empty threats as it turned out, but the occasion was surely momentous. Entertainment facilities were meager; it was a time of silence. It would be many years before the Big

Sound, before radio, television, motion pictures, even automobiles. Not until that very summer had the first transcontinental rail line been completed, and railroads were a thing of wonderment, the arrival of the daily train at the local depot an exciting event. And when it had pulled out and the sound of its whistle had died away, the clop-clop of a horse, the rustle of a tree, could be loud in the stillness. It was the time of the magic-lantern slide, the piano in the parlor, and band concerts on the village green. The coming of Harry Wright and his ball club was an event of enormous importance, and the local citizenry must have felt rarely privileged, even though the locals got beaten. Almost invariably the margin was one-sided, for the Red Stockings were the Yankees of their day, and the amateurs were usually no match for them.

Sixty-five games the Red Stockings played and sixty-four they won, the only blight on their otherwise perfect season being a 17–17 tie with the Troy, New York, Haymakers and this, according to one account, would have been a Red Stocking victory had it not been for "disgraceful action" on the part of the Haymakers. At the end of five innings the score was tied 17–17 when an argument broke out over a decision of the umpire. The captain of the Haymakers ordered the game suspended, whereupon a near riot broke out. "The crowd grew wild and jumped onto the field, causing a great disturbance, and it was only upon the prompt arrival of Chief Ruffin's police that damage was prevented. It seemed that a number of New York gamblers had placed large amounts of money on the Haymakers and, fearing a defeat, entered into collusion with the Haymakers to stop the game."

Aside from this game and a narrow squeak, 15–14, over the Rockford, Illinois, club, the Red Stockings won by enormous margins. Some of the more notable scores were:

Red Stockings 65, Omaha 1.

Red Stockings 103, Cincinnati Buckeyes 8.

Red Stockings 76, San Francisco Atlantics 5 (called at the

end of five innings).

In the game against San Francisco, the Red Stockings averaged better than fifteen runs per inning, while in the game against the Cincinnati Buckeyes the Red Stockings, in safe passage around the base paths alone, traveled more than seven miles! Meanwhile, in some of the games, the locals were also whacking Harry's pitchers (Asa Brainard and Harry himself) with good authority. It was hardly a pitcher's year.

There are several factors that may account for the huge scoring. Unlike the billiard-table-like surfaces of today, the playing fields were poorly kept and bumpy, making the ball hard to handle; there were no gloves; and the pitcher, even though he stood closer to the batter than pitchers do today, was severely restricted by a rule which prohibited him from swinging his arm above hip level.

Another clue may lie in the old-time approach to infield play. George Wright is described as roving far and wide, gobbling up everything in sight, which may have been what made him the "very beau ideal of a shortstop." Other infielders, particularly those grounded in amateurism, may have had a less dynamic approach. An old lithograph hanging in the museum at Cooperstown shows the batter up and the pitcher about to deliver the ball; the first, second, and third basemen are all standing squarely on their bags and the shortstop is standing precisely on a line between second and third. This particular infield, at least, was preserving Alexander Cartwright's concept of geometric symmetry to an extent far beyond that ever intended by Cartwright—an extent suggesting that old-time infielders may have covered very little ground.

Finally, in November, after seven months of baseball, the Red Stockings called it a season. They played their last game that year, on November 5 in Cincinnati, giving the Brooklyn Mutuals a return match and this time beating them by the conclusive score of 17 to 8.

The next year they were at it again. Not until June 14, 1870, were they beaten, meaning that from April 1868 to June 1870 they played 130 games and won them all except the tainted tie with the Troy Haymakers.

Perhaps fittingly, the scene of their downfall was Brooklyn, where so many months before they had scored their most illustrious victory. The Brooklyn Atlantics beat them 8 to 7, in eleven innings. George Zettlein, the Brooklyn pitcher, went the route, limiting the Red Stockings to two earned runs. After the game, Aaron Champion, the Cincinnati club president, "wept like a child."

Harry Ellard's saga of the Red Stockings was published in 1907. The author was apparently a direct descendant of one George B. Ellard, who was instrumental in rounding up the Red Stockings and getting them started as baseball's first professional team. Of George B. Ellard, the author says, not surprisingly: "He has been properly termed the 'Father' of professional baseball."

In 1908 *Baseball Magazine* featured an article by an old-time fan who set out to recall "the good old days," addressing himself to those who, unlike himself, were too young to remember baseball as it was played in the early 1870's.

"Far back in the mists of memory," he wrote, "I can see Harry Wright chasing fly balls with whiskers that must have tempted Aeolus. I can see George Wright playing . . . with a moustache equalling Jim O'Rourke's in size, scope and brilliancy. There was old Zettlein, the 'Lively Turtle,' pitching with a never varying straight-arm delivery the shoulder-ball, the waist-ball, and the hip ball, as the batter might require."

There are differences between today's game and Harry Wright's game, and yet the game Harry and his men played was baseball—baseball the sport and now, finally, in spite of the dilettantes, baseball the profession. After years of trial and error, there would be baseball the industry, baseball the national institution, and baseball the national mystique—a mystique so profitable, offering a national image so valuable, that by early 1969, one hundred years after the Red Stockings, the major-league owners would be concerned by a full-circle trend among the players toward long, bushy sideburns and other hirsute adornments which, although they might not be so abundant as to tempt Aeolus the wind god, were still so deviationist as to scare hell out of the magnates. What they feared was that the populace might no longer deem baseball a game for red-blooded Americans.

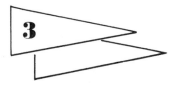

3

"The Black Shadow of Treachery"

IN THE YEARS TO COME, THE SPINDLY WOODEN BLEACHERS IN the ball parks of 1869 would be replaced by mammoth structures of steel and concrete in many of the principal cities of the nation. In the early 1900's, Malvina Hoffman, a noted sculptress of the era would spend day after day at New York's Polo Grounds mesmerized by the perfection of bodily form she found in a pitcher named Christy Mathewson. In the 1920's many of the country's leading newspapers would find front-page, banner-headline news in an ordinary stomach ache that an outfielder named Ruth brought upon himself by eating too many hotdogs. Still later Willie Mays, son of a Georgia sharecropper, would be paid at the rate of $770 per game, earning nearly as much for a few hours' work as most of the members of Harry Wright's team received for the entire 1869 season. In 1911 President William Howard Taft would belly-up to the box-seat railing and throw out the first ball in the American League opener. Rarely thereafter, except in wartime, would the President of the United States fail to grace opening-day ceremonies with his presence. (One—Dwight D. Eisenhower— who tried to skip the opener for a round of golf in Atlanta drew such pointed remarks in the press that when rain washed out the game he hurried back to town and embraced his second chance.) Statesmen and politicians alike would regard baseball as sacrosanct and so identified with America would it become that Japanese soldiers in World War II, stung by American insults against Emperor Hirohito, would shout into the night from their foxholes what they clearly believed to be a fitting retort: *The hell with Babe Ruth!*" Baseball would become part of American folklore, legend, and idiom. Along with jazz music and drinking, it would contribute perhaps more words and phrases to the American language than any other pastime. In the national idiom there would be, with the possible exception of apple pie, nothing that America was so American as.

The evidence indicates that baseball succeeded in spite of itself, for the history of its adolescence is the history of an enterprise self-maimed, over and over again, almost invariably by the very men who played and ran it. For it to win such fantastic acceptance took some doing. Clearly it had something going for it.

Among the many who have tried to explain baseball's mystique, a favorite theme has always been the identification of the game with the nation, with particular stress on democracy and on such qualities-in-common as lusty youth, brawling vigor, and American ingenuity.

One explanation published by *Baseball Magazine* in 1908 summed it up as follows: "Baseball is not merely an interesting and scientific game. It is the game which calls into play the dominant traits of Americans in its demand for agility, quick thinking, and a tremendous exertion and excitement. It is peculiarly popular and fascinating to us because it means a contest, a personal hand-to-hand encounter. Baseball has all the elements of the personal battle which makes every red-blooded American itch to see a glove-contest."

And again: "Baseball's chief clutch on the heartstrings of its devotees is the fact that it is played on the square, first, last and all the time. Baseball is an honest game. It is a clean game, played by little boys on the corner lots, and big boys on the well-kept grounds of the various leagues. It is played out in the sunshine where the blue sky looks down on the green grass. . . . Baseball is our one best pastime. We play it when schoolboys. We go to see it when we come to middle age. We send our boys and our office boys when we are grown old and fat and gouty. And when we have crossed The Home Plate, as some day we must, and when the children of our children fill the stands where once we cheered, perhaps our spirits shall be spectators."

By 1908, when these were published, the campaign to win popular acceptance for baseball had become near-evangelical in fervor as well as phraseology. It also contained a distinct note of triumph, for by 1908 the worst for a time was over. Much of the disreputable element had been eliminated and many of the game's bad actors had crossed The Home Plate and gone for the last time to The Clubhouse.

Baseball may indeed have been a game played out where the blue sky met the green grass, but all evidence indicates that for long years, certainly during its first quarter century, it was *not* a clean game, played on the square. It was often a crooked game, influenced heavily by professional gamblers, played in the main by alcoholics and roughnecks, controlled by slow-witted, insensibly greedy executives, and witnessed by rowdies to whom "Kill the umpire!" was sometimes more than a merely metaphorical aspiration.

Gamblers took extreme measures to protect their investments, making life hazardous for those intrepid enough to perform counter to their best interests. In the early days on the Pacific Coast, gamblers were not above using gunfire to rattle if not intimidate the players. "Just as a fly ball was dropping into a fielder's hands," according to Seymour Church's account, "every gambler who had bet on the nine at bat would discharge a fusillade from his six-shooter in an endeavor to confuse the fielder and make him miss the ball."

If we are to believe the accounts of widespread drunkenness among the players, a fielder might have had trouble handling the ball cleanly even without the distraction of gunfire. For those who might question whether the drinking habits of the players gave advantage to the offense or the defense, or to one team over another, we have *Baseball Magazine's* word that it was a standoff.

"As every team was composed of drunks, they were evenly matched in this regard," the magazine notes.

So freely were games thrown that at times the proceedings must have been highly confusing to the spectator, if one conceives of opposing gambling rings and their opposing apostles on the field of play, each soddenly trying to out-fumble the other.

None of baseball's venality, to be sure, was the fault of the exemplary Harry Wright and his blue-ribbon Red Stockings.

Invincible though they were on the field, and as impeccable as they may have been off it, the main contribution of the Red Stockings to baseball history lay in the service they rendered as trail blazers. They proved that baseball could succeed as a business. So tempting was the prospect of money-for-play that professional baseball clubs quickly sprang up all through the country, and although the dilettante amateurs might continue to grouse and sulk a while longer, their day was done.

So strong did the professional movement become that within less than two years it was possible to form a players organization known as the National Association of Professional Baseball

Players. The group was founded at a meeting in New York early in 1871 and that same summer took the field and played ball, operating as baseball's first major league.

The following clubs were represented: the Philadelphia Athletics; the Bostons; the Chicago White Stockings; the Brooklyn Eckfords; the Forest Cities of Cleveland; the Forest Cities of Rockford, Illinois; the Troy Haymakers; the Fort Wayne Kekiongas; and the New York Mutuals.

The league leader that year was Philadelphia, even then known as the Athletics, and thus the Philadelphia Athletics of 1871 were the first team ever to win a major-league pennant. Exactly seventy years later, in 1931, they would win their last and later would leave Philadelphia bound for Oakland by way of Kansas City.

In recent years organized baseball has been criticized for the frequency and impatience with which franchises have been shifted from one city to another, almost invariably because the club was either not making a profit or was not making as large a profit as the owners had hoped for. This turbulence seems modest indeed when compared to the confusion of the 1870's, 80's, and 90's. Teams took the field only to fall apart in mid-season, sometimes because the players were habitually too drunk to carry on. Players of higher principle, and even some owners, withdrew because they found the game offensive, particularly its gambling element and the widespread practice of contract breaking. As teams dropped out, other teams replaced them. Leagues were formed only to fold. Competition for the public dollar (or quarter or fifty-cent piece) was ruthless. Nationally it was a time of confusion and corruption. Ulysses S. Grant spent eight years presiding over a South floundering with reconstruction, a North riddled with the corruption of the spoils system. In the large eastern financial centers the world belonged to the Vanderbilts and the Jay Goulds. The very rich were getting very much richer and the poor be damned, while in the West the Indians and the buffalo were still getting it good and proper. For a nation bedded in the Puritan ethic, the spectacle was a sorry one, and baseball, as Lee Allen notes, offered in miniature a replica of the stained national portrait.

Much has been written about the nature of the public performer, and baseball players are public performers just as surely as are, say, actors and musicians. An athlete faces a unique problem, one shared by many in the entertainment field or by those who depend for their performance upon youth. Theirs is the short, happy life. More often than not they have lived out the most exciting part of it long before they reach forty and the rest is anticlimax. It is a problem not shared by those in careers that do not depend upon the physical agility and stamina of youth, or, in the case of motion-picture stars, upon youth's purported physical allure. In baseball it is a problem faced even by the game's very greatest players, and with them perhaps it is most acute of all because of the very brilliance of the careers they left behind. Most have a desire to remain a part of the game even though in a minor capacity. Rogers Hornsby, perhaps the greatest right-handed hitter in the history of baseball, happily accepted a job as a Chicago scout for the New York Mets at the age of sixty-five. "I've never been a scout before," he wrote, "but it keeps me close to the game I love. With the Cubs and White Sox in Chicago there's a game almost every day. And I'm back at the ball park every day—where I feel I've always belonged."

Yet coaching and scouting jobs are relatively few, and unless a retired player is lucky enough to land one—or one of the relatively far fewer managerial or executive jobs—he must spend his declining years in a business which in most cases cannot fail to strike him as far less glamorous than the game he played in his physical prime. He may be excused for feeling that he has had the best of his life and must now merely watch the younger men do what he is no longer capable of doing. The problem, largely a psychological one, of course, is one that a faded star must have strength of character to overcome, even today.. In those faroff days of the nineteenth century, when passions were more unbridled, education scant, and self-awareness hardly widespread, the problem must have been infinitely greater.

The unique nature of the problem as it relates to baseball players is noted by no less (and perhaps no less likely) a personage than the eminent composer of military marches, John Philip Sousa, who wrote for *Baseball Magazine* in 1909: "If baseball has a drawback, it is the early time of life at which the player is forced to retire and give way to younger blood. . . . The only thing that 99 per cent or more of the players have left of their individual connection with the game after they have passed their fortieth year is a happy memory of what used to be."

In his book *100 Years of Baseball,* Lee Allen states: "It has often been alleged that these early players were of the worst possible type and though there were notable exceptions the charge is generally true. . . . It must be remembered that many were alcoholics. Baseball was and is a perishable business. Conditioned as they were to good money and high living, they could not adjust to life after their skills were exhausted."

Records show that one of the early players was shot to death during a lynching attempt at Glens Falls, New York, after being accused of murdering a little girl. Another served a penitentiary term for arson after setting fire to a hotel in Pennsylvania. Another was arrested for highway robbery.

There were many who did not wait for retirement to demonstrate their venality. The so-called Players League made little effort to police itself. During its five-year life span its players apparently were free to show up loaded at game time and to traffic with gamblers almost as they chose. With their gambling spoils they lived high, Lee Allen writes, traveling "from city to city like princes, drinking champagne . . . every night, sporting diamonds and peeling off bills from huge wads of money."

Both the gamblers and players were in step with their times. Their profits were minuscule compared with the huge chunks being gouged from the public revenue by the big-time mulcters in Washington.

The Players League lasted five years. In its final season, thirteen clubs entered the field but only seven played out the schedule and it seems hardly an exaggeration to say that it was quite simply because the players were too drunk to play.

Little lamented unless by the gamblers, the Players League folded after the 1875 season. The following year, 1876, was notable in a number of respects. It was the year the catcher's mask was invented, although for a long while catchers refused to use it, finding it either cumbersome, unmanly, or both. It was the year the Republicans nominated Rutherford B. Hayes to succeed Grant. It was the year Custer and his men were annihilated by the Sioux. And it was the year the National League was founded, no doubt by coincidence exactly a hundred years after the founding of the United States of America. The National League would totter. Its executives would do their utmost to kill it, and to kill baseball. But it would survive, even as it survives today, marking in 1969 its ninety-fourth season of continuous service to a nation either grateful or oblivious, as the case may be.

In 1876 the mandate of the National League was clear: Get rid of the drunks. Get rid of the gamblers. Clean up baseball. To this end, it selected a man of stature as its first president, Morgan G. Bulkeley, later Governor of Connecticut and still later a member of the Spalding commission on the origin of baseball. He was succeeded the following year by William A. Hulbert, who, soon after taking office, struck a decisive blow for clean baseball by expelling four Louisville players for life after they were found guilty of taking bribes to throw games.

Casting about for other means of livelihood, two of the four became cops.

After twenty-five years baseball finally solved its organizational problems, but only after prolonged and bitter warfare during which the National League was assaulted time and again by those hoping to strip away its power and end the monopoly which its owners tried with all their granite hearts to maintain. The game itself produced some memorable players during that period—Cap Anson, Hoss Radbourn, Ed Delehanty, Bobby Lowe, Hugh Jennings, Wee Willie Keeler, John McGraw, and one with the memorable name of Orvall Overall —and it produced the game's first colorful executive, Chris von der Ahe.

For a panoramic view of the era, however, it might be interesting to review a study made by one Allen Sangree, a sportswriter, who saw the quarter century in terms of Five Wars, which he enumerated as follows:

1. War of the American Association.
2. War of the Union Association.
3. Revolt of the Baseball Brotherhood.
4. Second War of the American Association.
5. War of the American League.

Mr. Sangree's study was published in the August 1911 issue of *Baseball Magazine,* which gave the article, and Sangree himself, the sort of advance billing any writer might envy: "This is one of the grandest themes which has ever occupied the pen of a sporting writer and Mr. Sangree has given it full justice. His vivid sparkling style brings scenes to the eye clearcut as a picture in their terrible distinctness, fired with dramatic power. . . . A great story written in a great style by a great writer."

Mr. Sangree tells his story as perhaps no one else might have, before or since. He begins: "The grandest sport that ever inspired the human race with a broader vision of the boundless pleasures of life was not evolved in ease and luxury. Good things never are. The primal curse of Adam has rested too long on the face of the earth and her treasures are torn from her unyielding bosom only with unceasing toil."

That much out of the way, Sangree notes that one reason the game was slow in developing was the shyness of investors: "A new world in sport stretched before these old-time investors just as the new world lay far off beyond the sunset in the age of Columbus and his Spanish galleons but the prospective magnates were as timid as the courtiers of the ancient king. The progress of baseball was necessarily slow but it grew faster than its warmest friends had any right to expect. Then when it was scarcely out of the era of mere experiment it was plunged into a series of disastrous and wasting wars. . . .

"Envy and jealousy and selfishness, bitter and lasting, combined with the black shadow of treachery, were ever ready to light like a pestilence on the bloom of prosperity at the moment it seemed on the point of blossoming into full and complete success.

"Club after club was sacrificed to selfishness and narrow-mindedness. League after league began in the dawn of promise and struggled through a clouded noonday of partial success only to go down forever in the darkness of blasted hopes into the gulf of ruin which yawned pitilessly beneath. . . .

"The pages of baseball history have been rent and torn and blackened by strife. They present a picture which is unlovely to the eye, a picture of elemental passions turned loose, passions stalking like firm shadows against the flaring background of avarice and greed which raged throughout like a consuming fire. And yet the National Game was destined to emerge from its period of stress and strife stronger and deeper-rooted and more powerful than ever, a lasting tribute to the undying zeal for clean uplifting sport which is so much a fundamental demand of the American people.

"It has developed like one of those beautiful blossoms which unfold a world of fragrance and loveliness from the slimy depths of stagnant pools where all else is dismal and forbidding."

Without even flagging, Sangree goes on:

"Slowly and powerfully the germ of the great National Game began to expand. Finally it blossomed out in a genuine tangible organization, the old National League. The history of this league is a checkered one. Sometimes it was a 12-club league, then contracted into eight clubs, then expanded to 12 again and so on. . . ."

Once the haughty National League was firmly established, it became a fit target for those who wanted a slice of the action, Sangree says in effect, and then continues:

"There were too many brainy, energetic men outside the mystic circle who were willing to dare all things to break in. For these dauntless spirits the [National League] loomed up like some feudal castle with its donjon keep and its battlemented towers. Around its moated fastnesses they gathered— predatory magnates like plumed and helmeted robber barons in the old days. They knew that within those forbidding walls were stored all the treasures of their desires and they were ready and anxious to stretch every nerve in their attainment.

"Time and again they watched the sun of seeming prosperity gild those battlemented towers but when the fury of the conflict had passed they crept away through the tangled shrubbery of the low-lying hills and watched that same sun descending with the wrecks of their hopes beyond the black mountains of failure and disappointment. The National League, just like a stout old castle, had endured so many sieges that it came to be looked upon as impregnable."

Bringing his article up to date, Sangree states:

"The arrogant message which Alexander the Great sent to the prime potentate of the tottering Persian Empire that there could not be two suns in Heaven has been refuted, for in the baseball sky of the present, two luminaries of equal importance preside over the destinies of the National Game."

One sun was the American League, for after winning clearcut victories in the first four wars, the National League would surrender in the fifth, and baseball—quite deservedly in Sangree's opinion—would finally become the "world of fragrance and loveliness" which some might say, it remains to this very day.

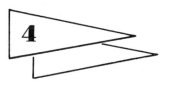

"Ve Lick der Stuffings out of Every Team in Baseball"

IN THE LIFE OF ORGANIZED BASEBALL, THE YEARS BEFORE 1900 may be viewed as a period of growing up, a time of experiment, of trial and error. Not only was it necessary to deal with the drunks and gamblers, but to experiment with the balance of power between pitcher and batter and see to it that the game was as sound and as workable as rule changes could make it. It was a period when—and none too soon—the poor umpire began to receive some measure of respect, and when the players were put in their places—which, in a legal sense, have always been and today remain the places of peons, however handsomely paid they may be.

In this sense, then, it was a time of preparation for the greater glory to come, and yet the years before 1900 produced some of the game's legendary figures, and in some cities the fans may never have had so much fun before or since.

Although Sangree saw it as a period "rent and torn and blackened by strife," and although the league structure before 1900 may appear to have been a jumble, once one gets past the old Players League's brief existence from 1871 to 1875, there have been only three major leagues in all baseball history that ever really mattered—the National, the American, and, for one brief, gaudy decade, the American Association.

For a full ten years the American Association vied with the National League on equal footing, and if in the end it lost the battle, the Association had a lot of fun and so, from all indications, did the populace.

The National League, confronted as it undeniably was with grave excesses when it was formed in 1876, took extreme measures to correct them. For widespread sin, it sought to substitute total rectitude. It decreed no gambling, no liquor or beer sold on the premises, no Sunday baseball. Fun was fun, but, on the other hand, baseball was baseball.

Perhaps fittingly, the National League's foremost player during much of its staid early history was one Adrian Constantine Anson, an upright and undeniably efficient young man who submitted to the nickname "Cap" for the understandable reason that for many years he was captain of the old Chicago White Stockings as well as their star first baseman and heaviest hitter. Anson was born in a log cabin in Iowa to a father "who himself was no mean knight of the sphere." He was, even for his time, an extreme racist, refusing even to appear on the same field with Negro players, of whom in that era there were almost none. In a class struggle between owners and players, he sided with the owners. He is also the author of a book in which he described a train trip he and other players took with their wives after the season of 1888:

"As we sailed along through the gathering darkness, over bridges and culverts and by stations that seemed like phantoms in the dim light, the song of the rail became monotonous in our ears and we turned for recreation to cards. . . . As the ladies in the party had given the boys permission to smoke where and when they pleased, the blue veil that hung over the various tables was soon thick enough to cut with a knife. A mandolin and guitar in the party added to our enjoyment and it was not until the midnight hour had come and gone that we sought our couches."

Although from time to time before 1900 innumerable cities in the East and Midwest were represented in the so-called major leagues, there were only a few teams that made any great impact on baseball history, among them Boston, Providence, the old St. Louis Browns, and the swashbuckling Baltimore Orioles. Another was Anson's team, the White Stockings, who in the National League's first eleven years won six pennants.

In those early years, just as other National League teams found it hard to match the brand of baseball being played by the upright Anson's White Stockings, so too did they have their troubles with the staid league fathers. In its first three years of operation, the National League lost ball clubs right and left, either by expulsion for misconduct or by withdrawal because they could not measure up to the exacting moral code prescribed for them.

The Philadelphia Athletics were kicked out after one season for failing to play out their schedule, and so were the New York Mutuals. Louisville quit after it lost the four players who were expelled from organized baseball for accepting bribes. St. Louis dropped out after two seasons, and Cincinnati was ousted after the 1880 season because it insisted on selling beer in the ball park. The latter three, being river-town clubs, acted just as the National League fathers might have predicted.

The National League, through its sheer virtue—understandable and necessary as a flight to virtue may have been—left a huge entertainment vacuum that the American Association moved gleefully to fill. In 1882, taking its stand in the heavily Germanic Midwest and using the three river-town teams as a nucleus, the Association opened up an eight-club circuit which the National League owners contemptuously dubbed "the beer and whiskey league," a nickname that Association club owners might have been excused for embracing with chortles of gratitude. They did their utmost to live up to it, and in the process they even served up good baseball.

In the years to come, indeed well into the 1900's, Sunday baseball was a subject of fervid argument. Magazines became forums in which fans and nonfans helped decide whether Sunday ball was a profanation of the Lord's Day or a blessing for a laboring class subjected to a work week which by today's standard, or any standard, was onerous.

To Chris von der Ahe and the other American Association club owners, the answer seemed simple: play ball on Sunday. Not only did the Association play Sunday ball, but its owners cut prices to twenty-five cents, although the National League was still charging fifty. They dressed their players in colors as vivid and varied as jockey silks. The sale of beer at the ball park was not only permitted, it was cheerfully encouraged, to such an extent that many of the league's ball parks must have resembled spacious beer gardens.

No fewer than three of the eight teams were owned by men who had made their money in the beer or whiskey business, von der Ahe being one and Harry von der Horst, owner of the Baltimore club, being another. The two men had more in common than the similarity of their names. Both they and the other Association owners were dedicated to the belief that baseball, to be profitable, should be fun, a belief that would be embraced with pleasure and profit some seventy years later by

Bill Veeck, who would be viewed in his day with the same disdain directed at the upstart owners in the old American Association.

Chris von der Ahe was owner of the St. Louis Browns. His life, with its colorful highs and its devastating lows, might well provide inspiration for tragicomic opera. A German immigrant, he settled in St. Louis, made a career for himself in beer and whiskey, and then invested his profits in a baseball club. For a time his team prospered, both on the field and at the turnstile, but by the end of the century he was broke and disgraced.

What manner of man Chris was seems to be a matter of debate. In some accounts he emerges as a lovable buffoon, the Happy Immigrant, guileless, naïve, open-hearted and open-handed. Among some of his contemporaries he may indeed have been regarded with affection, the sort of affection with which an audience regards a clown, a sober man the drunk, or a native the quaint foreigner. Facially, he fit the picture of a clown. His nose, we are told, was huge, red, and shaped like a turnip. He favored loud checkered suits and habitually wore the sort of flattened derby associated with burlesque comedians. His heavy German accent alone was apparently enough to fracture many of his contemporaries as well as a few of his biographers.

In no particular order, von der Ahe's consuming interests were baseball, money, whiskey, and women. Baseball at first was incidental. Among other enterprises, he owned a saloon and boarding house adjacent to the St. Louis ball park and he could not help noticing that baseball fans, both before and after the game, drank a lot of beer at his bar. Putting two and two together, Chris decided that baseball and beer might make splendid running mates. At first he was content to buy the beer concession at the ball park, and then he bought the ball club itself.

Although at first his interest in owning the club may have been largely economic, von der Ahe, like many other owners since, quickly found himself caught up with the team and the game. In the parlance of psychiatry, he identified mightily. He fell in love with baseball, with the St. Louis Browns, and, there is evidence to believe, with Chris von der Ahe.

So great must it all have seemed, and such a marvelous pageant, that von der Ahe added pageantry of his own. Over the Golden Lion saloon in St. Louis he ran up a golden ball inscribed "Game Today," or, if there was no game, a flag so informing the patrons, according to historian Harold Seymour. He took full-page advertisements in the newspapers proclaiming: "The Browns Are Here! The Hardest Hitters, the Finest Fielders, the Best Base Runners, the Coming Champions!"

In the days when the Browns were the class of the league, he often accompanied the players on their road trips. Arriving at their destination, the team walked single file all the way from the depot to their hotel, a bit of theatricality thought up by von der Ahe and one which he undoubtedly regarded as a recurrent victory parade. In Chris's order of march, he quite naturally was at the head of the line, being, as he called himself, "der Boss President of der Prowns." (As later quoted, his pronunciation is reminiscent of nothing so much as the long-running comic strip, *The Katzenjammer Kids*.) Following him in the line of march was none other than Charles Comiskey, who later went on to establish a dynasty with the White Sox in Chicago. Another of those marching was one Tip O'Neill, an outfielder who, in 1887, recorded the fantastic batting average of .492. (It should be noted that in 1887 walks counted as base hits, and a batter was allowed four strikes.)

Still another in the line of march was Arlie Latham, the team's third baseman, whom, we are told, Chris invariably referred to as "Latams," and who, being a noted prankster, delighted in putting Chris on. According to one account, Latham bought a fake nose closely resembling von der Ahe's real nose and also bought the sort of flattened derby that Chris wore. On the way from the depot, he would attach the nose, jam on the derby, and march behind the boss, imitating his walk. Von der Ahe was at a loss to understand the laughter of the crowd—

mystified as well as hurt, expecting not merriment but the respect he felt was the team's due.

"Vy do dey laugh at us?" he would ask Manager Comiskey. "Ve ain't funny! Ve lick der stuffiings out of every team in baseball!"

And so for four years in a row the Browns did indeed lick the stuffing out of their rivals, winning four pennants in a row under Comiskey, beginning in 1885 and ending in 1888. Even though sneered at by the National League, the American Association did not go unrecognized, and during these years there was a World Series of sorts. In the Series of 1885 the Browns tied Cap Anson's Chicago White Stockings, winners of the National League pennant, and the next year they beat the same White Stockings, becoming thereby the champions of the world. There seems little doubt that von der Ahe, in his glee, regarded it as a victory for the forces of drink over those of temperance. After the Series he handed over his entire profit, nearly $15,000, to the team. In 1888, when the Browns again won the pennant (but lost the Series to the New York Giants), he spent $20,000 on lavish accommodations for the club, including a special train for the trip east to New York and new clothes for all the Browns and their guests.

It is easy to picture Chris sitting day after day at the ball park, his own best fan, guzzling beer beneath the brim of his flattened derby, watching his beloved Browns, a man bedazzled by the American scene and intensely proud that he was, by God, a *part* of the scene. Yet for all his delight with himself and his world, for all his lavish generosity, he was capable of remarkably petty behavior. Upon occasion he could be both autocrat and penny-pincher. In the mid 1880's he advertised a free ladies' day but when the women of St. Louis showed up at the ball park they found they had the choice of sitting free on the hard board seats of the bleachers or paying the customary twenty-five cents to sit in the grandstand. On another occasion he got himself in trouble with a St. Louis union because he hired nonunion bartenders and waiters at underscale wages. And he once fired a good Browns right-fielder named Frank Genins for taking a blasé attitude when a rival batter knocked the ball over the right-field fence, demanding to know why Genins did not "spring mit yourself against dot fence and howl and shake your fist as dot ball vent ofer?"

Even in his days of high profits and lush living, he was not above petty mistrust and suspicion. His suspicions could be absurdedly off target, and so, for that matter, could his boasts, one of the latter being that his ball park had "the largest infield in the world." He came to regard his fellow magnates as thieves and crooks, "porch-climbers and sand-baggers," whose special delight was to make life hard for the St. Louis Browns, even in such unlikely areas as the weather.

After a financially indifferent season, when many of his normally profitable Sunday games had been rained out, Chris showed up for the league meeting in a rage. He greeted his fellow club owners with a sullen nod, one account recalls, and before they went into executive session to prepare the next season's schedule, he put his gold watch and pocketbook in the hotel safe. When the meeting began, he arose and made the following remarks (largely purged of Katzenjammerisms):

"Gentlemen, I would call you by your right names and speak of you as robbers, but I would not for anything hurt any man's feelings—but I want to have the schedule arranged to give the Browns a little chance for an even break. I was no hog and all I want is the square deal. For instance, I do not insist on the Fourth of Chuly at my grounds, for the last Fourth they setted the park on fire mit cannon-crackers and I lose money putting out the blazes. And as for Decoration Day, anybody what wants it can have it. In St. Louis they never decorate the box office mit any silver, so let some other club enchoy the big occasion.

"Where I have a kick coming, gentlemen, is this: Last year you arranged that fool schedules so that the Browns lose no less than twenty-four days by rain—twenty-four days and seven of them Sundays the rain breaks up mein games. Now that is not right. I don't want the best of things but I do demand an even break. I want you to schedule a few of the rainy days for Chicago and Zinzinnati and not to give the Browns any more rainy days than you hand out to oder beebles."

With a hurt expression, Chris sat down, undoubtedly to guffaws.

The foregoing seems absurdly apocryphal, and yet the pages of baseball periodicals are liberally sprinkled with similar examples of the man's massive naïveté. Under the circumstances there is reason to wonder if Chris, particularly in those, his happy days, was not deliberately creating the role of Happy Immigrant for his fellow owners and the beer- and baseball-buying public.

Meanwhile, in the eastern sector of the distillery circuit, Baltimore was winning no pennants, but Harry von der Horst was making life gay for its fans, and they for him. The Baltimore ball park not only sold beer, it also had picnic tables and for those who brought their own horses there was plenty of stable space. Once the ball game was over, a band began to tune up and the Baltimore fans, as the evening wore on, could stay right there in the park to dine and dance or listen to the music.

There is some reason to believe that the ball players, even during the course of the game, may have been tempted by the camaraderie of the picnickers, for in 1889 we find a rule change stating that henceforth all players "must come in from the field and seat themselves on the players bench at the conclusion of their half in the field."

Although it was still a few years before the famous Baltimore bully-boys of the 1890's would mop up the baseball world, the Baltimore fans of 1885 already had a man to yell about—a man as remarkable in his day as John Unitas, Frank Robinson, and Brooks Robinson are in theirs.

He was Matthew Aloysius "Matches" Kilroy, a left-handed

pitcher who, in 1885, to the intense satisfaction of those in the beer garden, struck out 505 batters—a record that has never been approached since, not even by the peerless Sandy Koufax, who holds the modern record of 382. In the following year Kilroy won forty-six games and dropped twenty, a fantastic number of decisions by later standards, but not startling in 1886.

The year 1885 was a pitcher's year. By then most of the restrictions on pitching had been removed, and the result, according to Henry Chadwick, was a "pretty state of things." In his book *The Art of Pitching and Fielding*, published in 1889, Chadwick complains that in 1885 the pitcher had things very much his own way, "one result being the fact that the monotonous and uninteresting 'pitcher's games' prevailed to a greater extent than previously known in the history of the game." During the 1885 season, he attests, there were no fewer than twenty-eight no-hit games!

Anyone with a passing interest in today's sports pages will find Chadwick's lament familiar, for the 1968 season was also very much a pitcher's year, so much so that the fans yawned and looked the other way and the alarmed club owners set about once more to see what could be done. Before the 1969 season began, they had reduced the strike zone and lowered the pitcher's mound.

Over the years baseball has experimented time and again with the delicate ratio of superiority between pitcher and batter, a ratio even more important to the dynamics of the game than the distance between bases. The advantage has fluctuated from pitcher to batter and back, occasionally settling into a satisfactory balance only to go out of kilter again. A number of factors affect this balance, the size of the so-called strike zone being only one. Another, of course, is the distance the pitcher must throw the ball—the distance between pitcher's mound and batter's box. Others have been the restrictions placed on the pitcher's method of delivery and on what he may permissibly do to the cover of the ball—nick it, scar it, grease it, spit on it.

Still other factors—and these, of course, have nothing to do with the rules—are the pitcher's and the batter's skill.

By and large, baseball fans are not defensive-minded. Although they enjoy a pitchers' battle, the evidence is that they enjoy one only once in a while. The overwhelming preference has been for heavy hitting, powerful offensive displays—slugfests, as they are called. Whether a psychiatrist might make a national ethos of this is a matter of debate.

It is conceivable that baseball's quick spurt to popularity in the early days may have been the sheer volume of the scoring. In some quarters the pitcher was thought to be of little importance, his function being merely to serve up the ball and set the game in motion. This conception of the pitcher's role is supported by a look at the restrictions under which he was forced to operate.

Perhaps most importantly, he was prohibited from swinging his hand above waist level, which meant that he had to pitch underhand. He was forced, moreover, to throw the ball where the batter wanted it. He was compelled to throw to the strike zone but the batter could, without penalty, refuse to swing until he got exactly the pitch he wanted; no strikes were counted until he swung and missed.

Pitching rules for the 1875 season are spelled out in a booklet entitled *Dime Baseball Player*, published in 1876 and edited by the seldom-idle Henry Chadwick:

"The batsman, on taking his position, must call for either a '*high ball*,' a '*low ball*' or a '*fair ball*' and the umpire shall notify the pitcher to deliver the ball as required. . . . A high ball shall be one sent in above the waist of the batsman but not higher than his shoulders. A low ball shall be one sent in not lower than within one foot of the ground but not higher than his waist. A fair ball shall be one between the range of shoulder high and one foot from the ground. All the above must be *over the home base*."

In the late 1870's a rule change permitted the pitcher to throw overhand. For a while longer the batter could still dictate where he wanted the pitch—that is, high or low—but by the early 1880's this rule had also been changed. Beginning in 1881 the distance between pitcher and batter was set at fifty feet; for years it had been forty-five feet, but even at fifty the batter must have felt the pitcher was virtually staring down his throat. (In 1893 the distance was pegged at sixty feet, six inches, and it has remained thus to the present day.)

In the earlier days, forced to throw underhand, most pitchers threw a simple straight ball with very little on it, including speed. Discovery of the curve is generally credited to one William Arthur (Candy) Cummings, who has written that he hit upon it in 1863 while "a number of boys and myself were amusing ourselves by throwing clamshells, and watching them sail along through the air, turning now to the right and now to the left." Cummings later pitched in pro ball and although he and a few others apparently managed to put a wrinkle on the ball while throwing underhand, the great majority of pitchers were throwing straight stuff. According to the straight-shooting Cap Anson, speaking in 1902, "It was a much easier matter to hit the old straight underhand delivery with its straight ball . . . than to hit the swift, curved ball of today."

By the early 1880's, with most of the pitching restrictions lifted, there was a sharp turn in the balance of power. Not only was there Matthew Aloysius Kilroy's strike-out feat, there were the accomplishments of Charles (Old Hoss) Radbourn, another of the game's legendary figures. Hurling for Providence, Rhode Island, which for eight seasons was a member of the old National League, in 1883 Radbourn pitched to seventy-two decisions, winning forty-four and losing twenty-eight. The following year he improved this record, placing in the record book the remarkable statistic of sixty victories and twelve defeats.

In 1884 the World Series pitted Providence, the National League pennant winner, against the old New York Metropolitans, who had won the flag in the American Association, beating out von der Ahe's Browns. The Series was for the best three games out of five, but only the first three games were necessary. Pitching on successive days without rest, Old Hoss Radbourn won all three, sewing up the Series for Providence; he didn't walk a single batter and gave up a combined total of only three hits.

Though it may have been a gilded age for many pitchers, there were some who fared poorly, among them the unfortunate T. J. Mullane, who hurled for Cincinnati of the American Association in 1885. In May of that year, pitching against Brooklyn, Mullane had a 7–0 lead after seven innings. In the eighth, Brooklyn belted his ears back and won the game 8–7. A few days later, against Philadelphia, Mullane again was leading by a big score, when again in the late innings he got pasted and lost.

Baseball—even in the free-and-easy American Association —was still touchy on the subject of dishonesty, and when charges were made that Mullane had purposely blown both games in collusion with gamblers, the charges were given serious attention and a thorough investigation. As it turned out, they were traced to a disgruntled Cincinnati newspaperman who had been expelled from the ball park for disorderly conduct, and Mullane was cleared. His only sin had been to lose his stuff and get knocked from the box, an everyday occurrence throughout baseball history. Members of the pitching fraternity, past and present, might well rejoice that T. J. Mullane, in out-facing the charges, helped eliminate an occupational hazard which surely would have made the job of a pitcher too risky even to contemplate.

With all the problems besetting organized baseball in its early years—the venality, the corruption, the dynamics of the game—it is perhaps understandable that baseball was very slow in doing anything for the poor umpire. Less understandable is why in those days anyone would have wanted to be an umpire in the first place.

Psychiatry has had little traffic with baseball as a game;

there is apparently only meager symbolism to be noted. Considering the rough treatment accorded him, however, there is a strong temptation to view the umpire as Father. A psychiatric case is not difficult to make. The umpire is implacable in his authority. His rulebook, from which he can quote chapter and verse, is his Bible. He is in favor of law and order. He is impatient with dillydallying. He has the authority both to recommend fines and to oust from the premises. He permits no back talk, frowns on profanity, reacts violently and swiftly against tantrums, and is, moreover, the only person on the field wearing long pants.

Although psychologists, perhaps with reluctance, have left the mechanics of the game more or less alone, they have had something to say about fans. In 1950 Bill Veeck, then owner of the St. Louis Browns, hired Dr. David F. Tracy in the hope that his men might become better ball players through psychology. They didn't, but in a book summing up his experiences, Dr. Tracy had this to say about fans: "The world is full of people who want heroes to praise and villains to hiss. Without heroes and villains they'd be unhappy. . . . The baseball fanatic imagines that everyone who opposes his hero is a villain."

Tracy was referring to the opposing team, and there have indeed been notable instances of fans' wrath being vented upon visiting players. But far more often wrath has been turned upon the umpire, who seems a far better candidate for the role of villain.

In 1909 *Baseball Magazine* carried an article entitled "Rooters You Have Met" in which it criticized the fan who "takes his spite out on the poor umpire," noting: "He has a very select vocabulary for dealing with this individual. 'You big rummy!' he yells. 'Open your eyes! You oughter umpire for a blind school! Where did you get that glass eye! Get your lamps trimmed!' "

The same magazine published a poem by the illustrious sportswriter Grantland Rice entitled "A Tip to Teddy." Addressed to Theodore Roosevelt, then president, it suggested that when Teddy was ready to leave office and wanted new thrills to replace those of San Juan Hill and big-game hunting, he would do well to take up the challenge of umpiring a big-league baseball game:

That's the only job for you, take your tip now, Theodore
Think of how your pulse will leap when you hear the angry
    roar
Of the bleacher gods in rage, you will find the action there
Which you've hunted for in vain, in the Presidential chair.
Chasing mountain lions and such, catching grizzlies will seem
    tame
Lined up with the jolt you'll get in the thick of some close
    game.
Choking angry wolves to death as a sport will stack up raw
When you see Kid Elberfeld swinging for your under-jaw,
When you hear Hugh Jennings roar, 'Call them strikes, you
    lump of cheese!'
Or McGraw comes rushing in, kicking at your shins and knees.

Even though the umpire's lot had somewhat improved since earlier days, the magazine still saw fit to editorialize about the practice of "yelling at the umpire."

"How ignoble," the editorial ranted, "to take a hand in the abuse of that individual, and call him a robber, a thief, or some other opprobrious epithet! Those that stoop to such practices ought to be speedily removed from the field."

To an umpire of the 1870's, 1880's, and even the 1890's, the epithets causing concern in 1909 surely would have seemed mild. In those early days, reviling the umpire gave many of the fans more pleasure than the game itself. They sat waiting for a suitable provocation and when it came, as it usually did, they worked themselves up to a frothing, stomping rage and often came slavering from the stands down onto the field, not unlike a bunch of Indians peeling off over the brow of a hill after working themselves up with war dance and fire water.

Now and then an umpire would strike back. In an exhibition game at Chattanooga in 1889 a certain Umpire Magill picked up a bat and fractured a fan's skull when the abuse became intolerable, but for the most part it was the umpire who was on the receiving end, earning his pittance in durance vile, often at the risk of limb and even of life. He worked alone, responsible not only for calling balls and strikes but for rulings on the base paths as well as fair-foul decisions affecting the outermost reaches of the ball park. It was not until after 1900 that the two-umpire system was begun. It had been suggested earlier but rejected by the owners as unnecessarily expensive.

What it was like to be an umpire in the early days can be judged by the reminiscences of James Johnstone, a National League umpire around the turn of the century. In an article entitled "Mobbing the Umpire" he recalled a game played in Louisville. It was a crucial game, the fans' nerves were tingling, and unusual precautions were taken, although whether for his personal safety or for his successful prosecution, he does not make entirely clear. Before Johnstone was even allowed to enter the ball park that day he was searched by the local police, for what weapons he does not say.

"A patrol wagon was driven inside the grounds," he recounts, "and I was given to understand that if there was any trouble, the conveyance would be for my special benefit."

Trouble was not long in coming, in the form of a close play at first base. Johnstone ruled the runner out, a decision that went against the home team. The Louisville manager headed for first base in rage. On cue, the fans poured out of the stands. Johnstone and the Louisville manager stood chin to chin. Egged on by the fans, the manager moved to the attack.

"He gave me a violent shove," Johnstone recalled, "I fell heavily on my right hand, injuring myself severely. In a jiffy I was put into the patrol wagon and driven to the jail. I must admit that I felt rather down-in-the-mouth.

"The crowd swarmed to the jail and made some little racket. Word was passed around that they were going to lynch the umpire, but I felt no uneasiness."

Omitting to explain why he felt no uneasiness, Umpire Johnstone goes on to say that about six o'clock that evening he was turned loose, whereupon he sneaked off to the local telegraph office and wired league headquarters that he was forfeiting the game to the visiting team on grounds that he had been refused police protection, even though it might appear that he had been given a reasonable amount.

"Here another hitch came up. The telegraph operator made public the contents of my message."

Word quickly got around, and the effect on the Louisville fans may be well imagined. By this time Johnstone had taken refuge in his hotel room, and none too soon, for he had been there only a few minutes when the president of the Louisville club and the still-irate manager "came to the hotel and told me I would have to go back to jail—for inciting a riot. The cloud loomed up pretty black, I tell you."

Avoiding his persecutors, Johnstone waited until dark and slipped out of town by rail, with no further damage except to his nerves. For his day's work, including the thrills and chills, he was paid $5.00, the customary fee per game for many years. In addition, according to the *Reach Baseball Guide* for 1883, he was entitled to the following expense money:

"Each regular and substitute umpire shall be allowed all legitimate hotel and traveling expenses while on active duty, viz: Railroad fares, sleeping car fares, price of station meals, omnibus tickets to and from depots and hotel bills not to exceed three dollars per day."

Umpire Johnstone and his fellow arbiters might well have looked back "through the mists of memory" and gazed with envy upon the umpire who stood in dignified ease along the first-base line, wearing his shiny silk hat and resting one foot on the stool so thoughtfully provided for his greater comfort and insouciance.

A union might also have been of help, but it was not until

1968, after ninety-nine seasons of professional baseball, that umpires would make any serious attempt to organize.

The players tried much earlier, but might as well not have bothered, for all the good it did them.

In Mr. Sangree's catalogue of baseball wars, the second is listed as the War of the Union League, which was quickly over. In 1884 the Union League operated in effect as a third major league, challenging the National League and the American Association for the customers' favor. The public demonstrated, as it would demonstrate in the years to come, that three major leagues were too many, and the Union League folded after one season, never to be heard from again.

The third war, however, would be of much greater importance. It would involve a massive revolt by the players themselves. It would arouse fury and fear among the club owners and even cries of bolshevism. Its effect on baseball history would be far-reaching. The National League would put down the revolt and then, with a discreet whoop and holler, would kill the old American Association as well.

As Sangree recorded, after a decade of being warmed by the "sun of seeming prosperity," Chris von der Ahe and his fellow owners would now creep away "through the tangled shrubbery of the low-lying hills and watch that same sun descending with the wrecks of their hopes beyond the black mountains of failure and disappointment."

And von der Ahe himself would be kidnaped from Missouri, spirited into Pennsylvania and thrown into an Allegheny County jail.

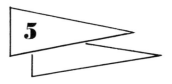

Order out of Chaos

WILLIE MAYS, THE ILLUSTRIOUS CENTER-FIELDER OF THE SAN Francisco Giants, received as high as $125,000 a year for playing baseball. Mickey Mantle, last of a dynasty, last of the great Yankees, received $100,000 a year even after his knees buckled and he played only part time.

Yet Willie and Mickey were peons.

Don Drysdale, a peon known in the sports world as a tireless right-handed pitcher, toils approximately every fourth day during the six-month season for the Los Angeles Dodgers and for this toil he receives about $100,000 a year. Peon Drysdale drives expensive sports cars and consorts with a Hollywood, California, element often described as swinging.

Carl Yastrzemski was raised to $100,000 a year by the Red Sox largely because in 1967 he won the American League batting championship, along with the home-run and runs-batted-in championships, leading the Red Sox to a pennant. In 1968 he won the batting championship again, this time with a mark of .301, the lowest winning average in the history of baseball.

Yastrzemski, Frank Robinson, Hank Aaron, Dennis McLain, Frank Howard—all in supersalary brackets, yet all peons, as every player in organized baseball throughout the game's history has been, except for a brief period at the very beginning and a brief interlude in 1890, the year the players rose up in revolt.

It is hard to feel sorry for them, and it seems unlikely that they feel sorry for themselves—yet from time to time throughout the game's history someone cuts loose with a blast against baseball for giving America something so un-American as a peonage system.

In doing so, the game's critics are on strong legal and economic ground. Ball players are in effect paid slaves. Unlike the rest of American wage earners they cannot move about freely in the labor market and sell their services to the highest bidder. They must play for the club that holds their contract or they do not play at all. They may not switch teams unless, at the owner's discretion, they are traded. Their salary is the salary they are able to wangle from the owner. In no other branch of American industry is this true, and what it means is that baseball players, no matter how enviously one may view their high wages and short hours, are in the legal sense owned for the duration of their baseball career.

The source of ownership is something called the "reserve clause," and in the power structure of organized baseball there is no weapon so valuable—nor indeed so essential to the preservation of baseball as the nation has known it.

As far back as the late 1870's—very soon after the National League was formed—club owners found to their dismay that players' salaries could be a most expensive item. What made them so was competition—players were selling their talents to the owner willing to pay most for them. To kill competition the owners agreed among themselves that after each season an owner was entitled to "reserve" the right to rehire a given number of players for the following season. These players were in effect his property and, by agreement, no other club

Connie Mack managed the Philadelphia Athletics for half a century, directing a cavalcade of brilliant players, winning nine pennants, and trying almost twenty years for a tenth—which never came.

Connie Mack and John McGraw, the two Irishmen who so excelled at managing baseball teams, pictured during the 1911 World Series in which Connie bested McGraw in a battle of wits.

Walter Johnson, a gentle, modest man whose smoking fast ball paralyzed American League batters for years.

Eddie Collins, a brainy, speedy, all-round performer, one of the 1919 White Sox players untainted by the Black Sox scandal.

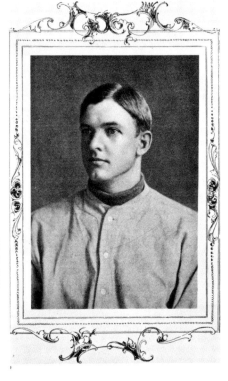

Christy Mathewson, gentleman and pitcher, for years the idol of New York and the nation. Gassed while in training for World War I, he died young of tuberculosis.

Napoleon Lajoie, a bad-ball hitter whose peak batting average of .422 was unequaled even by Ty Cobb.

Napoleon Lajoie in the winner's circle with a horseshoe made of silver dollars bestowed by grateful fans.

The young John McGraw, who later would write: "With my team I am an absolute czar. My men know it. I order plays and they obey. If they don't, I fine them."

Lajoie and Cobb in the tonneau of a snappy Chalmers touring car. In 1910, when Cobb beat out Lajoie for the batting title by a mere seven-tenths of a point, the Chalmers company gave each man a car as a sort of unofficial Most Valuable Player award.

Joe Jackson could neither read nor write but he was perhaps the best natural hitter in the history of baseball. It was his misfortune to be competing in his peak years with Ty Cobb. "What a hell of a league this is," he once moaned to Cobb. "Ah hit .387, .408, and .395 the last three years and Ah ain't won nothin' *yet!*" Jackson ruined his career by taking a bribe in the Black Sox scandal.

Christy Mathewson excelled not only in baseball but in football and checkers. Here he vanquishes the checker champion of Indiana, while the champion of Ohio awaits his turn.

When Rube Waddell died, *Literary Digest* called him
"one of those characters, at once the most enviable
and the saddest in the world, who are too great at
heart for the civilization in which they live."

Rube Waddell, incorrigible eccentric and
sterling southpaw who pitched for Los
Angeles in 1902 before joining the Athletics the same year. He loved baseball but
might have been just as happy as a bartender or fireman. He once pitched and
won both ends of a doubleheader and then
turned cartwheels all the way to the clubhouse.

For Ty Cobb, generally considered the greatest player in history, there was no substitute for winning.

In the view of some, Ty Cobb was a cruel, hostile man who spiked infielders for the pleasure of it. "I may have been fierce," he wrote, "but never low or underhand."

owner might hire or even approach them.

The number of "reserved" players originally was five. Over the years it grew and today the reserve clause covers each club's basic squad of twenty-five men, plus an additional fifteen, a total of forty in all. These men are owned.

The reserve clause is clearly a restraint upon individual freedom. By condoning monopoly, it clearly violates the antitrust act. Yet it has never been upset in the courts, and although Congress has done some probing from time to time it has always seen fit to let baseball alone.

In defense of the reserve clause, one may picture the alternative, something that club owners never tire of asking the courts and the public to picture. If, they say, the players were free to sell themselves to the highest bidder, the club with the most money would own the best players. League standings would be highly predictable—they would correspond in descending order with the size of bank accounts. One or two teams would dominate all the rest, and instead of seeing competition the public would see nothing but an exhibition.

It is tempting to note that the New York Yankee dynasty dominated baseball for the better part of four decades, reserve clause or no, and it is also worth observing that wealth alone does not guarantee pennants. Yet it does seem likely, as the owners contend, that if the reserve clause were outlawed and all the peons went free, baseball as we have known it would be finished, and from all indications there are many in the country who would view its demise with regret.

Hatred of the reserve clause helped fire the player revolt of 1890. Other provocations were unique not so much to baseball as to the era, for it was a time when management in all branches of industry could be merciless without attracting a great deal of attention. The owners of baseball clubs probably were no more and no less oppressive than owners in general.

From the viewpoint of the players, one of the most cruel offenses was the so-called blacklist. A player blacklisted by one owner automatically was blacklisted by all and hence, during the period of his disesteem, had no way of earning his living. He could be blacklisted for any one of a number of misdemeanors in the areas of insubordination and moral turpitude, and owners were not above shadowing the players with private detectives to get the goods on them, whatever the goods might happen to be.

There was also an attempt to place a top limit of $2,000 a year on player salaries and for a time the limitation was nominally in effect, agreed to by the owners in solemn conclave. The owners themselves, however, made a mockery of the rule, and knaves of themselves, by slipping additional money under the table to players of high ability.

More irksome than oppressive was the attitude of the owners toward the use they could make of a player's time. Utility players were commonly put to work taking tickets at the gate and sometimes were even obliged to help sweep up after the game.

Perhaps the most insulting of all management brainstorms was a salary-classification plan devised by John T. Brush, who in the early 1900's was to become owner of the New York Giants. Under this plan, a player's salary was equated with his grade—A, B, C, D, or E. What grade he was given depended to some extent upon his playing ability but also upon his deportment and general attitude. Players who received A's qualified for the top salary of $2,500 a year. Those who got as low as E had to be content with $1,500. If an E player mended his ways and earnestly tried to be a good boy, he might win a higher grade.

It may be worth noting that in this period of its history the United States was far more class-conscious than it ever has been since. Privileges of wealth, birth, and education were claimed without question and pursued and expressed in ways that today seem revolting or laughable, or both.

There was indeed a gulf between the owner class and the laboring class, and most owners of the time were determined to keep that gulf wide and deep. By tradition and custom, they felt totally justified. Their attitude was hardly paternal, as it lacked the benevolence associated with paternalism. It was more as if they were dealing with a class of primitive, coarse beings from a world their parents had warned them about. Baseball-club owners were not without justification in this view of their underlings.

In H. C. Palmer's *Stories of the Baseball Field,* published in 1890, we find this attempt to describe the nature of a baseball player: "As a rule there is little of the serious in a ball player's makeup. . . . Being engaged in a business that is really a pastime and unquestionably a pleasure, there is small wonder that the life of the average professional ball player is full of good things; that his spirits are almost continually effervescing in practical jokes and clever stories; that humor with him is in the ascendancy and that each season is prolific of laughable incidents."

This was one view, and if it is not apocryphal it is surely antiseptic. Ball players of the era may have been jolly, but they were also for the most part abysmally educated, and there were still many drunkards. The fact that they were on the road a great deal, away from their families, made it easy for them to indulge in hanky-panky. And they were as superstitious as the most primitive tribesmen. Even today ball players are notoriously superstitious and will take the most bizarre means to end a batting slump, for example. At one time, when clubs traveled by train and often by bus, passing a wagonload of hay was considered just about the most fortunate thing that could happen. If a player happened to be in a slump he was sure to break out of it that very afternoon. Today, in the taxi from air terminal to hotel, a player is unlikely to overtake a hay wagon so he must get along as best he can, contenting himself with knocking on wood, refusing to step on a crack, and making sure that no one steals his favorite bat. In the days before 1900 the players had a broad range of fetishes and phobias. Among the latter, the most certain harbinger of doom was seeing someone with eye trouble—a man with one eye or with a wall-eye or an artificial eye. The game was as good as lost, and at the sight of such a man the players reacted in the manner of a Transylvanian peasant who sees Count Dracula chancing by at twilight. Some indeed may have quickly made the sign of the cross. Perhaps others went off in search of a hay wagon.

When Karl Marx called on the workers of the world to unite, it is unlikely he had in mind a laboring class wearing knickerbockers and peaked caps and earning a living by swatting a small white ball. Yet the player revolt was a genuine head-on clash of labor and capitalism, and the players departed from classic lines only in that they took on other capitalists as partners, principally as financial backers and advisers.

After muttering at first with bewilderment and then with anger throughout the 1880's, by the end of the decade the players were ready to make their move. In 1890 they put teams on the field in eight cities, calling their organization the Players League and competing smack-up against the National League and the American Association, both of which continued operating with the largely ragtag collection of performers left to them.

The Players League had widespread public sympathy, it had most of the good ball players, and it might have succeeded. One strong reason for its failure was that the players started squabbling not only among themselves but with their backers. Another was inexperience. A third was the entrenched administrative strength of the National League, which had the sort of "solidarity" that Marx recommended for the proletariat. Finally, three leagues meant that there was just too much baseball for the public to swallow.

The *Reach Guide* intoned that the season of 1890 "will go down in the annals of professional baseball as the most disastrous in the history of the game in America." Of the twenty-four major-league teams on the field that year very few even managed to clear expenses, and most took enormous losses. Among Players League teams, the average attendance per game in Cleveland was 927, and in Buffalo, 942. In the National League average attendance in New York was 919; Cleveland, 668; and in Pittsburgh a miserable 411. And in many parks the price of admission was still only twenty-five cents a head.

With cool acumen (and the financial reserves to absorb its own losses), the National League sat back and waited for signs of weakness, watching the cripples fall one by one, sometimes giving them a little shove. At the end of the season the Players League was dead.

During the 1880's the National League and the American Association had co-existed, not amicably but with a sort of wary equilibrium that on the National League's part was highly grudging. By and large, each league respected the other's player contracts and territorial rights, and they also of course vied in the World Series. The rise and fall of the Players League upset the status quo and things were never the same again.

Some owners doubtless would have liked nothing better than to take all the insurrectionist players and put them on a perpetual blacklist, but this would have presented a major problem: it would have left nobody worth mentioning to play baseball.

In this spirit of forgiveness, the owners agreed that in the main the players were to return to the clubs that owned them as of the end of the 1889 season. A great many players were involved and the reshuffling process was far from orderly. Very quickly it became cutthroat. After some preliminary filching and counterfilching, the National League and the American Association gave up all pretense of decency and began stealing each other's players left and right. Inevitably, the two leagues spent the 1891 season in open battle. Payrolls were at an all-time high, mainly because the clubs of both leagues

had engaged in a wild bidding match for the available players. Attendance again was low, partly because the public was
disgusted with the way baseball no longer seemed to be a
game played on the field but an economic battle royal waged
furtively and greedily behind closed doors.

After the financially ruinous season of 1891 the two leagues
knew they had no choice but to make peace, and their rep-
resentatives met to talk it over. What the National League
demanded of the American Association was not quite uncon-
ditional surrender but it was very close to it. Under the peace
terms, the National League remained intact, merging with
four American Association teams to form a twelve-team league.
The other four American Association teams were dissolved.
Although the process was called a merger, the American Association was just as dead as the Players League. If ever there
had been any doubt that the game was big business, it was
now resolved. Baseball's incisors were showing and they
looked bloody.

The Gay Nineties were not uniformly gay, although they
still are in television beer commercials. If that decade gave
us the Floradora Sextette, Gibson Girls, barbershop quartets,
and bicycles built for two, it was also a time of poverty and
unemployment. It saw the Panic of 1893, the great Pullman
strike of 1894, the March of Coxey's pitiable army of unem-
ployed on Washington, and the Spanish-American War. It was
also a decade when the United States, as never before or since
in its history, was controlled by huge business trusts, among
them the National League.

With the total control it so long had sought, and with its
clumsy twelve-team loop, the National League proceeded to
prove that monopoly could be ruthless, unprofitable, stupid,
and often extremely dull.

After suffering the tedium of baseball's business problems,
the public in the early 90's searched hopefully for a little fun
and excitement. Here and there they found it, perhaps most

notably in the old Baltimore Orioles, who swashbuckled, cursed, clawed, and kicked their way to a species of baseball immortality, although there is still some question whether the mark they left in the sands of time was that of a baseball shoe or of a cloven hoof.

Even though the Orioles played the game like a band of bloodthirsty Saracens, they may be rightly regarded as baseball pioneers just as surely as the more decorous Cincinnati Red Stockings of Harry Wright.

In the language of the diamond, "inside" baseball is a sort of thinking man's game, as distinguished from the slam-bang style of indiscriminate power and chance. Instead of standing up and flailing away, an exponent of inside baseball takes a thoughtful look at the game's rules and dynamics and then uses the opportunities they offer for outwitting the enemy. Inside baseball thus is a game of nuance and precision. Two of its prime weapons are the bunt and the so-called hit-and-run play, or, as some insist it be called, the run-and-hit play. Bunting, of course, involves deftly nudging the ball a short distance and beating the throw to first base. The hit-and-run play is an offensive maneuver requiring not only finesse but a runner already on first. As the pitch is delivered, the runner starts for second. The second baseman, assuming the runner is going to steal, rushes over to cover the bag. The batter thereupon reaches out and slaps the ball into the outfield through the corridor just vacated by the second baseman (or shortstop, as the case may be, although it is usually the second baseman). The result is a safe hit for the batter and in most cases a safe trip all the way to third base for the runner.

This is one form of "hitting 'em where they ain't," a dictum attributed to one Wee Willie Keeler, a small man who played the outfield admirably for the old Orioles. Keeler was perhaps the most accurate place-hitter in the history of the game, hitting for no great distance but for high averages. Asked what advice he might offer for success in batting, Keeler once replied forthrightly: "Hit 'em where they ain't."

Although the Orioles of the 90's may not have originated
all the elements of thinking man's baseball, they are perhaps
its most renowned practitioners. They may not have originated
the bunt, but they bunted the opposition silly. They may not
have originated the hit-and-run play, but they used it with
tremendous success. Another offensive maneuver was known
as the "Baltimore chop," and one might be pardoned if one
guessed that this expression was used to describe what the
Orioles enjoyed doing with their spikes to opposition flesh. In
fact, however, it was a sort of chopped bunt which took a
very high bounce, giving the runner time to beat it out for
a hit. As thinking men, the old Orioles were also adept at
out-psyching the opposition, rattling them with taunts, revile-
ments, intimidation and worse. Although they may not have
originated dirty baseball, they perfected it to a high degree.
In a National League filled with dirty players they were undoubtedly the dirtiest of their time and may well have been
the dirtiest the game has ever known.

The Orioles' success with the hit-and-run play has been
attributed largely to the place-hitting skill of Wee Willie
Keeler and to the highly specialized talents of their third baseman, John McGraw—the same John McGraw who with the
New York Giants was to become one of the most successful
managers in baseball history. McGraw, who batted in the
lead-off spot for the Orioles, was renowned for being tempera-
mental, and employed almost any means, savory or unsavory,
for getting on base. Batting second was Wee Willie, with his
ability to place the ball beyond reach of the opposition. Together they made an effective duo.

An appraisal of the old Orioles was made in 1908 by Wilbert
Robinson, who was catcher for the team in its heyday and
later for many years managers of the Brooklyn Dodgers (in
fact, the Brooklyn team was so identified with him that for a
time it was known as the Robins). It is worth noting that
from the ranks of the old Orioles there came no fewer than
three renowned major-league managers: in addition to Mc-

Graw and Robinson, there was Hugh Jennings, the Oriole shortstop who later became a highly successful manager for Detroit in the Ty Cobb era. Thus the Orioles helped set the stage for the game's future not only with their innovations on the field but by providing some of the men who would be big names in the new, brighter era just ahead.

Robinson claimed that the Orioles revolutionized the game by introducing "modern, scientific baseball."

"Take the bunt," he wrote. "It may have been seen occasionally somewhere before, but if so it made no lasting impression. The first men to realize its practical value were Keeler and McGraw. Both were fast runners. Dumping the ball was an astounding thing to players of those days. Unprepared as the third and first basemen were for a thing like that, before they could handle the ball, fleet Keeler or McGraw were across the bag, kidding the other fellows. . . . Yes, there were great old days and great old teams, but I'll always swear to the end that Baltimore had all the others skinned."

In the light of other information available on the speech and mores of the old Orioles, it might be interesting to know what sort of "kidding" Robinson had in mind. In many accounts, one finds the Orioles accused of the dirtiest play and "vilest obscenities" imaginable, and of using their spikes on opposing players and umpires alike. John Heydler, one-time president of the National League, once wrote that he had seen "umpires bathe their feet by the hour after McGraw and others spiked them through their shoes."

It is clear that for the old-time Orioles it was not so much how you played the game as whether you won or lost. Of their success there can be no doubt. In the twelve-team National League they won the pennant in 1894, repeating in 1895 and again in 1896. Seeking to make it four straight, they were nosed out by Boston in 1897 on the final day of the season, but then proceeded to polish off the Bostons in the post-season "Temple Cup" series, a tepid substitute for the World Series, which was necessarily in abeyance because of the National

League monopoly. There was no other major-league champion to offer World Series opposition during the 90's, and the Temple Cup series was played between the first- and second-place National League teams, an event that seldom set the public pulse atingle.

When Boston beat out the Orioles for the pennant in 1897 the *Reach Guide* termed it a popular victory "because the Boston club had won many admirers and supporters by its exceptionally good deportment." Not only did the Bostons display gentlemanly behavior, they also contributed a fine brand of baseball, winning five pennants during the 90's to the Orioles' three. The two teams dominated the game for a full decade, and in the public view it was always the good guys against the bad.

Villains though they were to the rest of the league, at least for a time the Orioles were heroes in the city of Baltimore, which, after 1896, had to wait seventy years for its next major-league pennant. The *Reach Guide* tells of the reception given the 1894 Orioles after they "surprised the country and knocked out all predictions by winning the pennant."

"The team reached Baltimore on the evening of October 2nd by special train from Chicago," the *Reach Guide* recounts. "From the time the train entered Maryland until it arrived at Camden Station [in Baltimore], the trip was one triumphal march. At Cumberland, thousands greeted the pennant-winners, and at Martinsburg, Harpers Ferry and Washington the scenes of enthusiasm were repeated. As the special train pulled into Camden Station, hundreds of track torpedoes were exploded, and a multitude limited only to the capacity of the surrounding streets cheered the players as they left the train. The players took carriages and led a procession of enthusiasts and rooters through the business district of the city, ending up at the Fifth Regiment Armory. The line was divided into six divisions with floats and decorated wagons distributed throughout. Fireworks were discharged from an enormous platform-wagon. Mounted police and a band of music preceded the marshal and his aides mounted on horseback. Along the route of the parade, the houses were gorgeously decorated and illuminated. A terrific jam of humanity was on the streets from start to finish. When the armory was reached, there were more fireworks and the reception lasted nearly two hours."

Two years later public enthusiasm had dwindled, not because the Orioles were less proficient but because the people of Baltimore took the team's winning ways for granted and became bored. Even though the Orioles remained big road attractions in other cities, where the fans came out hoping to see them beaten and perhaps maimed, attendance at home declined sharply.

It is ironic that this team, a team so invincible as to create boredom, was the direct forebear of none other than the New York Yankees. After the 1899 season Baltimore was dropped from the National League. In 1901 and 1902 it became a member of the new American League and before the 1903 season its franchise was shifted to New York, where it was vested in the New York Highlanders, who later became the Yankees.

Long before this, for all the heroics of Baltimore and Boston, the twelve-team National League had proved itself a stodgy failure. Right from its very first season—1892—it was clear that twelve teams were just too many. If it was difficult for the fans to work up rooting interest in seventh- and eight-place teams, it was even harder to sustain enthusiasm for those finishing in slots nine through twelve.

In a rather wistful footnote to the season of 1892, the *Reach Guide* found another reason for poor attendance around the league—the mediocre playing of the New York Giants. Warning that as New York goes so goes baseball, it asked vaguely that the Giants be given aid and comfort.

"Queer as it may seem," the *Guide* states, "it has become a recognized fact that baseball as a business is, to a great degree, governed throughout the country by the success or non-success of the New York club in attracting the lovers of the game. Last year the team was a failure from April till October, and the attendance at the Polo Grounds decreased to alarming proportions. Immediately the slump began to affect all other cities. It is this peculiarity of the New York center which has induced all those interested in the business success of baseball to join, so far as each one can, in helping New York to put and keep in the field a team worthy to represent the metropolitan city of the United States."

An even more succinct appraisal of baseball in New York during the 1890's was made by *Sporting Life*, a popular journal of the day devoted to "baseball, trap shooting and general sports": "It is to be hoped that the New York Club will start the new year on a new line, and this time make good the oft-repeated promise to give a hungry public such baseball as befits the first city of the land. Surely we have had enough tailend ball to last us a century."

John McGraw, Christy Mathewson, and others very soon would bring to New York the brand of baseball some felt it deserved. But even had the Giants played good ball in the 90's it is doubtful that the National League would have been strong or savory enough to prosper. By the middle of the decade, the nation was undergoing a severe economic depression, and in 1898, according to the *Reach Guide*, the Spanish-American War "wrecked the game for months." Although the top teams continued to meet expenses, the tail-enders lost heavily.

Among those to suffer were the once-mighty St. Louis Browns and their once-jolly owner, Chris von der Ahe. The Browns were never the same after the player revolt; they were losers throughout the 90's, and so ultimately was Chris. Trying desperately to offset heavy losses at the gate, von der Ahe turned his stadium into an amusement park, even including a short-course race track, which operated during the off season. He came under heavy criticism from the other club owners and from members of the press, who not only criticized him for carnival tactics but also took pleasure in uncovering often titillating details of his personal life.

In one account, we find this summation of von der Ahe's decline: "Clear up to the last of his baseball career, Chris was a dead game sport. He was a royal spender and a champion of good fellows when his Browns were winning flags and raking in the money. When the evil days came, when his club was a regular loser and the money began to dwindle, Chris was still the same old Chris and he accepted his downfall as gallantly as he did the good fortune of his earlier years."

A St. Louis newspaper, on the other hand, found Chris neither gallant nor appealing. The clown mask, if it was a mask, had come unstuck, revealing a sour, crabbed old man.

What happened to him at the end of his career was enough to make him so. He was heavily in debt, hounded by creditors, and considered such a poor financial risk that the other National League magnates, through more or less legal means, stripped away his ownership of the ball club. *Sporting News* called his private life "an affront to the community," making much of the liaisons he carried on with certain gay ladies of the Nineties.

One of his creditors was W. A. Nimick, president of the Pittsburgh ball club, who, according to historian Harold Seymour, once posted bond for him and who, to recover the money, found it expedient to get Chris into a Pennsylvania court. "By a ruse, Nimick's agents lured von der Ahe into a carriage, spirited him out of Missouri and had him thrown into an Allegheny County jail where, disheveled and disgraced, he reposed for several days."

As Chris lay there waiting for his lawyers to bail him out, he might be excused if he recalled the days when as the Boss President he adjusted his flat derby, banded his players together, and led them in a triumphal march up from the depot.

It seems remarkable, in retrospect, that as the National League foundered the men who controlled it should have taken measures that only compounded their mistakes. To cure the evils of monopoly, they sought stronger and still stronger

monopoly, even combining in a series of interlocking ownership deals. Seldom was "conflict of interest" so flagrantly illustrated as in the National League of the 1890's. The estimable
A. G. Spalding, who owned a large block of stock in the
Chicago club, also owned stock in the New York Giants, and
others were also guilty of this sort of dualism. Even so, the
owners bickered constantly among themselves. Some accused
others of cheating on the gate receipts. They cut salaries ruth-
lessly, even whimsically, losing the respect of the players and
the public alike. The press became increasingly critical, and
in 1900 Cap Anson himself wrote: "Baseball as at present
conducted is a gigantic monopoly, intolerant of opposition and
run on a grab-all-there-is-in-sight policy that is alienating its
friends and disgusting the very public that has so long and
cheerfully given it the support that it has withheld from other
forms of amusement."

Drunk and stupefied by the power and greed of its owners,
organized baseball was staggering to the end of the nineteenth
century—and there were some who doubted it would make it.

Clearly baseball cried out for a savior. He came in the person of Byron Bancroft Johnson, who, although he too in time
would have his critics and even his enemies, performed a
service for baseball in its hour of need. What he brought to
baseball was competition, and never was the salubrious effect
of competition more dramatically illustrated.

Not, of course, that Ban Johnson was moved by altruism or
necessarily even by idealism. Like others, he was influenced
by a desire for profit, but he had the vision to see that great
profit did not necessarily follow from great greed, and he had
the strength to fight the National League head to head and the
intelligence and endurance to win.

Using the teams of a minor league (the Western) as his
nucleus, in 1900 Johnson formed what became a new major
league, calling it the American and demanding equal status.
Predictably, the National League moaned and groaned, whined
and kicked. Three years of warfare ensued. Not only did John-

son refuse to give ground, but he invaded some of the National League's best cities and stole many of its best players.

When it was over, there were two major leagues and baseball was finally out of the dark ages.

THE

GOLDEN DAYS

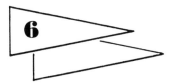

The Blue Sky and

the Green Grass

BASEBALL HAS BEEN CALLED A GREAT MANY UNCOMPLIMENTARY names. It has been reviled and lampooned because of its performers, its owners, and its fans. It has been called a game played by the largely ignorant for the easily excitable. It has been called tedious and dull. Bill Veeck warned long ago that baseball was killing its clientele with boredom. As far back as 1916 one Louis Graves, a critic of the day, was saying somewhat the same thing, although his desire was not to save baseball but simply to damn it.

"Having acquired a national flag and a national anthem," he wrote in *Harper's Weekly,* "these United States of America decided some 40 years ago that they needed a national game. Up to that time, sport of an individual character had sufficed; but now no longer could horseback riding, boxing, hunting, running and jumping meet the demands of a society that was rapidly becoming effete and citified and whose tastes were becoming communistic. Some substitute adapted to new conditions had to be found.

"In an aimless spasmodic sort of way, a game played with a ball and bat had come into favor. . . . In an evil hour for this land of the free, some busybodies who ought to have been occupying their time in a better way, pounced upon this new game of baseball and decided it should be the national sport. . . .

"The time had come when people demanded the privilege of sitting inert in great crowds and seeing a few less lazy human beings go through physical exercises. . . . They knew they wanted something and they easily hypnotized themselves into thinking that baseball filled the bill. It was all they had to choose, and they chose it.

"The worst fault of baseball—and it is an unpardonable fault in any game that pretends to be a spectacle—is that it is not lively. For vivacity I would compare baseball with chess or billiards. It is somewhat less exciting than a spelling bee.

"Tell a fan that baseball is not lively and he will bid you remember such and such a moment in some famous contest when three men were on base and Christy Somebody was pitching and Hans Who's-This cracked a grounder to the shortstop and so on. . . . But the moments like this are abnormal. You go and sit through an hour and a half of dullness to get your one thrill. And you are lucky if the thrill comes then. I've lived in New York 13 years and have seen about 13 games (I went to nearly all of them because of the good company, for some of the most likable men have the baseball delusion) and in only one have I seen anything half as interesting as the balancing acts one can see the steel riveters do any day free of charge. . . .

"Though unquestionably the most ardent rooters of baseball do go to see it played, I have found that a great number of citizens extol it as a patriotic duty. It's a habit—like rising for the Star Spangled Banner.

"To put it briefly, baseball is the dullest of sports. I have never been able to understand why the clergymen want to prevent its being played on Sundays. There is so little about the game to distract one's attention that the grandstand is an ideal place for meditation and prayer."

Baseball indeed is a game of deadly lulls. It is a game which can drone on for hours in the heat of the afternoon while the home-town fan, his team down 8–1, yawns and feels the summer's somnolence steal over him, with little to break it but the dubious refreshment of a Coke in a paper cup, an enigmatic beverage, watery and faintly tan. His team is in eighth place. His team has *always* been in eighth place. But he sits there and his kid, his boy, wearing his Cub Scout uniform, sits beside him, pounding a small fist into the oiled pocket of the big glove he has brought along from home in the hope that a ball may come his way and that he will, like Nap Lajoie before him—like Eddie Collins, like Tris Speaker, like Joe DiMaggio —glove it cleanly, gracefully, heroically.

I like baseball, our man Charlie Hawkins thinks, purchasing a hotdog, rubbery and not quite cold. I've always liked baseball. His wife has asked him why he likes baseball but it's a foolish question with no real answer, a question no one should ask. Charlie likes baseball because it's baseball—hell, even Walt *Whitman* liked baseball. The home-town pitcher is being changed. The new pitcher comes shambling in from deep center field, walking as slowly as mortal man can walk. Finally he makes it to the pitcher's mound, where he is greeted by the manager who speaks a few words, presumably of encouragement, hands him the ball, and pats him about the haunches. This accomplished, the manager heads back to the dugout, the catcher returns to his post, and the pitcher, who has been warming up out in the center-field bullpen on and off throughout the long afternoon, now proceeds to warm up some more. This little pageant in nondynamics has now consumed anywhere from six to ten minutes. Charlie Hawkins yawns. His son Kevin thumps fist into glove and asks for another Coke. He asks the time. Charlie looks at his watch and says it's four-thirty. The game by now is two and a half hours old. Charlie belches and wishes he hadn't eaten the hotdog. Kevin thumps his glove. The pitcher pitches. Charlie belches and wishes he hadn't named his son Kevin. It's a bad day for the home team, as it so often has been during the past seventy years.

The relief pitcher walks the first two men he faces and out from the dugout comes the manager, glancing toward the center-field bullpen where the next relief pitcher is not yet warmed up, insufficiently alerted—although God knows why not after seventy years. The manager plays for time, as the rules allow. He circles the pitcher's mound. The pitcher paws the dirt with his spikes and glances toward center field, looking neither chagrined nor surprised at his own instant ineptitude. The manager paws the mound with his spikes, making a neat little pile of dirt. The catcher, who by now has joined the group, starts to paw the dirt with his spikes but there is no room for his foot. All three look toward center field, where the new pitcher by now is warming up at a furious rate.

Finally, giving the pitcher a pat on the haunches, the manager heads back toward the dugout as if he had decided to leave the pitcher in the game after all, but this of course is a ruse. No sooner has he crossed the foul line than back he comes, this time signaling to the distant reaches of center field for the new pitcher, who, having been given the few additional minutes of warm-up time, now comes shambling in from center field, walking as slowly as mortal man can walk without actually coming to a full halt. Charlie Hawkins against his will buys a bag of peanuts. It's a dream game, baseball—a game made to order for TV commercials.

It was a bad day for the locals and on the way home, lurching through the Sunday traffic, Charlie and Kevin speak of better times to come, of better luck next time. That there will indeed be a next time Charlie has no doubt, although if he thinks about it he may admit that what he witnessed was an essentially boring spectacle, one-sided, noncompetitive, nondynamic, a thing of lulls and pauses and rancid light refreshment. Yet Charlie feels satisfied and even fulfilled, for he has done a fine thing—he has taken his son to a baseball game and he knows there is no finer thing a father can do for his son. Why? Well, just because, that's why. For decade after decade it's what fathers have been doing. His father took him to baseball games. It's a link to the past, baseball. He has a comfortable feeling, a feeling of security and of continuity. He is linked with the past, with an earlier America—linked not only with his father and grandfather but linked with Christy Mathewson and Walter Johnson and Napoleon Lajoie, Honus Wagner, Rube Waddell, Ty Cobb. Is that it? He doesn't know, doesn't ask, probably doesn't care. He drives, and Kevin thumps his fist into the pocket of the big glove. Together they talk of how, with better luck, the home team might have bailed it out in the ninth, instead of falling thirteen runs short.

Charlie at some point much earlier in his life had been caught up in baseball's mystique, just as his father was before him, and just as now his son Kevin is.

For all its splendid moments, and it has had many, baseball can be a tedious game. It is a game that got off to a horrible start, with its drunkenness, crookedness, squabbling, greed, and stupidity—and by 1920 it would be facing its greatest peril, the Black Sox scandal, which threatened to carry it all the way back to the dark ages and perhaps snuff it out forever.

In the years between, baseball indeed must have had much going for it.

The game has had its periods of glory but in searching for the origin of its mystique it seems not unwarranted to cite the years following the creation of the American League. If one looks for the time when baseball made its magic, when it entered the marrow of the national bone, when it became established as the national pastime or national quirk, national stupidity or national strength, it was here—the golden era of roughly a dozen seasons beginning in 1903.

Although the world was approaching the end of the Edwardian era of peace and grace, many things were new. The nation was finally complete—in 1912 New Mexico and Arizona were admitted as the forty-seventh and forty-eighth states. The West had been won and more or less secured. By 1912 the population of the United States, rising with the waves of immigration, was approaching the 100 million mark. The nation was at peace and so for a while longer would be the world. The century was new. The automobile and the telephone were new. The American League was new—and so, it seemed, was baseball itself.

If these years may be thought of as a stage, it is remarkable that so many of the game's truly great figures were on stage during this era. Some were already there when it began, some entered just before it came to a close. The careers of still others spanned it almost precisely. Napoleon Lajoie, a second baseman of enormous natural grace and a truly great batsman, began his major-league career in 1896 and was still on stage through the golden era, not passing from the scene until 1918. Roughly the same years are covered in the career of Honus Wagner, the greatest of all shortstops, an ungainly-looking man with huge hands, gorilla arms, bowed legs, enormous speed and strength, and such a keen eye that he led the National League eight times in batting. Denton True Young, a farm boy known as Cy, started his career in 1890 and by the time he had finished in 1911 he had won 511 games, a record that surely will never be equaled. Ty Cobb, a man with a savage will to win, began his major-league career with the Detroit Tigers in 1905, ended it with Philadelphia in 1928, and during those twenty-four seasons established so many records that he is generally regarded as the greatest ball player in the history of the game.

The list is long. It includes Tris Speaker, one of the greatest of center-fielders and a batter during his era second only to

Cobb. It includes Walter Johnson and Christy Mathewson—who, with Cy Young, comprise perhaps the greatest pitching threesome the game has ever known—and such other pitching greats as Jack Chesbro, who in 1904, pitching for the New York Highlanders (later the Yankees), won forty-one games, an American League record that still stands; and such others as Rube Waddell, Mordecai (Three Finger) Brown, Ed Walsh, Rube Marquard, Smoky Joe Wood, Grover Cleveland Alexander, Jack Coombs, Chief Bender, and Eddie Plank. It includes such batters as Eddie Collins, Frank (Home Run) Baker, and Sam Crawford; such managers as the peerless Frank Chance, who led the Chicago Cubs to three consecutive pennants in 1906–8, and John McGraw and Connie Mack, who were the dominant managers in baseball for almost a quarter century.

Also on stage, prophetically, was Shoeless Joe Jackson, one of the game's greatest natural hitters, who joined Cleveland in 1911 and who eight years later would be the most prominent of those involved in the Black Sox scandal.

Toward the end of the era there was yet another entry—George Herman Ruth, who joined the Baltimore Orioles, then a minor-league team, in 1914 and was sold the same year to the Boston Red Sox. After the Black Sox scandal, when baseball desperately needed another golden era, Ruth would be instrumental in providing it.

But the Chicago Black Sox and the Age of Ruth were still far in the future. In the early years of the century, the stage belonged to Cobb, McGraw, Mathewson, Johnson, Speaker, Wagner, Lajoie, and all the others whose greatness on the field of play made them legendary figures and helped give baseball the strength and magic that would make it a national phenomenon.

These were the years of the first hooked generation—the generation that would first absorb the mystique and then pass it on to sons and grandsons, a generation for whom the game was played in a hopeful, more naïve America, and was identified with railroads and trolley cars, with the ebullience and confidence of Teddy Roosevelt, the values of Horatio Alger, the atmospheres of Booth Tarkington. These were the years long before television or even radio, a time when, for special events such as the World Series, people stood in throngs outside cigar stores, clustering around a blackboard and watching as a man in an alpaca jacket came out with a piece of chalk to record the score, half inning by half inning. And although America is none of that today, baseball perhaps profits by the perseveration just as movies and television profit by the public's whimsical desire to think of the West as still wild and to squirm with pleasure at the legendary feats of its folk heroes.

Baseball's folk heroes not only became legends, they were cheered and idolized in their own time. The focus was finally on the field of play, and the game belonged to the players and to the fans who watched them. The owners at last were in the background, giving the game its head and no longer imposing their business problems upon the public.

It was in this era that the structure of major-league baseball finally became stable. The National League, in the years 1892 through 1899, was made up of twelve teams. Before the 1900 season the league dropped four—Baltimore, Washington, Cleveland, and Louisville. This left Boston, Brooklyn, Philadelphia, and New York in the East, and St. Louis, Chicago, Cincinnati, and Pittsburgh in the West. Not for another forty-eight years would there be a change.

The American League, after shifting its Milwaukee franchise to St. Louis in 1902 and its Baltimore franchise to New York in 1903, had the following roster of cities: Boston, New York, Philadelphia, Washington, Cleveland, Detroit, Chicago, and St. Louis. It was a roster that would remain intact for exactly half a century.

During baseball's early years, rickety wooden stands had sufficed to hold the crowds but now these were torn down and replaced by the great stadiums that would become familiar landmarks and familiar names in many of the nation's principal cities for years to come.

To some, the new stadiums were a reason for enormous excitement, a sign of national progress and a cause for rejoicing. How great had the nation become and how bright was its future! Any American with a tendency to be despondent about his country was called upon to contemplate the new ball park that was completed in Pittsburgh in the summer of 1909. *Baseball Magazine* described it enthusiastically:

"The second grand division is the balcony, supported and suspended on steel trusses, the front row being over the fifth row of the lower deck. Here there are twelve tiers or steps rising more rapidly than those below so as to provide a perfect view of the diamond. The seats in this balcony, numbering 5,500, are also approached by level ways or passages from the rear and to the center of the deck in a manner similar to those below. This deck is also provided with toilets.

"The new park is the greatest achievement in civil engineering—and as beautiful as well as secure and comfortable a construction—as has been undertaken in this country since baseball first began to be the national pastime."

The new stadiums were built, of course, not to provide a memorable achievement in civil engineering but because money was being lost in paid admissions. The crowds were now so great that the old ball parks could no longer accommodate them. Public interest had become intense. The "fan" was a new breed and it was considered fashionable, even thoroughly American and indeed Americanizing, to become one— as dedicated and emotional as the fan who sued a local trolley company because the motorman took the wrong turn and made the plaintiff late for the ball game.

The language of fandom was a common language. There was by now a huge network of healthy, thriving minor leagues which touched upon almost every town and hamlet, so that the country was linked by baseball almost as it was linked by its telegraph and its railroads. An Iowa farm boy could know as much about Christy Mathewson as the New York boy who was able to go out to the Polo Grounds to watch him pitch.

For country boys, baseball offered an opportunity to get rich and famous in a hurry. For late-coming Americans—Irish and German, in the main—it provided a gateway, just as it would provide a gateway to Negroes years later, once they were finally admitted to the major leagues. The field was open to most, just as later the movie industry might be open to a high school girl if she wore a tight enough sweater and appeared at the right time in the right Hollywood drugstore. A boy could play baseball without any particular education, without wealth or privilege or class or breeding. What it took was a clear eye and coordination and the ability to knock a ball the length of a city block—or the length of a meadow, over the barn and far away.

All over America there was the sound, the crack, of bat meeting ball, a sound impossible to duplicate, just as it was impossible to mistake.

The national game had broken from its dark corridor and was running out in the sunlight "where the blue sky meets the green grass," and although the phrase is lush and extravagant it had special meaning in the early 1900's. Many many people worked as many as twelve hours a day, six days a week, in the darkness of factories and sweatshops. One has only to glance at the old dark-red derelict buildings in eastern-seaboard cities to realize that it might well have been an occasion for a factory hand to sit out in the open air and watch men in white uniforms perform where the blue sky came down to meet the green grass.

The fan was a curio, something new in America and something peculiarly American, the subject of endless articles in the periodicals of the day. People were taking him seriously—with delight, but nonetheless seriously—just as they were taking baseball and their relationship to it seriously. Some found the fan a phenomenon, a fit subject for somber reflection. Others viewed fandom with giddy delight—most notably *Baseball Magazine,* which bowed to none in its estimate of the benefits that baseball conferred upon the human lung and soul. Speaking of the fan, the magazine chortled:

"Watch him when he begins to enthuse. Is he pleased? He laughs, shouts, bestirs himself anxiously and gesticulates wildly. Is he displeased? He jeers the officials and indulges in hot arguments with his neighbors, stamping and ranting. . . . All the time his vital organs are summoned into strenuous sympathy with his frame of mind and he draws deep breaths of pure air. He may be weary when the game is over but for it he will eat and sleep better, his step will be more determined, his eyes will cease resembling those of a dead fish. . . . He goes to his desk or bench next day with a smiling face."

Baseball Magazine, while delighting in rabid fan enthusiasm —as well it might have—now and then exhorted the fans to behave themselves. In an article entitled "Rooters You Have Met," it noted: "Some fans never knock and no matter how bad a player may show up they are always on deck with their pleasant hearty cry: 'All right, old chap, all right. Don't mind that, old chap. Do better the next time.' These fans though are in the minority. Pity it is that there are not more of them."

The magazine also offered its pages as a forum for complaints and suggestions on how the National Game might become ever more attractive. The magazine, it may be noted, never called the game baseball when National Game would do —and National Game was invariably capitalized.

In 1908 it printed a letter from a fan who expressed his vexation over having his view obstructed by concession butchers: "As an exciting play looms up, along comes a lad yelling out, 'Popcorn, candy, cigarettes, etc.' and he places himself in a most disagreeable position and it's up to the fans to rout him out, in which way half of their attention is distracted from the National Game."

In the same year, a lady reader from Minot, North Dakota, suggested more ladies' days, asking: "Wouldn't there be a big turnout though, if a lot of pretty girls sat in the grandstand

and waved their handkerchiefs when a good play was pulled off? Doubleheaders could be played right along if a boy and girl sat side by side without the slightest mumble of complaint. Admission of women would tend to eliminate foul language and make the game cleaner in every way."

Whatever foul language there may have been on the field, in the dugout, and in the locker room, the game off the field was developing another lexicon, one all its own, coined by sportswriters, who, with very few exceptions, found baseball as exciting as did the most rabid fan. Month by month, year by year, they kept dropping new words and new phrases into the language, contributing to the ultimately massive baseball idiom. The "initial hassock" was first base. The "hot corner" was third. The pitcher was the "twirler" or a "southpaw" or "portsider" if he happened to pitch left-handed. He worked on the "mound," toeing "the slab," and his catcher was "the backstop." To the batter, who stood at the plate or "dish," there might befall an endless variety of fates. He might "fan" or "whiff"—meaning that he had struck out. He might be given a base on balls—"a free trip." If he were "redoubtable" enough, he might very well come through with a "circuit clout"—a home run, of which, in the early 1900's, there were very few. He might also "lay one down," meaning that he had elected to bunt, or he might hit a "can of corn"—an easy pop fly.

Sportswriters vied, and often strained, for color. To understand them took a special knowledge, which fans of the day happily—patriotically—acquired. Even the most knowledgeable, however, might have been hard put to decipher the following, published in 1909 and purporting to be an account, admittedly exaggerated, of a game played at the Polo Grounds between the New York Giants and the Pittsburgh Pirates.

"With the third inning faded into the dim and forgotten past, the fourth spasm in the afternoon's matinee of Dementia Baseballitis hopped into the glare of the calcium glim. It was the Giants' turn to paddle the pellet, Murderous Michael Donlin taking his turn beside the glad gum. Mike biffed the bulb on the proboscis and sent it gleefully gliding to the distant shrubbery. . . . Bresnahan managed to get next to the seamy side of a floater and the Toledo kid sent the denizens of Coogan's Bluff into Seventh Heaven of Gleefulness by starting the pulsating pill on a line for the extreme backyard. But they reckoned without the mighty Wagner. The Carnegie Dutchman extended a monster paw, the near-two bagger was cleverly captured by a dainty dab of his lunch hook and before you could bat an eye he had whipped the globule over to Abby, who made an earnest effort to put Donlin down and out but missed by a fraction of an inch."

(Actually, not a great deal happened. In the New York half of the fourth inning, Mike Donlin singled and catcher Roger Bresnahan lined out to Wagner, who almost doubled up Donlin at first base.)

Yet for all the evidence that baseball in many quarters was viewed as a marvelous new national toy, there is also ample evidence that it was taken seriously by men who had given it long and careful thought.

One of these was the drama critic of *Harper's Weekly,* who urged the national theater to pattern itself after baseball, calling "the one a tremendous national success, the other almost as tremendous a national failure." In a lament which continues to be heard up to the very present, he denounced a theater which was concentrated in a few hands and in one principal locale. The result, in his opinion, was a theater always out of touch with the people, and mass unemployment of actors:

"To one who has seriously considered the matter, it is as plain as day that those points in which our present theater has failed most conspicuously are the very points in which it has diverged furthest from the natural lines along which baseball has developed.

"Every city, every town and every village, almost every crossroads, has its one or more baseball teams. Think of the thousands of boys and men to whom this gives recreation and employment. Think of the wonderfully free outlet it affords for baseball talent, great and small. From his earliest years in many parts of the country, the boy with the liking for baseball has a chance to try himself out and if he makes good and cares to become a professional player he can pass by a natural process of growth to the best league in the nation.

"The shouts that go up from the bleachers all over the country, great and small, spring from the instinctive feeling that the game is the people's own. Likewise the apathy of the people toward the theater is due very largely to the conviction, equally well founded, that the theater is not the people's own."

Those interested in social problems were already advocating baseball as a cure for delinquency. In June 1911 *Collier's* offered a stark snapshot of the deprived children of that earlier day. "Sometimes on a walk in New York's east side," it said, "it seems as if every chasm of the whole district has a bonfire, with children dancing around it, jumping over the flames, stamping brands or weaving in procession with torches. . . . When you see children risking their lives with bonfires of pulling a chair from a van to smash it to pieces, with the avidity of a pack of wolves, or when you hear the crash of window glass followed by the patter of boys' feet and an enraged baker sprints down the avenue, scattering flour and profanity, you behold the pathological symptoms of a lack of good games. There is no inbred viciousness in tenement children. These simply are the evidences of an unsatisfied hunger for play."

The article advocated providing slum children with a large indoor-ball, or softball, which would enable them to have a game within the cramped space of tenement streets.

"Few spectators," it remarked, "who have watched one of these contests fail to remark on the combination of picturesqueness and danger involved. On the floor of an artificial canyon, in a faint fog and the rumbling traffic, behold some wildly animated small athletes pitching a grotesquely large ball, swinging a bantam-sized bat with an iron manhole-cover for home plate and first base the gridiron of a sewer catch-basin. Trolley cars dart and clang near the players' backs, un-heeded. The batters knock out liners under the very noses of draft horses."

For baseball to be taken so seriously, on so many levels, was an indication that it finally had matured. It always had taken itself seriously as a business. Now it seemed to take itself seriously both as a game and as an institution with responsi-bility to the public. It had become at least reasonably clean, certainly cleaner than it ever had been. By 1907 even the players were becoming gentlemanly, according to a National League umpire of the day, who reported there never had been a season when he heard "so little abuse of the umpire, so little bad language." Although he conceded that players were still "up to every trick imaginable," an umpire needed only to dis-play firmness. He no longer needed to flee for his life.

Baseball in any case had lost its ugly crust and was looking better all the time. No longer did the players stagger drunk-enly about the field, no longer did they commit mayhem on umpires. Whatever they might be doing, they were doing it more circumspectly, and a better public relations job was easy to perform. Above all, during this period baseball was no longer crooked. There was every evidence that it was being played on the level, and nothing was so important as this to its success.

In assessing the effects of crookedness, it is doubtless accu-rate to say that many people, sports fans among them, are dis-turbed and offended by the dishonest act itself. Of equal pertinence, perhaps, is the confusion which, in the case of the sports enthusiast, means not knowing where he stands. It can be disconcerting to assume that a game is bound by precise rules and then find that it was not. For the fullest enjoyment it is necessary to presume a desire to win on the part of the combatants. To yield one's essence, one's very stuff and mar-row, to give one's all as a rooter for a team or individual and then to find that the team or individual was not really trying is to be left feeling foolish, empty, and downright furious. For some sports fans, it seems safe to say, the venality is a minor affront compared with the displeasure of having been duped.

In the golden years of the early twentieth century fans at last knew or could believe that baseball, whatever else it might be, was on the up and up. The players, though many might be ignorant bumpkins, were nonetheless on the field for a purpose —to excel, to win; and to win they would contribute all the talent and energy fate had dealt them.

Thus the game had the form and coherence that only a strict code of rules could give it. Feeling this to be true, the fan could give his all, could yell and scream from his seat in the bleachers, could gather around the cigar-store scoreboard, lap up the information offered in the sports pages, write letters to *Baseball Magazine* and even go down to the depot to watch his heroes arrive or depart, without ever feeling that he would become a cuckold. He loved baseball and baseball would be true to him.

There are some who say that baseball has always been lucky. When it needed a Ban Johnson it got him. Twenty years later, when it badly needed a savior for a second time, it would get him, too—a savior with a doughlike face, a powerful torso, and dainty legs—Babe Ruth.

Baseball was also fortunate to get a Christy Mathewson and a Walter Johnson.

"From the false environment of low-browed gentlemen with hard fists, from the atmosphere of stale tobacco smoke and the fumes of liquor, with all the showy gilt and glitter of a thousand vanities, the sporting spirit of the age is emerging on a broad pedestal of wholesome and healthful influence. . . . To be a sport now no longer necessitates an acquaintance with flashy jewelry and champagne suppers."

This was written in 1911, and what the writer was saying was that the major-league professional baseball player had a clean new image. Two of the men who did most to create it were Christy Mathewson and Walter Johnson, who also happened to be two of the very greatest pitchers the game has ever known.

Johnson was a mild man with a smoking fast ball. He had in fact probably the greatest speed of any pitcher in the history of the game. Fortunately, he also had pinpoint control. Such was his gentleness that his brilliant career might have been disrupted, even ended, had he ever suffered the agony of striking and seriously injuring a batter.

Mathewson was a college man, rare for a ball player in his day. He was a graduate of Bucknell, where he had starred in football as well as baseball. He was also addicted to checkers, at which he was said to be both excellent and indefatigable.

In 1909 a writer of the day summed him up as follows: "Christy Mathewson talks like a Harvard graduate, looks like an actor, acts like a businessman, and impresses you as an all-round gentleman."

Mathewson and Johnson were among the first five players selected for membership in Baseball's Hall of Fame. Although Mathewson closed out his career with Cincinnati, he spent most of it with the Giants, a consistently successful team, while Johnson's was spent with a persistent tail-ender.

Johnson always pitched for Washington, and until the very end of his career the club was always heartbreakingly inept, just as for the most part it has been ever since. Even so, he left glittering statistics in baseball's record book. His career began in 1907 and ended in 1927, and in those twenty-one years he recorded 416 victories, an American League record. His 113 shutouts are a record for both leagues, and he shares the American League record for consecutive victories—sixteen.

Mathewson recorded 373 lifetime victories, all but one with the Giants, and holds the all-time "modern" National League record for most victories in one season, thirty-seven in 1908. In Mathewson's day, the New York Giants had an age of gold of their own, and it was Mathewson, perhaps, who did more

than anyone else to make it possible. It is worthy of note that
Mathewson, the consummate gentleman, always worked for
the same manager, the tough John McGraw, but McGraw de-
ferred to him, perhaps as much out of consideration for his
popularity as for his pitching prowess. For years Mathewson
was the idol of New York and indeed of the nation.

From all reports, we may judge that it was an age when the
youth of America admired and respected gentlemanly behavior, particularly when it was associated with the fame and
brilliance of a Mathewson or a Johnson. It was long before the
age when an unsavory reputation lent luster to a public performer. The heroes of the day were the good guys. In novels
and elsewhere, boys were taught right thinking and fair
play and to beware of the evils of drink and loose women, lying
and cheating. They read Frank Merriwell and Baseball Joe
and Horatio Alger. They were asked to drink Moxie so that
they, like their favorite ball players, might "eat better, sleep
better and feel better." They were bombarded with advertisements from something calling itself the Baseball Correspondence School, which invited them to "become professional
ballplayers—join the big leagues. The most profitable and
fascinating profession in the world. If you have any ability
whatever, our course of mail instruction will bring it out and
therefore qualify you for the big leagues." Enticing glimpses
of life in the major leagues were offered in juvenile fiction.
Baseball Joe Matson pitched for the Giants and was a character patterned, hardly loosely, after Christy Mathewson. He was
the idol of the Polo Grounds and had a place on Riverside
Drive, a neighborhood of quiet grace, where he lived a clean,
unassuming existence. Never was there a finer gentleman or
finer pitcher than Baseball Joe—even though he was once
stupid enough to sign his name at the bottom of a blank sheet
of paper, which came back to him as a completed contract
requiring him to jump the Giants and pitch in an outlaw
league. Baseball Joe rightly concluded that it was the work of
cheats and bullies with whom, one idle night, he had been

comparing samples of penmanship.

The Frank Merriwell books were written by Gilbert Patten, under the penname Burt L. Standish. Glimpses of fictional big leaguers are offered in *Top-Notch Magazine*, which Patten edited in 1910 and which there is some reason to believe he wrote almost singlehandedly. In his editorials, addressed always to "Top-Notch Fellows," Patten expressed his credo: "I have no word of praise for the tricky, treacherous, contemptible fellow who wins at anything by underhand methods. Play Fair! Win on the Level!"

In the October 1910 issue there is a story purportedly boasting an authentic major-league background. The blurb reads: "Andy Nesbitt is a good sort and an exceptionally clever outfielder, but he has a bad attack of bulging ribs. He's chesty; thinks himself the only chap who can play ball. How that notion is knocked out of his head makes a bully tale of the diamond."

With his first major-league club, Andy promptly blows it, offending his teammates by his chestiness. He is traded to another club, where, chastened, no longer chesty, he saves the pennant on the final day of the season with an incredible catch and then wins it with a home run.

"But it was all for you," responded the young ball player without any of his old-time arrogance. "And now remember what you promised me if I played on the winning team."

May Sherwood blushed "but bravely smiled."

There is no mention of what May had promised him; in fact, there is virtually no prior mention of May Sherwood, except for a two-line entry narrating that Andy had taken a May Sherwood to a movie entitled *When Love Comes.*

In another issue of *Top-Notch* there is a story entitled "How Dugan Regained his Nerve," blurbed as a "short story of the professional diamond showing that players in the Big Leagues are often upset and 'put to the bad' by jealousies and heartburnings. Dugan finally demonstrated that he was built of the right stuff and by a single stroke of the willow again became the idol of the Chicago fans."

Bit players set the stage with a smattering of expository dialogue:

" 'Why the young beggar has gone half daffy about a girl and he is thinking of her when he ought to be playing ball. When a player under twenty gets dotty over a skirt, it seems to be all up with him.'

" 'Is it as bad as that with Dugan?'

" 'Pretty near. He plays like an inspired fanatic when the girl smiles upon him but I hear they had a tiff last night and she threatened to come to the game with Jim Saunders, whom he hates like poison. If the minx carries out her threat, I'm afraid it's all up with Dugan and the Chicago team.'

" 'Let's hope she'll change her mind.'

" 'Hang her! She hasn't, for there she goes into one of the boxes now, and suffering Jehosaphat, that's Jim Saunders with her!' "

Dugan, as might be expected under the circumstances, flounders his way through the early innings and then breaks all bounds of common sense by getting himself hit in the head with a pitched ball, thus: "Dugan, in an attempt to dodge, stepped squarely into the path of a swift curve and fell senseless."

Ruth, with a "startled smile," flees from the stands down to the dressing room. "Danny, Danny, speak to me," she cries as she bends over him, regardless of the staring, grinning bystanders. "Are you hurt?"

Dugan, who to judge by his reply may or may not still be senseless, states: "Just winded a little, Ruth. All right in a minute."

Even though some little time has elapsed and the proceedings presumably have been going on in his absence, Dugan is permitted to get back into the game and the climax is not long in coming:

"And then something happened. The next ball came straight toward the plate. Dugan stepped forward and hit it fair and square. Up and up it sailed until it finally dropped over the left field fence. . . . The ovation that broke loose for Dugan put in the shade everything of the sort that had ever before been seen on the Chicago field."

Although the author has not seen fit to say so, Ruth, in spite of the emotional rapprochement with Dugan in the dressing room, was perverse enough immediately thereafter to resume her seat in the box with Jim Saunders.

As Dugan circled the bases and dented home plate, "Ruth sat quiet with tears of joy shining in her eyes while Saunders wisely looked elsewhere."

Even in this its golden era baseball did not run unopposed. There were forces at work to undermine its popularity. Among them surely must be included the stories of Andy Nesbitt and Danny Dugan.

And in his frontal attack, in which he called baseball "somewhat less exciting than a spelling bee," Louis Graves struck a mighty blow for those who hoped, even at such a late date, that baseball might somehow be headed off. There is nothing in the record to show that Mr. Graves was maimed, but neither is there evidence that his acid commentary on the National Game had any effect whatever in holding back the tide.

He was competing against too many voices, great and small. One small voice of protest was raised in the same issue of *Harper's Weekly* by W. B. Hanna, a sportswriter. In rebuttal to Mr. Graves, Hanna stated his belief that "a great beauty of baseball is that it contains just the right proportion of action and inaction. That is one of its chief charms. Nothing palls so quickly as continuous action. The times between innings in baseball, bringing relaxation amid the whirl and excitement, are restful and pleasant."

He was competing against the greater voice of Walt Whitman, who said: "I see great things in baseball. It's our game— the American game. It will take our people out-of-doors, fill them with oxygen, give them a larger physical stoicism. Tend to relieve us from being a nervous, dyspeptic set. Repair these losses, and be a blessing to us."

Other and perhaps even more formidable opposition to the Graves viewpoint came from the clergy. *Baseball Magazine*, which recognized a good thing when it found one, was continually running articles with such titles as "Why Our Pastor Likes Baseball"—and the duo of clergy and magazine made for a breathless combination, as witness the following by the Reverend Roland D. Sawyer, a New York clergyman:

"At the baseball match, we encounter real democracy of spirit; one thing in common absorbs us; we rub shoulders high and low; we speak without waiting for an introduction; we forget everything clannish—all the pretty conventionalities being laid aside; individual experiences submerge in union of human feeling; we are swayed by a common impulse; we are all equal; the pressure of the crowd makes us one—the office boy who has stolen away, the businessman from the counting room, the clergyman from his study, the clerk from his desk, the girl from the factory, the wife from the home—all are on equal footing. Barriers are forgotten and how good it seems for us to be just human beings. It was just this experience which must have moved Ernest Howard Crosby of New York to explain: 'I find more genuine religion at the baseball match than I do at my father's church on Fifth Avenue.'"

Mr. Graves was fighting a game that could produce legends, although admittedly none so bizarre as the one that grew out of a contest between the University of St. Joseph and the Chatham Stars for the championship of Northern New Brunswick—a game in which a run was scored by a dead man. In this game, as recounted by *Baseball Magazine*, Chatham was leading 2–0 and two were out in the bottom of the ninth when O'Hara, a weak batter, doubled to left. He was followed by Robidoux, "a scrappy young Arcadian," who hit a long ball over the center-fielder's head. As O'Hara reached third base, he collapsed and died. Robidoux, rounding third, picked

O'Hara up and carried him down the base line, touching home plate first with O'Hara and then stepping on the plate himself. The game was tied 2–2.

The spectators went wild until it was announced that O'Hara was dead, and then they "stood with bared heads while the village doctor worked to restore life. O'Hara had scarificed his life that his team might win. He had scored a run while dead and thus made the most solemn, most dramatic and greatest play that baseball has ever seen!"

With something like this going against him, Mr. Graves clearly never had a chance.

He and others like him who wished the game ill, who felt it was a silly game and a glaring example of national values gone wrong, were fighting a public opinion which seemed convinced that baseball was the cure for the nation's ills and the best safeguard of its future.

As stated by the notable Allen Sangree, writing this time in *Everybody's Magazine* in 1907: "So long as it remains our national game, America will abide no monarchy—and anarchy will be too slow."

Or by H. Addington Bruce in *Outlook*, in 1913: "The little red school house has long been extolled as a prime factor in the republic's progress. I for one am firmly convinced that the lessons taught in it would have lacked much of their potency had it not been for the reinforcement they received from the lessons learned on the baseball field nearby. Long may Uncle Sam play ball!"

It was destiny. It was inevitability—perhaps even a national chemistry.

Baseball and the United States were made for each other.

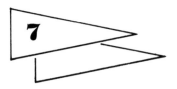

The National
Folk Drama

ALONG WITH SUCH OUTSIDE INFLUENCES AS SOCIOLOGY, PSYCHOL-
ogy, religio-public relations flak, and a puzzling offshoot of
chauvinism, what baseball also had going for it in its golden
age was the game, the men who played it, and the way they
played it. The nation may have been ripe for baseball and
may have given it unreasoning, dim-witted, mother-and-flag
adulation, but baseball gave the nation the brilliant exploits
of brilliant performers, fierce rivalries, illustrious World Series closely contested by great players and masterminded by
great managers. It was the age when John McGraw pitted
wits against France Chance and Connie Mack; when Chance,
the "Peerless Leader," matched strategy against Hugh Jennings; when Christy Mathewson pitched against Honus Wagner, Cy Young against Nap Lajoie. It was the age when

Walter Johnson, perhaps the greatest pitcher of all time, tried to blaze his fast ball past Ty Cobb, doubtless the greatest batter—dream encounters, and yet in that era something that could be watched on an ordinary weekday afternoon.

What baseball was giving the United States was its own national folk drama.

In this era there were six teams that dominated baseball—the New York Giants, Chicago Cubs, and Pittsburgh Pirates in the National League; the Philadelphia Athletics, Detroit Tigers, and Boston Red Sox in the American.

Most of baseball's dramatic moments, most of its star actors, were provided by those six teams.

It is entirely possible that when the 1892 *Reach Guide* lamented the low estate of baseball in New York and warned that as New York goes so goes baseball, it was not far off in its appraisal. For the rise of baseball to national popularity coincided almost precisely with the emergence of New York as a baseball power.

In the early 1900's, however, the best in New York baseball was represented not by the Yankees but by the Giants. The Yankees—as Yankees—did not even exist. The American League entry in New York was the team known as the Highlanders, who for a few years made a respectable enough showing in their own right, twice finishing second in the four years beginning in 1903, and vying with the Giants for a share of New York patronage. But the Highlanders were up against devastating odds. The hearts of New Yorkers belonged to the Giants.

After so many years of mediocrity, the city of New York finally had a team to be proud of, a team befitting the metropolis, a team which for year after year would make a trip out to the Polo Grounds at the foot of Coogan's Bluff an experience to be craved and remembered, to be recaptured with pride and delight the next day in the sweatshop or on Wall Street or while holding the reins of two huge Percheron draft horses with beer kegs rattling behind.

It was John McGraw who gave baseball to the city of New York.

When one speaks of the "McGraw years" in New York baseball, it is not immediately apparent which years are meant. The early years were the years of Christy Mathewson and Iron-Man Joe McGinnity, a pitcher of the stripe of Old Hoss Radbourn. McGinnity in 1903 started forty-eight games and completed forty-four, and three times in August pitched and won doubleheaders. Then there were the years of Roger Bresnahan, Mike Donlin, Arthur Devlin, Larry Doyle, Fred Tenney, Rube Marquard—and, until 1916, Mathewson. Later, in the early 1920's, there were Melvin Ott and Bill Terry and Fred Lindstrom and Travis Jackson—and, still later, Carl Hubbell.

And through all the years there was John McGraw, a short, irascible, ultimately pot-bellied, crafty, dedicated, autocratic man in whose life nothing mattered so much as winning a baseball game.

Before the arrival of McGraw the Giants were a very poor baseball club. In 1900 they finished dead last, in 1901 they were seventh, and in 1902 last again.

In 1903, McGraw's first year, the Giants had the unusual experience of a second-place finish. In both 1904 and 1905 they won the pennant. McGraw was off to a roaring start. He had a long way to go. Not until 1933 would he step down as Giants manager. At that time professional baseball in the United States was just over sixty years old. John McGraw was a manager for exactly thirty years.

In all the history of baseball, only one man ever managed longer—Connie Mack, McGraw's managerial counterpart in the American League and his polar opposite as a man.

John McGraw was known as "Little Napoleon" and the nickname is well founded, in terms of both his autocratic methods and the impression he gave as he directed his team from the third-base coach's box—a short, stumpy figure assuming an attitude that seemed always to be the same as the years passed, even when the pot belly became more pronounced and the hair turned gray and then white, the face became grizzled and the small eyes seemed to grow even smaller as they became hemmed in with wrinkles.

Almost always McGraw managed his team from the coach's box, and it was characteristic of him that he should have done so, for his philosophy of management was one always of direct confrontation, head to head, jaw to jaw. He was his own man, and in all the years of his stewardship there was never a doubt of who was boss of the New York Giants.

"Did you ever meet him?" a sportswriter asked his readers in 1908. "Did you ever come face to face and shake hands with the most unpopular man in the baseball business? If you did, the first thing that crosses your mind is that the person who introduced you is putting up a joke on you. It doesn't seem possible that the mild-mannered, gentlemanly, quiet man who shakes your hand is John McGraw. I have seen this John McGraw time and again give up his lower berth, or his stateroom, on a train to a woman and her children who had an upper or perhaps no berth at all. I have seen him do the same for an old man—and then sit up all night in the smoker."

Whether the writer was giving an accurate account or whether he was simply trying to make a story by portraying the "other" John McGraw is conjectural. Either way, it would have meant little to McGraw. Although he was doubtless unpopular around the league, he was extremely admired by the New York fans because of what he had given them and continued to give them year after year. Yet this too probably gave him little concern. He cared about winning ball games.

He had firm convictions on how ball games were won and lost, and on the responsibility for winning and losing them. It was his, the manager's. He left nothing to chance, shuffled off none of his chores, watched his players every second with his glittering hawk's eyes, and his brain kept whirling. He was always playing the angles, looking for openings, using strategy that was unorthodox for its day and might still be. There was a game in which the Giants, trailing 8–1, managed to fill the bases. The next batter singled and two runs could have scored easily but McGraw, coaching at third, prevented the second runner from scoring, holding him up at third. In his reasoning, there was nothing so upsetting to a pitcher as to look around and see the bases loaded with Giants. He kept them loaded, even at the expense of the additional run. Just as his old Baltimore Orioles had played thinking man's baseball in the 1890's, so was John McGraw a thinking man's manager—and an autocrat.

"With my team," he once said, "I am an absolute czar. My men know it. I order plays and they obey. If they don't, I fine them."

His credo, as offered to *Literary Digest* in 1914: "Learn to know every man under you, get under his skin, know his faults. Then cater to him—with kindness or roughness, as his case may demand."

Once during a game in Philadelphia, Rube Marquard and Josh Devore, roommates on the road, were sitting in the dugout talking of the fine hotel room they had. This sort of thing to McGraw was unthinkable. During a ball game his players were to think and speak of nothing but the ball game.

In McGraw's own account:

" 'Say Rube,' began Devore, 'ain't that room of ours a dandy?'

" 'Best in the lot,' replied Marquard.

" 'It's got five windows and swell furniture,' continued Devore.

" 'Solid mahogany,' I interrupted, 'and that will be all for you fellows. If I hear any more of that talk during this game I'll fine you $10 apiece.' "

Devore was a batter who always had trouble hitting against left-handed pitchers, mainly because, in McGraw's opinion, he was afraid of getting hit by the pitch. One day during a game with St. Louis he instructed Devore to let the pitcher hit him.

Devore looked flabbergasted.

"If you don't, it will cost you $10," McGraw said.

Devore let a couple go by and then took one on the hip. "Say, Mac, that was a cinch," he called as he ran, grinning, to first base.

From that day on, according to McGraw, Devore was always able to hit against left-handed pitchers.

With McGraw, by his own ready admission, there was no such thing as an honor system for ball players. To him, the honor system was an absurdity and a failure on his own part to accept responsibility. He treated his players like children and for the most part made them like it. "He'd walk up and down the dugout and yell, 'Wipe those damned smiles off your face,'" recalled Rogers Hornsby, who played for him. "He'd warn players against becoming buddy-buddy with sportswriters. One rookie was really scared. When a writer asked, 'Are you married?' the rookie answered, 'You'd better ask Mr. McGraw.'"

"I believe in the watch-dog policy whenever it's necessary," McGraw himself said. "I have always made it a point to maintain strict surveillance over my players when they are off the field."

On the field, he watched their every move, plotted the action to the last detail, always standing behind them if they followed orders, never absolving himself of blame if his orders proved wrong.

Billy Evans, for years an American League umpire, summed up McGraw's managerial philosophy as follows: "The theory on which the McGraw school of baseball is run is that the manager must be absolute in his leadership. He must never consult with his players. He reasons that the manager should take the entire responsibility and shoulder all the blame. McGraw never censures his players for making errors but let one of the players pull a boner and he never forgets it. Indeed, he makes it a point to mention it at stated intervals."

Over the years, one of the very few Giants McGraw ever took into his confidence was Christy Mathewson, and for seeing Matty as a man apart McGraw had good cause. Not only was he tractable and gentlemanly, he was also the greatest contributing force in McGraw's passionate desire to win baseball games. To have treated him as a minion would have been rankly ungrateful as well as unintelligent. He also had value as a go-between—when McGraw bawled out his players, it was Mathewson who healed the wounds, acting as counselor, particularly to the young players confronting the salty McGraw for the first time. For years and years the history of Giants baseball was focused on these two, the manager and the pitcher, and there was no player so instrumental as Mathewson in creating the glamor that became associated with the New York Giants.

Perhaps fittingly for such an exemplary young man, Mathewson began his baseball career by pitching for the YMCA in Scranton, Pennsylvania. The Giants acquired him from Norfolk of the Virginia League, where he had recorded an eye-popping season of twenty-one victories against two losses.

Mathewson's first season with the Giants was 1900, and within a very short time he was the idol of New York and soon of the nation, a man whose "photo was pasted up in the rooms of a million-odd men and boys." He must surely have been the most photographed ball player of his day, because he was a star pitcher, of course, but also because he was photogenic and generally considered handsome. His face showed the sort of "breeding" many associate with career State Department employees—square jaw, chiseled lines, everything indeed but horn-rimmed glasses. Most often he was photographed wearing one of the heavy cardigan sweaters with stand-up collars that most ball players of that day wore as windbreakers. Off the field he dressed like the businessman he was soon to become. "The fit of his coat shows that a Broadway tailor has taken careful measurements." In one photograph we see him with jacket off, wearing a wing collar and a necktie with a huge knot, looking supremely confident as he vies at checkers with the checker champion of the state of Indiana, who looks harassed. Sitting by, waiting his turn, is the checker champion of Ohio, looking anxious. Matty, we are told, drubbed them both. An interviewer wrote that his head was "a Saint-Gaudens head," and the sculptress Malvina Hoffman must have thought something of the sort, for she did a celebrated sculpture of him. She came out to the Polo Grounds time and again to watch him perform, just as, years later, the poetess Marianne Moore would go to Ebbets Field to watch the Brooklyn Dodgers.

Mathewson, we are told, was sober and industrious and thoughtful both off the field and on. Within a few years after joining the Giants he was in the insurance business with an office at 20 Vesey Street in Manhattan, parlaying his success on the diamond into security for the future, and counseling other ball players to do likewise; he also counseled parents on how best to fit their sons for a baseball career: "A boy cannot begin playing ball too early. I might almost say that while he is still creeping on all fours he should have a bouncing rubber ball."

Big Six, he was called, the man who gave the nation a new word—"the fadeaway," a perverse curve never before mastered by a right-handed pitcher, one that broke down and toward a right-handed batter. Schoolboys as far away as Nebraska, although they might not have understood the precise dynamics, knew the fadeaway was a pitch originated by Christy Mathewson and used by him with deadly effect. Year after year the victories mounted—twenty-nine in 1903, thirty-six in 1904, thirty-seven in 1908.

As pitching careers go, Mathewson's was by no means the longest. He ended it after the 1916 season. Yet into his seventeen seasons in the major leagues he packed a tremendous amount of pitching. There were some years when he was

McGraw's only dependable pitcher and he became, year in, year out, the workhorse of the Giant staff. For his major-league career, he averaged a bare fraction under twenty-two victories a season, while Walter Johnson, by comparison, averaged just over nineteen. As a moundsman, Mathewson was deceptive in more respects than one. Working as frequently as he was forced to work, he became a master at pacing himself. Instead of trying to mow down each opposition batter in turn, he eased up when there were no men on base or when the Giants had a commanding lead, saving his energies for the points of crisis. In the pinches, he was superb.

Some of baseball's greatest pitchers—and, for that matter, greatest sluggers—spend their entire careers without ever getting into a World Series. Mathewson pitched in no fewer than five, and it would have been six had the National League not been guilty of the sort of preposterous pettiness that the fans hoped it had left behind forever.

After the 1903 season, Boston, as the American League pennant winner, had the temerity to take on the National League winner, Pittsburgh, in the World Series. According to one account, when Boston won, the National League owners were so miffed over the loss they decreed the predictable: in 1904, no World Series. The Giants were the 1904 pennant winners, and according to another account it was McGraw himself who refused to enter his team in the Series, sarcastically referring to the Bostons as a minor-league team unworthy of the Giants' attention. In any case, the Giants sat it out and there was no Series. The public uproar was so great that the Series was resumed in 1905, and the World Series of 1905 was one of the game's most historic, partly because of the feats of Christy Mathewson and partly because it marked the first encounter between John McGraw and Connie Mack.

The life of Cornelius McGillicuddy, the name Mack was born with, covers an enormous span of baseball history, reaching far back into one century and stretching deep into the next. Mack was seven years old the summer that Harry Wright's old Cincinnati Red Stockings barnstormed the United States. He was seventy when Jimmy Foxx, Al Simmons, Lefty Grove, Mickey Cochrane, and the other Philadelphia Athletics of 1931 captured the third of three consecutive pennants. Not until 1950 did he end his managerial career, when he was eighty-eight. By then he was dealing with players whom he kept hoping to the very end he might somehow mold into a team that would give him the one last pennant that he sought but which never came. He won nine. Only McGraw and Casey Stengel won more.

It seems unreasonable to believe that a man who spent so many years as a major-league manager could ever have been anything else, but Mack, before taking over at Philadelphia in 1901, had had a ten-year career as a player, a catcher, doing a three-year hitch with Washington in the 1880's. Ironically, and perhaps absurdly, it was as a catcher that he gained entry into Baseball's Hall of Fame. As a catcher he is carried on its rolls; as a catcher he had a career batting average of .249.

When Mack became a manager he was thirty-nine years old, and already he seemed patriarchal. He fits the picture of a long, lean Mr. Chips of Baseball, with his mild eyes, slightly sunken cheeks, genteel manner, and his patience with the men who learned baseball under him during the long years of his career. Side by side, John McGraw and Connie Mack were like Mutt and Jeff, and the contrast between them did not end with height. Rarely did Mack become angry, rarely did he raise his voice. Instead of remaining gruffly aloof from his players, instead of operating as a one-man gang, he always had three of four of his brainiest and most experienced players as lieutenants, regularly seeking their advice. Seldom did he appear on the playing field. He directed his team from the dugout, looking always the part of a gentleman, dressed in a business suit, keeping the jacket on in early spring, taking it off when summer came and even then wearing a necktie and most often a detachable collar with rounded tabs, shirt sleeves rolled to the elbow. His hats were derbies or straw skimmers. In his hand there was a scorecard and the scorecard was his trademark. Some baseball fans knew that he used it to record every play of every game. Many more knew that he used it as a direction finder for misplaced outfielders. For fifty seasons he sat in the Philadelphia dugout, flicking, wigwagging with his scorecard, motioning an outfielder to move in, move out ("Look at old Connie with his scorecard!" the fans would say), move a little closer to the foul line or a little more toward center. From the shade of the dugout he sat squinting out over the field, squinting at a cavalcade of some of the greatest players the game has ever known—as far back as 1902, and doubtless with despair, at the incorrigible Rube Waddell; and almost thirty years later flicking and wigwagging to catch the attention of Al Simmons, Mule Haas, and Bing Miller, the outfield of his last great team; and, toward the end, at outfielders whose names no longer matter. And by then the veins in his thin arms stood out like cords and the hand that held the scorecard trembled a little.

Mack was unique in that he not only managed the Athletics, he was also part owner of the franchise. He was also the first manager to see the college campus as a proving ground for major-league ball players. Using full-time scouts, he scoured the college ranks. The dividends included Eddie Plank and Jack Coombs, two of his all-time great pitchers, as well as Eddie Collins and Jack Barry, half of the so-called "hundred-thousand-dollar infield" that would play for the Athletics a few years later.

For whatever reason, he also attracted two of the game's all-time incorrigibles—one of its most notorious villains, Joe Jackson, and perhaps its greatest comedian, or at least its most uninhibited eccentric, George Edward Waddell, known as Rube.

Although Jackson became a star with Cleveland and corrupted baseball as a member of the White Sox, he began his career as a rookie with the Philadelphia Athletics. For a time

Connie Mack coddled him along, struck and tempted by his enormous talent but disheartened by his primitive code of behavior. By his own admission, Jackson broke Mack's rules when he saw fit. Once, in his phrase, he "did a Waddell"—on his way to the ball park for the game he was seized, as he said, with a gripping desire to go to the theater, whereupon he hopped off the trolley and spent the afternoon at a burlesque house.

After other such episodes, Mack despaired and sent him to New Orleans, whence he was sold to Cleveland, a purchase which in the perspective of baseball history may not have been in the best interests of the National Game.

In some respects Rube Waddell's code of self-conduct was as loose and as naïve as Jackson's. He was self-indulgent, freewheeling, a child-man bent upon joy. It is difficult to think of him doing anything so covert as conniving with gamblers to throw ball games, and yet long after his career was ended there would be rumors.

The young Waddell seems to fit precisely the classic mold of country yokel, of raw rookie, and to read some contemporary descriptions is to wonder if he may not have been overdoing it, but it seems likely that his rustic, uninhibited mannerisms were real and not artifice. He applied on his own for his first major-league pitching job—with Louisville, then still in the National League—and when he showed up at the ball park he was wearing "a dinky little cap, country-cut clothes" and carrying a suitcase hardly larger than "the ordinary yellow collar-boxes." His walk, according to the *Baltimore Sun*, was a "typical country long-gait, with an accompanying swaying of the shoulders." When he walked to the pitcher's box, he had the look of a man walking over a plowed field. When the fans yelled, "Hey, Rube!" he bowed from the waist. Bestowing his nickname required little imagination.

In the lore of baseball, Waddell is famous for chasing fire engines (once during a game he vaulted the center-field fence

to chase one) and for the day he called in all three of his outfielders and all his infielders except the first baseman and
made them all stand by while he struck out the side.

He loved baseball but he might have been equally happy
as a fireman or a bartender. Once when he was scheduled
to pitch and failed to show up, he was found wearing a
white apron, tending bar. Lost to the Athletics for three days,
he returned as the drum major of a band marching up Main
Street. He posed in a show window as an automaton. One
winter he broke into the theater as one of the stars in a
melodrama called *The Stain of Guilt*. His part called for
him to save the girl and beat up the villain, which he did with
such realism and exuberance that it was necessary to work the
villain in relays. Tiring of his role, he walked out on the cast
and showed up tending bar in Camden, New Jersey, a city he
seemed to love. Once during a game at St. Louis he leaped
into the stands, beat up a gambler who had been taunting
him, returned to the field, struck out the batter, and then hit
the double that beat the Browns. In his final contract with
Connie Mack, he insisted upon a clause prohibiting his catcher
and roommate, Ossie Schreckengost, from eating crackers in
bed. Once, drunk at midnight, he invaded Mack's hotel room,
roused the sleeping manager, and tossed a rancid-smelling
onion-and-limburger-cheese sandwich on the counterpane,
telling Mack he had not been looking well and suggesting that
the sandwich might help perk him up.

Rube was strongly attracted to women, but their attraction
quickly wore off and he apparently chased them—and married
them—as whimsically as he chased fire engines and retreated
to bartending. "Thoughtless about married life," according to
the *Columbus Dispatch*, "he took frequent wives and led an
exciting life with them and with their relatives, being in
and out of jail for non-support and occasionally varying the
monotony by shying a flat-iron or other missile at one of his
parents-in-law."

Yet he once jumped into an icy river to save a man from

drowning, and was credited with saving the life of a teammate, Danny Hofman, after Hofman was hit in the head with a fast ball thrown by a Boston pitcher. An ambulance was summoned, players stood about indecisively, and a doctor expressed doubt that Hofman could survive if he wasn't gotten to the hospital immediately. At this, Waddell lifted the senseless Hofman gently to his shoulders and ran with him off the field and out of the park to the street, where he commandeered a passing carriage, got Hofman to the hospital, and, still wearing his baseball uniform, sat up with him all through the night, holding ice to his head.

When he died after a short, flashing life of thirty-seven years, the *Literary Digest* found him poignant, calling him "one of those characters at once the most enviable and the saddest and most pitiful in the world, who are too great at heart for the civilization in which they live. They are affectionate, good-hearted giants . . . too impatient and too full of animal energy to stop and work out all the little tricks and artifices that would bring them gain . . . angered only as a child is angered by the sting of little annoyances and sobered only in the presence of the genuine distress of others. Most of these giants die young."

It is unlikely that Waddell found his own life poignant. There is every evidence that he loved it—the pitching, the applause, the fan worship, sitting around in hotel lobbies waiting for people to recognize and admire him. In the words of another newspaper of the day, he was a "sworn enemy of gloom, a joyous wastrel, the boy that never grew up"—as well as one of the greatest of all pitchers. There were days when he had it all—the day when he pitched and won a fourteen-inning game and then kept right on pitching to win a nine-inning game, ending up by turning cartwheels all the way to the clubhouse.

The World Series of 1905, then, pitted the New York Giants of John McGraw against the Philadelphia Athletics of Connie

Mack. And it was to have pitted McGraw's star performer, the urbane Christy Mathewson, against Connie Mack's bad boy, Rube Waddell.

In that World Series Christy Mathewson did something that no pitcher since Old Hoss Radbourn had done, and something no pitcher has ever done since. Mathewson won three victories, all shutouts. The Athletics faced him in twenty-seven innings and scored not a run.

Of the five games played, all five were shutouts. The Giants won the Series, four games to one, their other victory going to Iron-Man McGinnity. Philadelphia's lone victory was pitched by Chief Bender, who shut out the Giants in the second game, 3–0.

The goat of the Series was Rube Waddell, even though—or because—he never pitched to a single batter. Counted upon as Mack's mainstay, he claimed to have injured his arm in a fall on a train. Years later there would be rumors that he had been bribed and that the injury was a fake. Whatever the truth, he was out of action for the entire Series, and the first encounter between McGraw and Mack was a victory for McGraw—and for Christy Mathewson. Not until 1911 would they meet again, and for a time they were forced to yield the stage to the Detroit Tigers of Ty Cobb and Hugh Jennings in the American League, and to the Cubs of Frank Chance in the National.

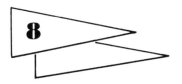

Golden Bats,
Golden Arms

FRANK CHANCE, FIRST BASEMAN AND MANAGER OF THE CHICAGO
Cubs, was neither the game's greatest first baseman nor its
greatest manager. He was merely excellent in all respects. His
contemporaries found it difficult to portray him as colorful,
for he wasn't. He was all business, all excellence, a college
man, a Californian, wealthy for his day, who approached
baseball, it would appear, as a project to be consummately
mastered. For McGraw baseball was a passion, for Waddell
the escapade he loved best and most enduringly, for Ty Cobb
an alleyway where he could slash his way to superiority—
but for Frank Chance baseball was a game he had chosen as
his occupation. He chose well and performed admirably,
making John McGraw's life miserable year after year while
the Cubs, under Chance, won three consecutive pennants,

gave way to Pittsburgh in 1909, and took it again in 1910. Not for nothing was he known as the Peerless Leader.

Unlike McGraw, unlike Mack, Chance was a playing manager, the first great one. He managed from his position on the diamond, first base, where he excelled as a fielder, just as he excelled as a batter and as a stealer of bases. One season he stole sixty-seven. Nor was he a slouch in the countinghouse. The Cubs' owner called him the "greatest manager in the past quarter century" and paid dearly for his services, not only in salary but in a share of the profits, for Chance owned a slice of the franchise.

Frank Chance was by no means a one-man team. He directed some splendid players. On Cub double plays, the ball traveled from shortstop Joe Tinker to second baseman Johnny Evers to first baseman Frank Chance—and Tinker to Evers to Chance became and has remained the most famous double-play combination of all time. He had one of baseball's greatest receivers, Johnny Kling. When Kling sat out the 1909 season because of salary squabbles, many felt it was his absence that cost the Cubs a fourth consecutive pennant, and he was chosen to at least one all-star team for that season even though he hadn't caught a single game. Their leading pitcher was the biblically named Mordecai Brown—also called Miner Brown because he had worked in the Indiana coal mines as a youth, but known most often as "Three Finger" Brown because the index finger of his right hand, his pitching hand, was a mere stub, causing the ball to perform strange dips and turns. Gripped in Brown's three fingers and thumb, and nudged by the stump, the ball twisted so puzzlingly that Mordecai was one of the most formidable pitchers of his day. To the extreme distaste of McGraw and the New York fans, he seemed always to be at his best against the Giants and particularly against the great Mathewson, usually beating him when they met head to head. Brown's moundmates included the well-known Ed Reulbach and the pitcher named Overall, whom his parents had chosen to name Orval. In 1908, when the Cubs edged the Giants for their third consecutive pennant, Brown, Reulbach, and Orval Overall contributed sixty-nine victories. In the National League's list of leading pitchers for that year, Brown, Reulbach, and Overall took down three of the four top spots. The only non-Cub was, as might be expected, Christy Mathewson, with a record of 36–11.

In 1906 the Cubs easily won the pennant with the astounding total of 116 victories, a total never equaled even by the New York Yankees at their most invincible. In the World Series, however, to the great surprise of the baseball world, the Cubs met their match, losing four games out of six to their cross-city rivals, the Chicago White Sox, who won it with a pitching staff headed by Big Ed Walsh, another ex-coal miner and a glutton for work, who depended upon a delivery that baseball has often tried to outlaw, never with success—the spitball.

The White Sox of that era were known as the "hitless wonders" and it was a phrase that might well have been applied to the teams of both leagues—by all standards except those of 1968, when the hitters, particularly in the American League, made the men of the hitless-wonder era seem fine hitters by comparison. Nonetheless, by the standards of the earlier day, the hitters were considered to be in a decade-long slump, bringing gloomy predictions for the game's future.

In the checks-and-balances ratio that baseball continually manipulated, now for the pitcher's benefit, now for the batter's, the last significant change had come in 1893 when the pitching slab was moved back five feet.

"The object of the change," as noted by the *Reach Guide*, "was to increase the batting, handicap the pitcher, and add to the interest of the sport. Each object was attained. The batting was materially increased. Whereas only twelve batsmen reached an average of .300 or over in 1892, more than 60 batsmen reached that percentage in 1893 under the new rule. Pitchers were astoundingly handicapped by the extra five feet. In many notable instances, pitchers were driven out of the business, or their effectiveness was so weakened as to make them of little or no worth to their respective clubs. The public interest in the game was thereby most certainly stimulated."

By 1898, however, the *Guide* reported that the game again was marked by "weak hitting all around the circuit—almost every one of the heavy sluggers, the men who sting the ball, fell off in percentage." When it got down to statistics, the *Guide* noted that in 1898 there were "only" forty-five men who hit .300 or better, a lament most puzzling to the fans of 1968, when Yastrzemski was the only man in the American League to reach .300, a mark traditionally observed as the point of separation between the game's good hitters and those who, at least in terms of hitting frequency, are among the also-rans. To record an average of .300 means that a man has averaged three safe hits in every ten times at bat.

The *Guide's* explanation for batting's low estate was that the pitchers had grown accustomed to the greater pitching distance and had once again mastered the hitters—if mastery it could be termed when forty-five of them batted over .300. In 1900 the *Guide's* sympathy for the batters intensified. They had a poor year indeed, it said, "the pitching of the season being altogether too good for them." A mere thirty-five reached the charmed .300 figure.

In the early years of the new century the decline became real, dramatically emphasized by the every-game-a-shutout 1905 World Series, and again by the World Series of 1906, when Ed Walsh and his pitching mates Doc White and Nick Altrock won it for the "hitless-wonder" White Sox by making the Cub batters look silly. All through both leagues, low-score games were the rule, teams scrapped hard for a single run, and the scoring of one was a rarity. In 1905 the American League batting championship was won by Elmer Flick with a mark of .306, lowest in history until Yastrzemski recorded .301. By 1905 home runs were almost extinct. The league-leading

total that year was eight, and a few seasons later Frank
Baker, the Philadelphia Athletics third baseman, could win a
reputation as a slugger, could win himself the nickname
"Home Run" Baker, by hitting two home runs in the 1911
World Series and winning the home-run championship four
years in a row with totals of nine, ten, twelve, and eight. In
1905 the White Sox hit only three home runs the entire season.

What to do about batting's low estate? It seemed unfeasible
to move the pitching slab back yet again. Many complaints
were directed against the size of the gloves being used. "Their
size," it was written in 1908, "should be kept down to reasonable proportions as a means of increasing hitting. Something
should be done at once in this matter. Run-getting has become more and more scarce and nothing has contributed
more to this fact than the cutting-off of hits by the use of these
enormous gloves. Nothing of this kind prevailed in the early
eighties and people who remember those days say the abuse
of the glove privilege has in large measure spoiled the game
for them."

An article written in 1909 by one James Lovitt might well
have been written following the season of 1968. Asking "Shall
batting be doomed?" Lovitt declaims:

"It takes no close observer of the game to see that batting
is being smothered out more and more by the modern style
of pitching. One might almost say that in a short time batting
will be only of the past tense. It is certainly a pity that batting—the life of the game—should be relegated to the background. Batting is the blood of the game. Every fan can testify
to the lackadaisical quality displayed . . . in a thirteen
inning game with neither side scoring. Some will say that
even though no runs are made, such a game is exciting. To
him, I say, you are not a true sport!"

If a true sport may be defined as one who wants more
hitting and less pitching, there are true sports by the tens and
hundreds of thousands among today's baseball fans. Once
again it is being asked if batting shall be doomed and once

again there are attempts to explain its decline. Large gloves are cited, just as they were seventy years ago. Another popular explanation is that kids, Little Leaguers and sand-lotters, enjoy being pitchers and many, a disproportionate number, turn to pitching at an early age, resulting in a bumper pitcher crop. Mickey Mantle advances the suggestion that kids interested in pitching have become smarter pitchers for having watched so many baseball games on television.

In the early 1900's, for all the talk of big gloves (which in fact were much smaller than those of today), the main reason for pitching superiority seems to have been the freedom of the pitchers to tamper with the cover of the ball. Not only could they spit on it, some coarsened its surface with sandpaper and even nicked it with knives or razor blades. These practices were gradually outlawed but in the end what seemed the real cure was the use of a more resilient ball, one with more cork in the center, and it would be ironic if the ills of baseball today could be cured with a fraction of an ounce of cork.

For all the talk of the dead-ball era, for all the low-scoring World Series and regular-season games, it is remarkable to note that dead ball or no, Age of Pitching or no, there were men in that time who pulverized the ball with amazing frequency, so that it may be reasonable to wonder if there may not simply have been better hitters in that day. For in that earlier time there were not only pitchers who recorded great feats by standards of measurement that are timeless, there were batters even in the dead-ball era whose feats were tremendous by standards equally timeless.

For all the memorable pitching feats of Christy Mathewson, Walter Johnson, Ed Walsh, Mordecai Brown, Rube Waddell, or Cy Young, there were remarkable displays of batting by such marvelous hitters as Napoleon Lajoie, Honus Wagner, and Ty Cobb. They stood up at the plate, looked at the dead ball, the scarred, nicked ball, and knocked it all over the lot—or, as in the case of Cobb, called upon cunning, craft, and

Walter Johnson, perhaps the game's greatest pitcher, hurling against Ty Cobb, its greatest hitter—a dream encounter that could be witnessed on an ordinary weekday afternoon during baseball's Golden Age.

GEORGE WRIGHT AND THE GOLDEN GATE
From a Painting by Carl Dahlgren, executed for S. R. Church

George Wright, a member of baseball's first professional team, the Cincinnati Red Stockings. George in his day was acclaimed as the "very beau ideal of a shortstop."

Delirious over the feats of the 1869 Red Stockings, the fans of Cincinnati were hard put to find a token of suitable magnitude. They settled on this huge bat.

The Elysian Fields, a gladed meadow near Hoboken, New Jersey, where the first recorded game of baseball was played in 1846.

John (Honus) Wagner, an ungainly-looking man of enormous strength and speed, was one of the few ball players of his day with careful regard for a dollar.

Wagner in his prime was considered the finest player on spikes. He is generally ranked just below Cobb among the all-time greats.

Denton True (Cy) Young, whose 511 pitching victories are a major-league record. His success maxims contrast with those of the remarkable Satchel Paige.

In baseball's early days, the umpire was considered fair game **for players and fans alike.**

Adrian Constantine (Cap) Anson, a **magnificent** player in the old days of barehanded baseball.

Rapid Robert Feller, a great right-hander. In 1948, while Feller helped pitch the Cleveland Indians to the pennant, Bill Veeck was giving away orchids and listening to the click of the turnstiles.

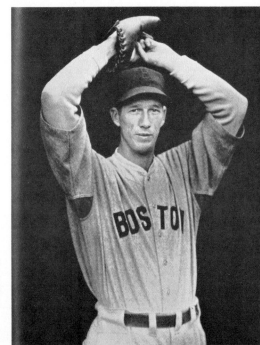

Robert Moses (Lefty) Grove was still pitching at forty-one. In 1931, as a member of Connie Mack's last great team, he chalked up a record of 31–4.

Jerome (Dizzy) Dean, who like Joe Namath and Cassius Clay had the talent to back up his mouth.

Dizzy and Paul (Daffy) Dean, a superlative brother act. In 1934 they brightened the dark days of the Depression by offering the public an epic, day-to-day suspense story.

Rogers Hornsby, the much-traveled player and manager who cared more about winning batting titles than about winning friends. One player said that playing under Hornsby was like being in reform school.

Jimmy Foxx, a Maryland farm boy whose powerful biceps and keen eye made him one of the best sluggers.

desire to record fabulous batting averages, placing the ball, chopping it, bunting it—when he wasn't lining it between the outfielders. Honus Wagner, playing for Pittsburgh, in the heart of the dead-ball era, rattled off, beginning in 1900, consecutive season batting averages of .380, .352, .329, .355, .349, .363, .339, and .350. He was hitting against the likes of Christy Mathewson, Ed Reulbach, Joe McGinnity, and "Three Finger" Brown. Napoleon Lajoie was cleaning harness and feeding oats to the horses in a Woonsocket, Rhode Island, livery stable when he was offered his first professional contract with Fall River, Massachusetts. He went on to a big-league career of twenty-one seasons, performing blazing feats with his bat—in spite of the fact that he was said to be a "careless" hitter, a bad-ball hitter, with a habit, like Yogi Berra years later, of hitting at anything he could reach with his bat. In 1901, when the ball was dead, he recorded the highest batting average in American League history, .422—a mark unequaled even by the great Ty Cobb.

Basically, conditions were the same. The distance from pitcher to batter was sixty feet, six inches, just as it is today. The speed of Walter Johnson's fast ball was computed at 120 feet per second, and certainly the batters of today are required to face none faster. At the rate of 120 feet per second it still takes half a second for the ball to travel from pitcher to batter. Batters then, just as batters now, have that same half second to act upon their recognition of the fact that the ball is coming, is already there, and the bat must be swung.

Of Ty Cobb, whose reflexes were surely among the greatest in history, Walter Johnson himself wrote: "If you put the ball on the outside where he likes it, he will drop it into left field. Keep it inside and he is liable to kill your first baseman. About 'the best way to fool him is to get the ball up there faster than he can get his bat around."

Cobb was one batter who hit Johnson with fair regularity, partly because he was the best hitter in the game but also because, by his own admission, he took advantage of John-

son's fear that he might some day hit and injure somebody
with his devastating fast ball. Cobb accordingly crowded the
plate, knowing that Johnson would ease up, which he always
did even though he knew what Cobb was up to. "When I
began hitting him," Cobb wrote, "he'd look upset and I'd hear
him say, 'Gee whillikins.'" When Walter Johnson was angry,
according to Cobb, he would exclaim "Goodness gracious" and
when he was extremely angry he would explode, "Goodness
gracious—*animal!*" For a man with such a mild vocabulary
and so gentle a manner, Johnson was an object of fear all
through the league. When Cobb was managing Detroit, he
recalled, his players, particularly on murky days, would seek
him out and moan, "'Ty, I've got an awful bellyache today,
mind if I lay off?' You could tell Johnson was slated to work
that day. The boys were scared and they begged off in
bunches. . . . I can't say I blame them. A sidearm Johnson
fast one looked about the size of a watermelon seed and it
hissed at you as it passed."

In the rise of the Detroit Tigers to interrupt Connie Mack's
domination of the American League, it was Cobb who took
down most of the credit—Cobb and Sam Crawford, the slugging outfielder, as well as Hugh Jennings, who directed the
Tigers to their first pennant in his very first year as manager,
1907. Jennings was still another ex-coal miner and later a
practicing lawyer. As a member of the old Baltimore Orioles,
he brought special qualifications for handling a slasher such as
Cobb and it was under Jennings' soothing guidance that Cobb,
after a particularly stormy freshman and sophomore year in
the big leagues, managed to compose his nerves and settle
down, at least frequently enough to give most of his attention
to baseball.

Cobb, on more than one count, was a man apart. In the faroff days of the early 1900's people enjoyed speaking of "hot
southern blood," and in Cobb's case the phrase was used frequently as an explanation for behavior that some chose to

explain otherwise—and which still others, Cobb among them, explained in terms of self-defense. In more than one view he was simply a cruel, hostile man. Some felt he had come north to refight the Civil War, to redeem the honor of the Southland by doing on a baseball field what the southern armies had been unable to do on the field of battle—not that he made any exception of southern players if they happened to be in his way. In a game at Philadelphia he spiked Frank Baker, whose native hamlet of Trappe on Maryland's eastern shore surely should have been southern enough in geography and sympathy for anyone who came north only to slash northerners. Although Cobb's blood was undeniably overheated, and although a behaviorist might have said his southern heritage had something to do with his makeup, it is also possible that he spiked opposition players simply because they were in his way and the base paths, he maintained, belonged to the runner.

"Starve and drive out the evil demon that lurks in all human blood and is ready to arise and reign. Be under the perpetual guidance of the better angel of your nature. Be good."

This was contained in a letter written to him by his "philosopher father," Cobb said, "and I lived up to it. I may have been fierce but never low or underhand."

A native of Royston, Georgia, Cobb came into the major leagues swinging—fighting with his fists almost from the very first day he entered the Detroit Tigers clubhouse, and he kept on fighting in one form or another all through his astonishing major-league career. With Augusta of the South Atlantic League, his first and only minor-league team (from which Detroit bought him for $700), he spent a good part of the season fighting, and when he joined the Tigers in August of 1905 he came into the clubhouse, according to one account, with a chip on his shoulder so pronounced that "discretion had to be drummed into him by the fists of his teammates." Other accounts maintain that he was a gentleman and a "well brought-up boy" who never deliberately picked a fight in his

life, and that he was set upon in the cluhouse as a rookie by
"bullies" among the Tiger players. To read some versions of
the Cobb saga is to picture a weak but fierce young man,
animal eyes darting, determined not to have his weakness
exploited, and yet Cobb was far from a weakling physically
and in no time at all his fantastic strength and ability in his
chosen field should have given him enormous satisfaction. One
night in Cleveland, however, he got into a fight with a hotel
night watchman, according to *Baseball Magazine,* and when
the watchman wielded his billy club over Cobb's head, Cobb
drew a knife, stabbed the watchman, and was arrested for
slashing. After he spiked Frank Baker even the mild Connie
Mack was aroused, calling Cobb the dirtiest player the game
had known, and with the old Orioles in mind this covered a
lot of ground. After the spiking incident, on Detroit's next trip
to Shibe Park, another of the proud new stadiums of the era,
the Philadelphia management coaxed City Hall to station
250 policemen in the park, presenting a solid wall of blue
between the fans in the right-field stands—and Cobb, who
played right field. The fans had vowed to have his head, and
he had even received a number of Black Hand letters. Other
than a continuous hail of epithets there were no incidents, but
it was characteristic of Cobb that he played without regard
to personal threats. At one point during the game, according
to Cobb's own version, he crossed the right-field foul line in
pursuit of a foul fly, lunging into the cops and even some of
the spectators who had overflowed onto the field. In the
process he fell on one fan's straw hat and splintered it. When
he took up his right-field post in the next inning, he brought
the fan a five-dollar bill, which was gratefully received. According to Cobb, Baker's spike wound was only a scratch in
the first place, and the whole incident, he said, was blown up
by a Philadelphia sportswriter.

There is ample evidence, however, that for whatever reason Cobb was hardly the most popular player in the American
League. Toward the end of the 1910 season Cobb and Na-

poleon Lajoie were in a very tight race for the league batting championship, and riding on the outcome was a snappy new open touring car, donated at that time by the Chalmers automobile company as a sort of unofficial Most Valuable Player award. All around the league they were rooting against Cobb, and on the final day of the season the St. Louis Browns laid down flagrantly for Lajoie, letting him beat out bunts and giving everything he hit such a wide berth that he got eight hits in a doubleheader. Even so, Cobb won the batting championship, .3848 to .3841. The Chalmers company gave each man a touring car.

Popular or unpopular, Ty Cobb was giving the people of Royston, Georgia, something to talk about besides the Civil War, just as he left a career record that will be talked about as long as baseball exists. His accomplishments are superb. In his twenty-four seasons in the majors he led the American League in hitting no fewer than twelve times, compiling a lifetime average of .367, highest of all time. His record for total hits—4,191—seems as unreachable as the 511 pitching victories of Cy Young. Very few major-leaguers ever reach the 3,000 mark. He also holds the record for most games played—3,033; most lifetime runs scored—23,244; and is second in triples, with 297.

Cobb is generally described as an all-round ball player. The fact is that although good enough, he was hardly among the greatest as a defensive outfielder, hardly a Tris Speaker or Joe DiMaggio, nor did he have a great arm. His strengths were his batting ability and his base stealing, both of which were given added dimension by his fierce desire to win at almost any cost. Although he was capable of hitting home runs, he did not go for them as most batsmen do today, and he didn't hit many, only 118 in his whole career, and never more than twelve in a season. For Cobb, a home run might have robbed him of a good part of the thrill of the game, because in his case the term hit and run takes on different meaning from its usual tactical meaning. To Cobb, the joy of

baseball was to hit and then run, and one may even spec-
ulate that the hitting was subordinate, an expedient to permit him to get on base and once there to fly.

As long ago as 1914, *Literary Digest,* long departed, printed
an article on the factors of speed, distance, and human capa-
bility in baseball. It was written by Carl H. Claudy, who
also wrote fiction for *American Boy* magazine, likewise departed.

"When a man gets on first base," Claudy wrote, "his next
thought is of second—only 90 feet away, which looks so near
and is so far. A good base runner may be able to get a lead
of say 10 feet—immediately reducing the distance he must
travel to 80 feet. With a standing start, any good base runner
should make this distance in three seconds. Starting as the
pitcher begins to deliver the ball, it would seem easy enough
to slide into that bag in three seconds time well ahead of the
ball. Yet the pitcher who throws the ball 65 feet (60.5 to the
plate and another 4.5 to the catcher's hands), and the catcher
who must glove the ball, pick it out of his glove and fire it
124 and a fraction feet to second base, manage between them
to handle the ball so quickly that in the majority of cases the
ball is waiting for the runner when he arrives, giving the
shortstop or second baseman who caught it plenty of time to
reach forward and down, and touch the runner with the
hand which holds the ball."

Cobb made a mockery of the odds against him. Once he
reached base there was hardly any holding him. As a base
stealer he was fantastic and even though Maury Wills eclipsed
his one-season record of ninety-six by stealing 104, in 1962, it
seems almost certain that no player ever will approach his
lifetime record of 892. The bare figures, moreover, hardly reflect the extra bases he took with his speed, or all the times he
forced the opposition into fielding errors, or the psychological
effect he had upon opposing pitchers and jittery infielders. In
his own time, it was said that the only sure way to stop him
on the base paths was to throw to the base ahead of the one

he was approaching.

As is the case with many baseball stars, Cobb was disappointing in World Series play. In 1907 he and the rest of the Tigers folded up and the Series was described as "the veriest walkover" for Frank Chance's Cubs who took four straight. When the same two clubs met again the following year, the Cubs won almost as lopsidedly, this time four games to one.

Meanwhile, back in New York the Giants of John McGraw were playing consistently splendid baseball and in that year, 1908, the Cubs only made it to the World Series by an eyelash, or more precisely because of the mental agility of their second baseman, Johnny Evers, one of the brainiest players the game has known. It was Evers who made an eternal goat of the unfortunate Fred Merkle, the Giants first baseman whose failure to touch second base cost the Giants a run which would have given them the 1908 pennant. As it was, they had to be content with another second-place finish, but attendance and fan interest could hardly have been greater had they been winning the pennant year in, year out. By then, New York was a town gone mad for baseball. Although much of the credit went to the magic of McGraw and Mathewson, the catching of Roger Bresnahan, and the hitting of Mike Donlin, some went also to John T. Brush, author of the baseball-classification plan which had so infuriated the players in the 1880's. Brush's arrival as owner of the Giants coincided closely with the arrival of McGraw and Mathewson, good men to coincide with. He took over, furthermore, from one of the most unpopular executives in the game's history, Andrew Freedman, who waged a continuing vendetta against the New York press. Under Brush, the club's relations with public and newsmen improved. When he took over as president, according to one observer of the period, "baseball in New York was in a very bad way. Public interest was dead, and but 200 or 300 people attended a game. Rowdyism was rampant and even the president of the league, on hand to restore order, could do nothing. But with the arrival of Brush, a reform was instituted. The support of a heretofore hostile press was there for the asking. Rowdy players were given short shrift. Umpires no longer moved about in fear and trembling, ever on the lookout for a flying tonic bottle."

In his public relations campaign, Brush seemed to look with particular favor on theater people, so that we have the illustrious Douglas Fairbanks, most popular actor of his day, speaking of a regular colony of actors and actresses "who hie to the Polo Grounds at every conceivable opportunity and root for the Giants. . . . One is always sure to meet people there whom he knows and need never lack for company or a jolly time, even if things do go against his favorites."

Not only Douglas Fairbanks but his female counterpart in glamor, Lillian Russell, the sex-pot of her day, exclaimed over *baseball*, baseball at the Polo Grounds.

"The mystery of the thing fascinated me," she wrote for *Baseball Magazine*. "What was this terrible force that drew out such breathless and tumultuous interest? What genius of appeal had outlined this drama, had awakened an interest that awed you and battered down the walls of native reserve? Surely it was more than the mere efforts of eighteen plain everyday-looking men to strike at a small sphere and, having occasionally met it, go scampering about a square of prescribed confines. . . . No, it was more than this. There were the commingled elements of surprise, of eager expectancy, of emotional efforts to anticipate kaleidoscopic possibilities, of civic partisanship, or personal admiration for a favorite—Oh! There were so many contributors that the whole keeps you guessing."

"Whatever else it is," Miss Russell went on, picking up the magazine's lungs-and-fresh-air line, "the game is wholesome. Its very vital call is its unquestioned integrity and it gives one the chance to 'smile out loud' under God's clear sky and to take in life-giving breaths of fresh air every time one empties the lungs with a lusty cheer."

At that time the Polo Grounds could accommodate only a little better than 30,000 fans and turnaway crowds were becoming commonplace, so that it was in the end fortunate for the management when a year or so later, in 1911, the stands were destroyed by fire, permitting construction of the huge 55,000-capacity stadium that was the pride of its day and remained the home of the Giants until they packed off to San Francisco.

In 1908, as the Giants and Cubs came neck and neck down to the wire, fan interest became frenzied. In the final series of the season, played at the Polo Grounds, more people were turned away than got inside. In one game a man climbed up a telegraph pole just outside the fence and watched from there—until his legs tired and he fell to the ground and was killed. The ridge of Coogan's Bluff was lined with spectators and photographs show a dense crowd standing on the roof of the grandstand.

Current Literature, a high-tone publication of the day, remarked in November 1908: "Had Chadwick, who died a few months ago, lived until last month he would have seen a nation gone wild over the game, politicians forgetful of their campaigns, stockbrokers ignoring their tickers, well dressed women courting ruin for their gowns and more by the hundred risking their very lives in one mad scramble to see the closing games of the season. . . . Never has there been such a frenzied baseball year as the one that came to a close a few days ago. 'New York City,' says the Herald, 'forgot all else to note the progress of the game. . . .' The Herald's telephones at Herald Square and the branch offices were so cumbered with inquiries about the score that it was difficult to transact the customary business over them."

With the article is a photograph captioned "35,000 aching hearts—this is the scene just after the final game of the season between the New Yorks and the Chicagos. This is part of the crowd that was inside the grounds. Fully as many more were

outside on the elevated road, on Coogan's Bluff and elsewhere
—and the New Yorks lost!"

Under a photo of Frank Chance, the magazine proclaimed:
"It may be said without exaggeration that the pennant the
Chicagos gained this year was won by Chance. It was his
generalship that did it."

The game the New Yorks lost was a playoff game for the
pennant, and had it not been for Fred Merkle—and John
Evers—the playoff would not even have been necessary and
the Giants would have had the pennant wrapped up. With
runners on first and second, Giant shortstop Al Bridwell hit a
line single to right center, scoring the runner on second.
Merkle, the runner on first, started down the base path when
the ball was hit, but neglected to touch second. Evers called
for the ball and stepped on second; Merkle was a force out
and the run did not count. All this necessitated the playoff
game, which the Cubs won. Although Merkle has been ma-
ligned for posterity, there were many who felt it was not so
much a matter of Merkle doing something stupid as of Evers
being uncommonly quick-witted. Umpire Billy Evans said
that Merkle had only done what most ball players were in the
habit of doing and it was a play, he wrote, that "would have
been overlooked by 99 out of 100 players."

The Giants moaned that they had lost on a technicality—
John T. Brush said he had lost the pennant to "the law." He
had also lost it to the Cubs, who went on to the World Series
and knocked off the Detroits in short order, Frank Chance
leading all hitters of both teams, and Ty Cobb once more had
played on the losing side in a World Series.

When Cobb's right to be called the game's greatest player
is challenged, the loudest challenges come from the advocates
of Honus Wagner, a heavily muscled, ungainly-appearing
man who led the Pittsburgh Pirates to the pennant in 1909,
snapping the three-year streak of Chance and the Cubs. His

batting accomplishments do not have quite the high gloss of Cobb's, yet he won the batting championship eight times, a National League record; like Cobb, he was tremendous on the bases, stealing sixty-one in 1907; and in defensive skills, from all accounts, he far surpassed his rival.

Wagner was a sure-handed shortstop with tremendous range and a mighty arm. "At first sight," one of his contemporaries wrote, "as he lazily strolls from the bench and then takes his position in the field—in his half-stooped attitude—he would be taken for an awkward and possibly careless player. But with the crash of the bat every faculty instantly becomes alert, every muscle comes into play, and with the sprightliness of a cat he pounces on seemingly safe drives far to the right or left and with his steel arm nails the runner by yards."

Forsaking a career as an apprentice barber, Wagner rode a freight train to Steubenville, Ohio, for his first baseball try-out and began his major-league career with Louisville in 1897. From the very first, his style at bat was "awkward, nay abominable," yet his hands were so strong and his reflexes so quick that he terrorized National League pitching year after year.

"Men of the diamond are notoriously loose with their pocketbooks," it was written in 1908. "With them it is come easy, go easy. A glove and bat hero, more so than almost any other man, lives for the day—and when the day's work is done, he is willing to pass the evening in jollity, with the result that the next morning he begins the day with almost empty hands."

Wagner, along with Frank Chance a few other players, was an outstanding exception. He was a man of wealth who invested in outside enterprises, most notably chickens, and once a circus. In the prime of his baseball career, he ran a thriving chicken business near his native Carnegie, Pennsylvania, and even when the Pirates were on the road his morning mail included a letter from his secretary reporting egg production for the preceding twenty-four hours. After the 1907 season he threatened to quit baseball to devote full attention to poultry. After the 1908 season he made the same threat, this time to handle a traveling circus he had bought with his brothers. Yet it was not until 1917 that he would finally quit, after a career of twenty-one seasons, eighteen of them in a Pittsburgh uniform.

The 1909 World Series, pitting Cobb against Wagner, opened at Forbes Field, the grand new Pittsburgh ball park that had been completed only that July. Contemporary accounts tell of the occasion. Hotels were jammed and "telephone centrals" sorely pressed. "Throngs of fair rooters lined the sidewalks, displaying proudly, upon swelling bosoms, miniature Tiger skins." In shop windows there were signs exclaiming: "I love my wife, but oh you Hans Wagner!"

Detroit rooters countered with placards saying: "You're my honey but oh you Ty Cobb!"

Before the opening game Cobb and Wagner were introduced to each other at home plate and were introduced to something new on the American scene. "The motion picture man is trundling his machine toward the plate and there stand Cobb and Wagner, doing their best to appear unconcerned, while he grinds into the celluloid films hundreds of feet of their conversation in facial expression and eye and lip movements. . . . The two brightest stars in the baseball firmament, side by side."

Cobb that season had batted .377 and stolen seventy-six bases. In the second Series game he electrified the crowd by stealing home, but otherwise his performance was undistinguished. The Series belonged to Wagner and to young Babe Adams, the Pittsburgh pitcher, who stopped the Tigers three times. For the Series, Cobb batted .231. Wagner hit .333, and his hits included a double and a triple.

For the Tigers it was their third consecutive pennant and

their third consecutive losing performance in a World Series. They would not win another pennant until 1934, with Mickey Cochrane and Hank Greenberg. The Pirates would not win again until 1927, when they might wish they hadn't, for in 1927 they would play dead for Babe Ruth and the "Murderers Row" of the New York Yankees.

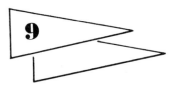

Scandal

THE SECOND DECADE OF THE NEW CENTURY HAD A BRIGHT ENOUGH beginning. Baseball was still a pageant, and it always has been at its best as a pageant. The stage for a while longer belonged to the players and the game. The household names were still Mack, McGraw, Mathewson, Cobb, Wagner, and Johnson, and now there were some newer ones: Rube Marquard, Eddie Collins, Smoky Joe Wood, Grover Cleveland Alexander, and George Stallings. Mack and McGraw resumed their mastery over their respective leagues and their World Series rivalry, and it was baseball at its best. But by the end of the decade the focus would be taken from the field of play and thence directly into the courtroom. The game would be blighted and the household names would be Eddie Cicotte, Chick Gandil, Joe Jackson, Claude Williams, and others of the White Sox who stupidly and indeed pitiably sold themselves down the river, ruining their careers and their lives.

But in 1911, as the decade began, it was still an age of innocence for baseball as it was for the world, and among baseball fans the important thing was that in 1911 both the Giants and the Athletics had won the pennant, insuring another World Series clash between the two Irishmen who so excelled at managing baseball teams.

Mack and the Athletics in fact had won the pennant in 1910, ending Detroit's three-year streak, and had gone on to whip the Cubs and Frank Chance badly in the World Series. It was the last pennant the Peerless Leader would ever win.

The Series of 1911 produced a battle of wits that fans and writers of the day considered as exciting as the feats on the field. Leading in the Series three games to two, Connie Mack, on the morning of the sixth game, found himself without a starting pitcher. Eddie Plank, his brilliant left-hander, had already been beaten. Jack Coombs was injured. Chief Bender had had only one day's rest and three were normally the minimum. For the Giants, even though they were trailing in the Series, the prospects looked excellent. If they got by this game, as they had every reason to hope they would, the great Mathewson would be available for the deciding seventh game.

Then and throughout his career Mack prided himself on pulling the unexpected. In the 1910 Series he had been credited with out-thinking the thinker, Frank Chance. Now, in the sixth game, he confounded McGraw and the public by sending Chief Bender to the mound, tired arm and all.

The battle of strategy began, and the prospect was that Bender would soon be out of the game. McGraw's thought, logical enough under the circumstances, was that Bender, after a single day's rest, would tire very early; hence he ordered the Giant batters to wait Bender out, to make him throw as many pitches as possible. Guessing this, Mack, in a counterdirective, instructed Bender to lay the first and often the second pitches right down the middle, knowing the Giants would let them pass and thus affording a quick one- and even two-strike advantage on each Giant batter in turn. This Bender did with success. In the middle innings, with things going against him, McGraw changed his strategy and told the

Giants to walk up to the plate and hit away. Again counter-punching, Mack thereupon ordered Bender to stop pouring the ball down the middle and to begin fuzzing up the corners of the plate instead. This too Bender did, again with success, as the Giants walked up and hit away at pitches that barely shaved the strike zone or were just beyond it.

Chief Bender ended up pitching a four-hitter, giving the Athletics the World Series, four games to two—and Mack had prevailed over John McGraw. Two years later, in 1913, he would prevail again, this time on the splendid abilities of Eddie Collins, Frank Baker, and other members of the team he had personally molded into the finest in the land. Thus Mack and McGraw had met for the third time, and Mack was the victor, two Series to one. In the years to come, each man would win more than his share of pennants but never again would they meet in a World Series.

Mack by now was being acclaimed as the paragon of managers, just as he was respected as a paragon among men. Articles were written remarking upon his patience, his decorum, the gentlemanly behavior of his players. He gave interviews extolling the virtues of clean living and total abstinence. Even then his players regarded him as fatherly, although as the 1911 season ended he would still be a major-league manager for another thirty-nine years.

It was the two Boston teams rather than John McGraw that proved the downfall of Connie Mack—first the Red Sox, who in 1912 nipped the Athletics at the wire, denying the clean-living Connie and his clean-living club a third consecutive pennant. But for that loss, they would have had five pennants in a row, a feat managed only by the New York Yankees, who did it twice.

The 1912 Red Sox were sparked by Tris Speaker, a complete ball player who blended remarkable defensive skills as a center-fielder with equally remarkable ability at bat, recording a lifetime batting average of .344, exactly the same lifetime mark achieved by Ted Williams, no defensive marvel, and almost twenty points better than the lifetime average of Joe DiMaggio, one of the very few players in history who matched up defensive and offensive skills at such a superior level as Speaker. On the mound, the Red Sox that year were led by Smoky Joe Wood, who had started pitching profession- ally at seventeen and who, even in 1912, at twenty-three, struck observers as a "small, frail-appearing, pale youth." For all his frail appearance, Wood had blinding speed. His fast ball was said to be the equal of the great Johnson's, and he used it on the league's batsmen that year with deadly effect, hanging up a won-lost record of thirty-four and five. Included was a streak of sixteen consecutive victories, an American League record that Wood shares with Walter Johnson, Lefty Grove, and Schoolboy Rowe. As for Boston fans, among the most rabid was John F. Fitzgerald—"Honey Fitz"—the Boston mayor who was President John F. Kennedy's grandfather.

The year 1912 was a great one for pitcher winning streaks. While Wood was pitching his sixteen in a row for Boston, Walter Johnson was winning the same number of consecutive victories for Washington, and Rube Marquard of the Giants was recording a streak of nineteen straight, a National League and major-league record that he shares with nobody.

Perhaps fittingly, it was the Boston Red Sox who staved off Johnson for Joe Wood, thwarting the great Washington pitcher in his bid for a seventeenth straight victory, although he missed but narrowly. The game was played in Boston late in the season and after ten innings the score was tied 0–0. To that point, Boston had achieved one scratch hit. In the eleventh inning, a hit-error-hit gave the Red Sox the winning run. Los- ing 1–0 ball games was the story of Walter Johnson's life.

With "Honey Fitz" riding the rooters' train back and forth between Boston and New York, the Red Sox went on to beat McGraw and the Giants in the 1912 World Series. Three pen- nants in a row the Giants had won, and three World Series in a row they lost. In the bottom of the tenth inning in the final game, Fred Snodgrass muffed a fly ball. On the next batter he made an incredible catch and came within an eyelash of doubling up the runner and ending the game. Instead, the Red Sox went on to win it, and once more the Giants had given to baseball history a "goat" of spectacular dimensions.

Already an event of national importance, the Series that year was avidly followed, according to *Outlook* magazine, "by many thousands standing in compact masses before the bulletin boards of city newspapers, or in little groups at the telegraph offices of remote and isolated villages"—and even the normal procedure of government was threatened.

"Unprecedented procedure was permitted in the Supreme Court of the United States," reported a Washington newspaper, "when the justices sitting on the bench hearing the government's arguments in the 'Bath Tub Trust' case, received bulletins inning by inning of the World Championship game in Boston. The progress of the play was closely watched by the members of the highest court in the land, especially by Associate Justice Day, who had requested the ball bulletins during the luncheon recess from 2 to 2:30 P.M. The little slips giving the progress of the play went to him not only during the luncheon recess but when the court resumed its sitting. They passed along the bench from justice to justice."

Before the 1913 season began, it was written that if any Boston baseball fan were to express doubt "as to the Red Sox ability to live up to their reputation as pennant winners and Giant beaters, it is likely he would be hanged in effigy, and Mayor Fitzgerald, perhaps the most enthusiastic rooter in the Hub, would make a denunciatory speech."

Nonetheless Connie Mack came back in 1913 to take another pennant, and yet another in 1914, his fourth in five seasons, only to run afoul this time of the other Boston team— baseball's "Miracle Team"—the 1914 Braves. A team with few standout players and in last place on July 19th, the Braves roared up the ladder to take the pennant, prodded, coaxed, harassed, and finally shoved over the top by their nervous, excitable manager, George Stallings.

In the World Series the Braves were up against the team almost universally acknowledged as the greatest in baseball, the Philadelphia Athletics. The Braves took four straight, and the effect on Connie Mack was profound. In Philadelphia baseball history, the aftermath would last for years.

What Mack did was to demolish the mighty machine, with all the splendid parts he had hand-picked and polished with such care. To the astonishment of the baseball world, he broke up the Athletics, selling off his stars, selling off the members of his "hundred-thousand-dollar infield" to rival clubs, deliberately resigning himself to building from the ground up, starting once more the job of fashioning another mighty machine. It took far longer than he could have anticipated before he would have the team he was seeking—the Athletics of 1929–31, the team which included among its ranks no fewer than four members of baseball's Hall of Fame: Al Simmons, Jimmy Foxx, Mickey Cochrane, and Lefty Grove. This team, too, in time, he would break up.

What Mack did in 1914 was done only partly because of the team's flat-footed performance against the Braves in the World Series. Another reason reminds one of the old Baltimore Orioles, whose fans became so casual about their winning ways that they stopped coming out to the ball park. For all the team's excellence, the Philadelphia fans had stopped supporting the Athletics, perhaps for the same reason but also doubtless because all through the country fan interest had begun to slacken. That year, 1914, was the year World War I began. Moreover, there was greater competition for leisure spending—something new known as the movies, along with a game of increasing popularity, golf, and for those who could afford them, automobiles.

Mack was influenced by all these factors and by yet another —the team in his estimate was no longer a team. Rather it was a collection of individual ball players of undeniable talent and skill but of little cohesive spirit, a team that took winning for granted, just as its fans did.

"The Athletics," said the *Literary Digest* in 1915 after the team was scrapped, "had begun to look like a team that could not lose—the mythical team of which every fan has dreamed. There was no hint of a flaw in the organization or at least no hint that one lacking Connie Mack's eye could see."

What Mack had seen, or sensed, he said, was a "strange feeling that crops out in great clubs." It cropped out, he thought, in the Orioles as well as in the Cubs when they became too successful under Frank Chance. What Mack surmised was that all great teams contain the seeds of their own collapse.

Even so, as he faced the future in 1915, Mack could say that it was "the happiest period" of his life: "I am broke financially but full of ambition. It is like starting all over again for me and I love baseball and I love to build up teams. I have done it once and will do it again."

Do it again he would, but not for fifteen long years.

The 1914 season can perhaps be called the last of the golden era. Even with the abnormal feat of the Boston Braves trouncing the Athletics in the Series, it was by many standards the last season that might be called normal, the last before the game's equilibrium would be jarred from outside. Once again the focus left the field of play. The year World War I began was also the year that marked the start of yet another war in baseball, this time the war of the Federal League. After calling itself a major league and operating with some success in 1914, the Federal League, loaded with money, demanded recognition as a co-equal. The pattern by now was predictable and the battle ran along traditional lines, just as it always had. The American and National Leagues refused recognition and the skirmish was on. The Federals raided the player ranks brandishing fat contracts, and some players jumped, among them "Three Finger" Brown; Joe Tinker, of Tinker to

Evers to Chance; and Hal Chase, a very good ball player but one always highly influenced by a dollar and seldom squeamish as to its source. Even Walter Johnson agreed to Fed terms but was dissuaded from jumping by Clark Griffith, who raised his salary, patted him on the back, and sent him forth to do service in a Washington uniform for yet another dozen seasons. For a third major league there never has been and probably never will be a good time. Even so, the timing of the Federals was particularly bad, for they not only ran into the war but into the attendance slump which had given every evidence of coming, war or no. After the season of 1915 the Feds called it a career—and once again it was proved that although baseball is indeed a popular game it is not so popular that its fans will support three major leagues.

In the years between the start of the war and America's entry in it, the Boston Red Sox remained a power in the American League, led by Tris Speaker, managed by Bill Carrigan, and now including on their roster a pitcher named George Herman Ruth. In 1915 the Red Sox won the pennant and trounced the Philadelphia Phillies in the Series. The year was notable for another event of considerable significance: in May 1915 George Herman Ruth hit the first home run of his major-league career. In 1916 the Giants performed a feat that to some seemed a virtual impossibility: during the season they put together two winning streaks, one of seventeen straight games and then, later in the season, another of twenty-six straight— the latter a major-league record—and yet they managed to finish no higher than fourth. The pennant was won by none other than the Brooklyn Dodgers—their first—and they promptly blew it to the Red Sox in the Series.

As the years passed, the game's greats were ticking off one marvelous season after another—Cobb, winning nine straight batting championships, yielding to Tris Speaker in 1916, and then coming back to record another three in a row; Johnson, pitching season after season for generally mediocre Washington teams but notching victory totals year after year in the high twenties and sometimes in the thirties. Honus Wagner had won his last batting championship in 1911, and after 1917 he would call it quits—ten years after he threatened to quit baseball for the chicken business. Napoleon Lajoie turned in his glove after the 1916 season. In the National League the Philadelphia Phillies had the spotlight at the expense of the floundering Athletics, and in 1916 they had a stellar pitching attraction in Grover Cleveland Alexander, who that season pitched sixteen shutouts, a major-league record. Christy Mathewson had pitched his last game for the New York Giants and for a short time would manage the Cincinnati Reds. In 1919 he would be sitting in the press box horrified at the spectacle of the Black Sox throwing the World Series, and in 1920 he would be spending Christmas at Saranac fighting tuberculosis, caused when he was accidentally gassed by his own army during a training program in France. As Ty Cobb relates the story, he, Mathewson, and other trainees were instructed to put on their gas masks at a signal, just as gas flooded an air-tight chamber. The entire group missed the signal. Eight men died, and Mathewson received such a suffocating dose that he contracted tuberculosis in both lungs.

America had entered the war in April 1917 and in that first season neither the caliber of the game nor attendance seemed markedly diminished, but in 1918 both were. Although ball players were called slackers, nearly 250 of them were in various branches of the service and the game was left in the hands of generally mediocre players, some of whom participated in close-order drills with bats over their shoulders to show that organized baseball was not unmindful of the war. The 1918 season was shortened by government order, ending on September 2nd and permitting the Red Sox to win the pennant with only seventy-five victories. Aided by the splendid pitching of young Babe Ruth, they went on to beat the Giants in the Series.

In both world wars, baseball was left pretty much alone by the government, and fan interest, particularly during World

War I, remained high.

As a writer for *Outlook* magazine commented in 1913: " 'Give us games!' was the cry of the Roman populace in time of disaster many centuries ago and it has been unconsciously echoed by many another people under the stress of some great crisis."

In Chicago, as the decade moved to a close, a very powerful baseball team had been assembled, one that was about to produce a crisis hardly related to war, a crisis that threatened to make "Give us games!" a cry that might become obsolete, so deep was the disgust of the American public.

For one of the significant facts about the White Sox who became Black Sox is that they were an extremely good baseball team, perhaps a great team, and one which might have gone on to win pennants in the 20's even in the face of the heroics of Babe Ruth and the Yankees. The White Sox had been built slowly and carefully by their Chicago owner, the same Charles Comiskey who performed with such success as playing manager of Chris von der Ahe's old St. Louis Browns. The White Sox had won the pennant in 1917 and trounced the Giants in the Series, and they had seen the Red Sox snatch it in the truncated season of 1918—but now with the war over and all the players back, the White Sox burned up the league in 1919. As they squared off against the Cincinnati Reds for the World Series they seemed to be sure-shot winners—and the betting odds so indicated.

Among their pitchers was Eddie Cicotte, a thirty-five-year-old veteran and the winner that year of twenty-nine games. Another was Claude (Lefty) Williams, still young but already a poised, careful workman with marvelous control. Cicotte and Williams were excellent pitchers, and two other members of the team were unquestionably among the greatest players the game has known. At second base was Eddie Collins, premier hitter, fielder, and base stealer, a charter member of the $100,-000 infield which had been scattered about the league by

Connie Mack when he broke up the 1914 Athletics. Collins, in a major-league career covering twenty-five seasons, would record a lifetime batting average of .333. In 1912, in the month of September, he twice stole six bases in a single ball game.

In left field was Joseph Jefferson Jackson—Joe Jackson, called by Walter Johnson the greatest natural hitter he had ever seen, and perhaps the only hitter ever envied by Ty Cobb. Among Jackson's many misfortunes, however, was to be playing baseball at the same time as Cobb. "What a hell of a league this is," he once moaned to Cobb. "Ah hit .387, .408, and .395 the last three years and Ah ain't won nothin' *yet!*"

The White Sox catcher was Ray Schalk, a scrappy, intelligent firebrand who excelled at handling pitchers. The team was managed by Kid Gleason, an astute veteran whose dreams of glory had crystallized with this dream team, the White Sox of 1919.

As told in Eliot Asinof's minutely researched and splendidly chronicled book, *Eight Men Out*, the story of the Black Sox is a drama of high suspense, filled with petty venality and epic villainy—and in the end, for the players, a tragedy. There was one, however, who would be hard to fit into the tragic mold. Unfortunately for the White Sox, for baseball, and for the United States, the White Sox first baseman that year was one Chick Gandil, a tall, muscular, tough ex-fighter and ex-boilermaker and a good ballplayer who apparently had been consorting with gamblers for some little time, as had other players in both leagues. After laying off for years, gamblers had begun to move back into baseball, partly because the race tracks had been shut down during the war and they had been forced to seek other betting outlets. During the 1919 season and even before, there were frequent reports of fixed games, but the baseball owners hushed them up as fast as they arose, and when they couldn't hush them, whitewashed them.

It was in the none too agile brain of Chick Gandil that the World Series fix was conceived. Gandil was incensed over what he considered the stinginess and tyranny of owner

Charles Comiskey, and his anger and resentment were shared by all the White Sox players, including those who had no part in the plot. From the evidence, Charles Comiskey was indeed remarkably close-fisted as well as despotic, and as the story unfolds he often emerges as the sort of villain one might expect to find in a melodrama. On the road, the White Sox had a meal allowance of $3.00 a day, when all through both leagues at the time it was $4.00. Often the White Sox were required to play in dirty uniforms so that Comiskey could save on cleaning and laundry bills. Whining about the falloff in attendance in 1918, Comiskey forced virtually the entire team to take cuts in salary for 1919—but attendance in 1919 was very high, which the players could plainly see, and his profits for the year were shown to be huge. A salary of $6,000 a year was tops on the White Sox, and most of the established players made somewhere between four and five thousand. When a player protested, he was told to take it or leave it, and if he left it he was out of baseball, because of the eminently reliable reserve clause. On the Cincinnati team, a run-of-the-mill team as pennant winners go, salaries were far higher, and the White Sox knew it.

For a long time after the fix was exposed, and even when it was merely suspected, the public assumed that it had been the gamblers who approached the players. It was in fact the opposite. As the 1919 season drew to a close and it became apparent that the White Sox had the pennant won, Chick Gandil took his brainstorm to a well-known gambler, one Sport Sullivan, offering to throw the Series if Sullivan would come up with $80,000, payable in advance, and guaranteeing to bring enough other players in on the plot to make certain that the fix would succeed.

Eddie Cicotte had been pitching in the big leagues for fourteen years. In 1917 he had won twenty-eight games, leading the White Sox to the pennant, and in 1919 he had won twenty-nine, again leading them to the pennant. For the 1919 season he had been forced to take a salary cut and was making less than $6,000. He hated Charles Comisky.

Cicotte was the first man Gandil approached. Cicotte said no—and then yes, for $10,000 payable before the Series began.

Gandil went after the team's number-two pitcher, Claude Williams, and got him. One by one he lined up the rest—Joe Jackson; Buck Weaver, an excellent third baseman; Swede Risberg, the shortstop; Happy Felsch, star center-fielder.

Seven including himself, Gandil felt, would be enough, but a utility player, Fred McMullin, overheard one of the conversations and wanted in. There was no choice but to include him.

As the Series approached, the eight conspirators at first found it possible to be rather carefree. Baseball games after all had been fixed before—not on such broad scope, true; not under such brilliant light, not in a World Series—but even so, what they were doing was not very much different from what other players were doing and they were confident they could bring it off fairly easily. Besides, over and above the money they would get, they were also getting nice revenge on Charles Comiskey and on their enemies among the other players. As the Series approached, the eight were constantly together, talking it over, sometimes even with a good laugh or two, and in their togetherness there was nothing unusual, nothing suspicious, because all season long they had been something of a clique, hating the likes of Eddie Collins; Ray Schalk; Dickie Kerr, a classy little southpaw; Urban Faber, a pitcher who would be disabled for the Series; and others among the good guys who were a clique in their own right. As students of the scandal have observed, it is remarkable that the White Sox played such very good baseball that summer, what with the cliques and the crisscross currents of hatred.

The fix was on. Where was the money? On the field, the action was relatively easy to follow. What the players did to lose was done where all could see, sometimes blatantly, sometimes with considerable subtlety, borderline in nature. To many of the fans it might have appeared that the White Sox were simply having an off day, a series of off days, and from the first this was what Gandil and the others had counted upon, for baseball, as often noted, is a game of inches. Breaking a second too late in quest of a fly ball, hanging a curve ball high where the batter would like it, getting a glove on a grounder but not coming up with it cleanly—this was the shadow area of doubt where Gandil and the others hoped to operate, and who would know? There were some who knew immediately—Kid Gleason, the manager, and Ray Schalk, the catcher. There were others who could not know for sure but who deeply suspected, and prominent among these was the sportswriter Hugh Fullerton and the man who sat in the press box with him to help him "expert" the Series—Christy Mathewson. Both were men of character and both loved baseball. They didn't want to believe in the fix but they couldn't ignore the possibility because even before the Series began there were rumors that the fix was on and to support the rumors there was a flood of money being bet on Cincinnati, so much that the Reds became betting favorites when only a few days earlier they had been, deservedly, the underdogs.

Off the field the story of the scandal is a labyrinth, an incredible maze of doublecrosses upon doublecrosses, of broken promises, of guileless stupidity among the players, of artful, cruel deceit among those who manipulated them—gamblers, baseball executives, and public officials alike. To follow the story behind the scenes is to walk dazedly through a Marienbad corridor, opening one door after another. In one room we find Sport Sullivan, in another Abe Attell, a retired prizefighter, an ex-champ. In yet another we find "Sleepy Bill" Burns, a former White Sox pitcher who had retired from the game after an indifferent career and gone off to prospect for oil in Texas. With him was an auto mechanic, a punk named Maharg whose real name may or may not have been Graham—Maharg spelled backward. Each had a part, but at the end of the corridor, behind the last door, in the last room, seated in the darkness, was Arnold Rothstein, the fabulously wealthy

New York gambler, who had not initiated the plot but who masterminded it and in the end controlled it, made a fortune from the fix and in the end went scot-free, as for that matter did Sullivan, Attell, Comiskey, and all the others—all except the players.

Of the promised $80,000, Gandil received initially only $10,000, which he gave to Cicotte, who sewed it into his jacket and went out to pitch game number one. Always acting anonymously, always through spokesmen and lieutenants, Rothstein had sent word that Cicotte was to hit the first Cincinnati batter as a signal that all was well. Cicotte hit him right between the shoulder blades, and Rothstein, in touch with the game by telegraph, went out and bet another $100,000 on the Reds. He had already bet $270,000, including a $90,000 bet with Harry Sinclair, who later would be nailed in the Teapot Dome scandal. With deceit hardly artful, Cicotte then proceeded to blow the game 9–1, pitching abominably and watching the White Sox hitters, most of them, play dead.

The pitching assignment in the second game went to Claude Williams, the poised master of control, the man who could nick corners with his curve ball. When it counted that day, Williams served up fat ones, giving the Reds a 4–2 victory, and after that game Ray Schalk knew and Kid Gleason knew. They didn't know about everybody but they knew about Cicotte, Williams, and Gandil, who had left men on base and had made a fielding misplay that was glaring. After the game, Schalk beat up Williams with his fists. Gleason went after Gandil's throat. They were told to lay off, that everybody has an off day now and then.

From Rothstein to Attell to Gandil came word that the White Sox were to win game number three, and it is likely that they would have won it anyway because Dickie Kerr, the Chicago pitcher, not in on the fix, pitched a masterful game, shutting out the Reds 3–0. Gandil obediently batted across two runs. In the fourth game, operating with much greater subtlety, Cicotte pitched well but made two deliberate errors, allowing the two runs that gave the Reds a 2–0 victory.

It was after the fourth game that Gandil received another installment, this time $20,000, from Sport Sullivan. Sullivan had gotten the $80,000 but was keeping the rest to place bets for himself. Gandil gave the $20,000 away—$5,000 each to Williams, Joe Jackson, Swede Risberg, and Happy Felsch. Fred McMullin, the utility man, would have to wait for his, and as for Buck Weaver, the third baseman, as far as Gandil was concerned he would never get a cent. Weaver had agreed to the fix but right from the first inning of the first game it was obvious that he had changed his mind. He loved playing baseball too much to play it poorly and he played on the level throughout the Series, receiving no money—but in the months and years to come this would get him nowhere.

In the fifth game Jackson and Felsch stood by and watched a fly ball drop between them for a triple and Felsch later misplayed a fly on his own. Once again the White Sox lost, this time 4–0, and what was incredible was that this team of great batters had in five games produced a total of only six runs. It is ironic to note that the great Eddie Collins, whose hands were clean, had a poor Series nonetheless, and equally ironic to record that Joe Jackson, who was very much in on the fix and at times acted it, and would suffer for it, still collected twelve hits and batted .375.

Normally, with the Reds leading four games to one, the Series would have been over, but 1919 was the first year in a three-year experiment that made the Series a best-five-out-of-nine affair. Player shares of the gate receipts were based on attendance at the first five games. To add yet another ironic note, it was announced after the fifth game that each player on the winning team would receive just over $5,000.

The White Sox won the sixth game 5–4 in spite of the fixers, and in game number seven an electrifying change seemed to take place. Whether out of remorse, whether they felt they were being doublecrossed on the amount still due them, or whether perhaps they simply knew they were too good to lose and were tired of losing, the White Sox played like a team in-spired, winning 4–1, and it was Eddie Cicotte who won it. Was the fighter who had been told to take a dive about to defy the mob?

Chicago now was trailing by a mere four games to three, and back in New York the mob was edgy. Rothstein summoned Sullivan to his apartment. The World Series, Rothstein said, would end the next day, and the Cincinnati Reds would win it, five games to three. It would end, moreover, in the first inning. Sullivan said he would see to it. He put in a long-distance call to a friend in Chicago. Although Claude Williams had no children, he had a wife, and that evening he and his wife were approached on the street by a man in a black derby who drew Williams aside and had a few words with him.

Next day in the very first inning, while Ray Schalk cursed and barked and demanded the low curve, Claude Williams threw nothing but medium-speed pitches straight down the middle, pitches known in the trade as cripples. The Reds teed off. They murdered the cripples.

When the World Series of 1919 was over, the winner was Cincinnati, five games to three.

It was almost another year before the players were brought to account, a year of profound fright on the part of Comiskey and others in the baseball empire—for what was at stake, and they all knew it as the rumors piled up, was the very structure of organized baseball, a multimillion-dollar edifice which could topple, wiping them out one and all. Did Comiskey want an investigation? He did, but mostly he didn't. He offered $20,-000 to anyone who might bring him the truth and he hired private detectives to shadow the suspected players. But when, a short time after the Series ended, he received a letter from Joe Jackson's wife (Joe could neither read nor write) saying that Jackson had information that would prove the Series was crooked, Comiskey filed the letter away and didn't reply. A one-man investigation was conducted by Hugh Fullerton, who wrote an exposé and persuaded the *New York World* to pub-

lish it. Another season began, the season of 1920, and seven of
the Black Sox were back with the team again, all but Gandil,
who had gotten by far the largest share of the bribe money
and skipped. All through the season, Fullerton pressed for an
investigation. Comiskey quailed. Baseball's then ruling body,
the National Commission, spoke out of both sides of its mouth.
Baseball Magazine became a vehicle of infamy, denouncing
Fullerton for daring to drag baseball's good name through the
mud. On the field, the White Sox, unbelievably, were in the
thick of the 1920 pennant fight, once again under the influence
of gamblers, throwing a game now and then but still in and
out of the league lead all through the season. Joe Jackson was
batting .380. Cicotte and Williams were winning twenty games
or so apiece but for all the games they won there was something about the ones they lost, and Eddie Collins saw it. He
was convinced, and he went and told Charles Comiskey so.
Comiskey said there was nothing to be done at that time.

But there was, and among those now pushing for the long-
delayed investigation was the righteous and often self-
righteous Ban Johnson, American League president,
a tough-minded man unafraid of the truth but one who also
undeniably had an axe to grind. At one time he and Charles
Comiskey had been friends and drinking companions. Together they had planned the campaign to set up the American
League, but over the years they had become enemies. Ban
Johnson hated Comiskey and would be happy to see him
squirm.

A Chicago grand jury was summoned on September 7, 1920,
and later the same month a Philadelphia newspaper printed
its own exposé. With this, Eddie Cicotte spilled his guts and
when he had told it all he said: "I'm through with baseball.
I'm going to lose myself if I can and start life over again." Joe
Jackson talked, and then Felsch. The *Chicago Herald Examiner* published its quickly famous colloquoy between Jackson and the small boy who trailed along after him as he left the
grand-jury room.

"Say it ain't so, Joe. Say it ain't so."
"Yes, kid, I'm afraid it is."
"Well, I never would have thought it," the boy said.

The nation read and watched with revulsion, sadness, and, ultimately, cynicism. Its revulsion was fed day after day by the newspapers, but the revulsion could stand alone. The nation had been proud. In 1918 it considered itself to have done a noble thing, helping to lick the Hun and make the world, it was said, safe for democracy. And now this, a spectacle of corruption, disgusting enough in any phase of American life, but it had happened to the National Game, the National Pastime, this thing that America was as American as—and had happened, moreover, in 1919, the fiftieth anniversary of professional baseball in the United States.

Horrified and fascinated, the public continued to watch. Attell squealed on Rothstein, and Rothstein went of his own volition to Chicago, where with a show of suave dignity he professed his innocence before a grand jury which seemed to believe him. He then returned to New York, and after seeing to it that Attell escaped extradition gave him $50,000 and told him to get lost. With the season about to end, and the White Sox still very much in contention, Comiskey, to his credit, suspended all the suspected players, surrendering any chance for the pennant. Cleveland won it, an indictment was returned by the grand jury, and in November organized baseball made a decision.

Kenesaw Mountain Landis was a federal judge in the district of Illinois. Once he had captured the public imagination by forcing John D. Rockefeller to come to Chicago to testify in an antitrust case involving his own Standard Oil Company, ultimately imposing a fine of more than $29 million. Landis was tough, fair, and honest. Baseball was running scared. On November 7, 1920, Kenesaw Mountain Landis was appointed baseball's high commissioner with autocratic power and the then mammoth salary of $50,000 a year. It was the smartest decision, one of the few smart ones, that organized baseball ever made.

The players were arraigned in February 1921, and the state asked the jury to convict them of conspiring with gamblers to defraud the public. Conviction could have meant five years in jail and a $2,000 fine for each. "Sleepy Bill" Burns, the former White Sox pitcher, was dug up by Ban Johnson to testify against the players, and he presented a damning case. But the players, for reasons that at first seemed mysterious, were represented by defense lawyers of great talent and prestige, high-priced men who, it gradually became clear, had been made available by organized baseball itself to see the players through their hour of need. When they were acquitted, as they all were, Chick Gandil bellowed: "I guess that'll learn Ban Johnson he can't frame an honest bunch of ball players."

The clear-cut victor was organized baseball. In his first official act, Landis had placed every one of the corrupted players on baseball's ineligible list, and after they were acquitted he threw them all out of the game for life. Organized baseball had conspired to save them from legal punishment —and then imposed punishment of its own. Never again would they play baseball in a major- or minor-league uniform.

Sullivan, Burns, Attell, and Rothstein all went unpunished. The players, most of them thirty or under, were dazed. What they knew best they could no longer do. Buck Weaver, eternally protesting his innocence, tried over and over again for reinstatement, but Landis was adamant. Gradually they drifted into other walks of life, taking modest jobs; some tried playing semi-pro baseball but not for long.

Joe Jackson went back to the South to stay, the South where he had spent his boyhood in ignorance and marginal living, working in a mill until the day he knew he had a special gift, knew he could knock a baseball the length of a meadow and far away. He ended his life in South Carolina running a dry-cleaning shop, and later a liquor store. One day, long after the World Series of 1919, a customer came in to buy a bottle. It was Ty Cobb. They talked, and Joe Jackson gave no sign of recognition. Cobb frowned. Finally he asked, "Don't you know me, Joe?"

"Sure," Jackson said sadly. "But I didn't think you knew me after all these years. I didn't want to embarrass you or anything."

"Joe, I'll tell you how well I remember you. Whenever I got the idea I was a good hitter, I'd stop and take a good look at you. I don't think I ever saw a more perfect swing than yours."

Ty Cobb's lifetime batting average was .367, the highest of any player in the history of the game. Next highest is the .358 of Rogers Hornsby.

Third on the list is the .356 compiled by Shoeless Joe Jackson, and he was getting better, they said, every year.

It would never get him into the Hall of Fame.

Part Three

THE RISE AND
FALL OF THE
NEW YORK
YANKEES

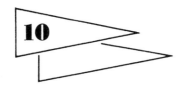

The Babe

IN BASEBALL'S HOUR OF NEED CAME THE BIG MAN WITH THE mighty bat.

Whud-duh Babe dooduh day?

What the Babe usually had done that day was hit one out of the park, something he did 714 times from the day he joined the Red Sox as a youthful pitcher in 1914 until the day in 1935 when he played his last major-league baseball game, not as a member of the Yankees but so unfittingly as a member of a National League team, the Boston Braves.

Whud-duh . . .

In the 1920's, in season, it was a question asked each day all over America . . . in late afternoon in the dim light of a speakeasy . . . on a front-porch stoop in the cool of evening . . . on subways and trolleys and trains and from the tonneaus of Hupmobiles.

"He hit another one . . ."

America, so it would seem, took unreasoning delight that a man, a rather fat man, a man who looked so out of condition that he seemed incapable of running the length of a city block or bending down to touch his toes, a rather ugly man with coarse pudgy features who wore a flapping camel-hair coat and a cap with a snap-button bill, who loved to eat and drink immoderately, who swore and murdered the English language—America took delight that such a man as this could stand up at the plate and day after day swing and send a baseball in a high arching parabola over a distant fence or into the distant stands, most often the right-field stands of Yankee Stadium, his stadium, built for him, built to accommodate his mighty swats, the House That Ruth Built. It was home, the most hospitable he had ever known and during the years of his glory as great, as hospitable a home as a man could ever ask. In it for long years he was the Babe, the Bambino, the Sultan of Swat, the king, his divine right challenged by his subjects only once and then by a man half his size, and then because he had gotten a king-sized bellyache. But he got over the bellyache and patched up his troubles with the little man, Miller Huggins, and went on with his career and for America life seemed good, because it had fought and helped win a war, because even though it was the time of Prohibition, a drink could be had and it was fun to sneak one under the old man Uncle Sam's nose and because Charles Lindbergh flew the Atlantic and because the Babe was hitting them out of the ball park and baseball in spite of the Black Sox was not dead.

"Sixty!"

He had come very close before, fifty-four and even fifty-nine—but sixty was magic. Sixty for the nation seemed to have a special significance, to bring a special thrill. It was an occasion for awe, for special rejoicing, the day in September 1927 when he faced Tom Zachary at New York and sent number sixty into the right-field stands. The banner headlines on the late-afternoon papers would say simply: "The Babe: 60" and people would know what it meant and would marvel.

In one and the same year, Lindbergh had flown the Atlantic —and Babe Ruth hit number sixty! A lucky nation, a nation of destiny, a marvelous time to be living. The reaction was as great as if, say, somebody had reached the moon.

"Who yuh think yuh are—Bay Bruth?"

The answer was yes. All over the United States, on its playgrounds, in its alleys, its city streets, its fields and its vacant lots, the kids were swinging from the heels and for a moment or two each day, yes, they were Babe Ruth. For America was the land of opportunity where even a poor boy could grow up to be Babe Ruth, who after all would earn more than the President of the United States, and Cal Coolidge, God knows, couldn't hit the broad side of a barn. All he could do was grunt. Cal Coolidge moved through life with careful sidesteps, smiling sour smiles. Babe Ruth laughed a mighty laugh, strode with the stride of a giant, slamming the door of his Stutz Bearcat and wading through the crowds, long camel-hair coat flapping near his ankles, big brown eyes shining, a long cigar stuck between the fat lips, and grinning as they all said, "Hiya, Babe," and yelling back, "Hiya, kid . . . sure, kid . . . attaboy, kid, keep swinging from the heels."

Ruth had been a special kid, raised in a Baltimore orphanage although he was not quite an orphan, but living in the orphanage was better, somebody decided, than living on the Baltimore waterfront where broken-down derelict ball players came to his father's saloon and where tough Chesapeake Bay oystermen came after a long icy winter on the bay, spending the money they had rightfully earned and some they would have had to pay in wages to deckhands they had knocked overboard to drown rather than pay—"paying off with the boom," it was called. So Ruth was raised in the orphanage, St. Mary's, a large, forbidding building of red brick looking very much like an orphanage might be expected to look—and he came out of the orphanage to earn more money than the President, to receive the awe of a flabbergasted na-

tion, flabbergasted and delighted that in its midst there could
be such a Charlemagne, such a Henry VIII as George Herman
Ruth, who conquered like Charlemagne and dissipated like
Henry; the Babe, who spent his energy as fast as it was re-
newed. The nation had Prohibition, a law it cheerfully flouted;
it was in a mood for irreverence, and in a mood to admire
this nonathlete who himself flouted all the no-tobacco, no-
alcohol, early-to-bed, early-to-rise dicta that athletes were said
to observe. For Ruth smoked and drank, he ate like a pig, was
seldom early to bed, and rose only early enough to get out to
the ball park for batting practice. Looking at him, old Harry
Wright might have said he needed a little ginger. Yet, hung-
over from drink, from food, from long early-morning hours of
card playing and carousing, he still had enough left the next
day to swing from the heels and more often than not hit one
into the stands and then move around the bases with the
dainty steps he reserved for the aftermath of his home runs,
and with his heavy upper body and his slim ankles looking always a little like a large pigeon, wearing a black baseball cap
inscribed NY, circling the bases slowly and looking down at the
steps he was taking.

He had two bad years, bad for him. In 1921 he defied the
new czar, Kenesaw Mountain Landis, and took a team on a
postseason barnstorming tour, whereupon Landis suspended
him. Not until late May of 1922 did he get back into the game,
and that year he didn't even win the home-run title. And then
in 1925, a man who could dissipate even with hotdogs and ice
cream, he flouted the training rules, got his big bellyache, ran
afoul of his tiny manager, Miller Huggins, again lost the
home-run title, and lost the Yankees the pennant. Finally
Jacob Ruppert, a beer baron who owned Ruth legally if not in
spirit and who marveled over him with all the rest, stepped in
and made peace—and on through the 20's and into the 30's
roared the Babe, and the Yankees roared with him.

In 1935 the sportswriters and the fans all said how strange it was to see Babe Ruth in the uniform of the Boston Braves, but he had started out in Boston and now he was finishing in Boston and after that year he was out of uniform forever—bitter because baseball never gave him the managerial job he said he wanted, and yet he probably would not have been a good manager. He spent aimless days, he aged, he developed throat cancer, he paid a farewell visit to Yankee Stadium and spoke a few words that were hard to make out because by then the disease had him, and when the afternoon was over he returned to the hospital. There came the day of August 16, 1948.

What the Babe did that day was die, and the flags in Yankee Stadium flew at half staff.

But in 1921 Babe Ruth was alive and drunk in New York City, if not on liquid joy then drunk with the glory of being Babe Ruth in the third decade of the twentieth century, the decade of Ruth, Dempsey, Tunney, Jimmy Walker, Charles Lindbergh, Cal Coolidge, of the fringed miniskirt, the Charleston, the rumble seat, and of the New York Yankees.

In the case of the Yankees it would be the first decade of many, far too many, some would say, because the Yankees dominated baseball on and off, but mostly on, for the better part of forty years, so that for better or worse the history of professional baseball in the United States was for four decades often the history of the New York Yankees. There were other teams and other players, good ones and even great ones, and they too have a place in history because they helped make it, but the Yankees made most of it. They were the centrifugal force, the standard, the gauge, by which other teams were measured and by which other teams measured themselves. To beat the Yankees in the World Series, to beat them out for the pennant, to best them in a three-game series, even to beat them in a single ball game—these were the goals to which other teams aspired, and too often they fell short.

It seems a matter of irony that as far back as October 1923 a national magazine should have asked: "Is New York Getting

Too Many Pennants?" Little could it have known that in 1923 the Yankee dynasty had barely begun, little could it have known what was in store for baseball. From 1921 through 1964, a span of forty-four seasons, the Yankees' proportionate share should have been five, at the most six, pennants. They won twenty-nine!

Yet even as far back as 1923 the point was well taken, for in that season, 1923, the Yankees had just won their third straight pennant—and the New York Giants of John McGraw had done likewise, trouncing the Yankees in the World Series the first two years and losing to them in 1923.

The article asked if it was money—the riches that came from representing the metropolis—that gave New York teams an advantage, and money of course helped, just as it would always help, but in the years ahead it would be proved that money alone could not topple the Yankees, no matter how much money a given club owner (Tom Yawkey of the Red Sox, for example) might be willing to spend. In the years ahead what the Yankees would have would be the most consistently productive farm system in baseball. What they had in the early 20's was a lot of good ball players and the home-run power of Babe Ruth, who upstaged the place-hit-and-slash-em tactics of Ty Cobb and made the country crazy over home runs. Home runs, as the *Literary Digest* said in 1921, were in season and they became an epidemic. In 1918 the major-league total was only 235, while in 1922 there were 1,055, and even though that season, the season of his suspension, Ruth lost out to Ken Williams' thirty-nine, the year before he hit fifty-nine and the year before that, fifty-four.

"The home run epidemic," the magazine said, "might better be called the Babe Ruth epidemic, for the habit began with the so-called and very much admired 'Bambino.'" It went on to quote a baseball critic of the day: "He has batted home runs at so dizzy a pace that he has fired the enthusiasm of the entire country. He has not only slugged his way to fame but he has got everybody else doing it. The home run fever is in the air.

It is infectious. . . . Babe has not only smashed all records, he has smashed the long-accepted system of things in the batting world, and on the ruins of that system he has erected another system, or rather lack of system, whose dominant quality is brute force.

"Most of us," the article continued, "plod along and seem to exert little influence on the scheme of things. But now and again a superman arises in the domain of politics or finance or science and plays havoc with kingdoms or fortunes or established theories. Such a superman in a narrow but nonetheless obvious field is Babe Ruth. He might not make much impression in the fine arts or classical literature. Doubtless Thomas Edison, applying his celebrated questionnaire test, would label Babe 'amazingly ignorant.' Nevertheless, in his own particular field, Babe is a true superman."

His fields were many. One was eating. Another was drinking. "He absorbed enough punishment off plates of food and out of bottles to have killed an ordinary man," wrote Ty Cobb, a Ruth watcher and Ruth baiter who infuriated the big man by calling him an egg on stilts, a beer keg on two straws. "I've never seen such an appetite. He would start shoveling down victuals in the morning and never stop. I've seen him at midnight, propped up in bed, order six huge club sandwiches and put them away along with a platter of pigs knuckles and a pitcher of beer. And all the time he'd be smoking a big black cigar. Next day he'd hit two or three home runs and trot around the bases, complaining all the way of gas pains and bellyache."

The year of the big bellyache was 1925, while the Yankees were in Asheville, North Carolina, en route back north from spring training. An ambulance rushed the Babe to the hospital and newspaper headlines all over the country heralded the national crisis. Ruth was still sick when the season opened, and it was not until he got back into the lineup that his differences with Huggins reached the point of blowup. Huggins fined him $5,000 for breaking training rules. Ruth, in a rage, directed owner Jake Ruppert to lift the fine but Ruppert stuck by Huggins. The Babe sulked and then, promising to be a good boy, picked up his big bat again but too late for a Yankee pennant that season.

In the decade of the 20's there were only two years when the World Series failed to include a team from New York. In 1925 the Series involved the Pittsburgh Pirates and, of all teams, the Washington Senators, or Nationals, as they were more often called then—or indeed, Champs, as the Washington papers referred to them all through that season of 1925, a title they had earned by edging McGraw's Giants in the 1924 World Series after winning the pennant under their "boy manager," Bucky Harris.

In the World Series of 1925 the great Walter Perry Johnson, gentleman and pitcher, was nearing the end of his remarkable career. Yet if he was now over the hill, he had given no sign in the first and fourth games of the Series, for in the first game he had beaten the Pirates 4–1 on a five-hitter, and in the fourth game, even with an injured leg, he shut them out 4–0 in what an overwrought Washington writer called "the greatest triumph that any man ever won upon the diamond." Leading in games at this point three to one, and in a fair way to repeat as world champions, Washington saw the Pirates take the next two and tie the Series at three games apiece.

For the seventh and deciding game, Bucky Harris chose Walter Johnson as his pitcher, a choice that would later be criticized by American League president Ban Johnson as one of sentiment rather than common sense. Yet for nineteen years Walter Johnson—the Big Train, old Barney—had been superb. As recently as the year before he had led the league with a pitching mark of 23–7, and against the Pirates to this point his performance had been just shy of perfection. Who better to rely upon in Washington's hour of need? Gone, it was true, was the smoking fast ball, the blue-ribbon pitch that enabled him to record a fantastic 1.09 earned-run average in 1913 and once gave him three shutouts in four days—the fast ball that Ty Cobb said "looked about the size of a watermelon seed and *hissed* at you as it passed." By now, this late in his career, Johnson was relying mainly on the curve ball he had developed over the years and the marvelous control he had had from the very first, since the day he had come to Washington as a young boy from Idaho. But his curve and his control had been all he needed in his first two victories and now he could be pardoned for hoping for another shutout, which would have given him, after all these years, a World Series performance comparable to the three masterpieces hurled by Christy Mathewson in the faroff Series of 1905. And that he should have been thinking of Mathewson was no accident, for Matty had died only a day or so earlier, even as the Series progressed.

On the day the seventh game was scheduled it rained in Pittsburgh, the game was postponed, and the sportswriters wrote of how fortunate this was because it gave Walter Johnson's aging right arm an extra day's rest. On the next day it was still raining but the game was played anyway—in semi-darkness, on a field, Ring Lardner said, that "looked like chicken à la king." The Series had started late that year, and with the postponement and the days off for traveling, it was by now nearly mid-October.

That day in the rain at Pittsburgh Walter Johnson pitched his heart out. Instead of a low-hit shutout he pitched a fifteen-hitter, yet he pitched the entire game. He was given leads of 4–0, of 6–3, and as late as the top of the eighth inning he still led 7–6. As he stood on the mound to face the Pirates in the bottom of the eighth, the clouds and the smoke of Pittsburgh hung low over the field and it was by now so dark that the fans in the distant bleachers could barely make out pitcher and batter. It was raining hard, and as Johnson took his warm-up pitches he slipped in the mud. Some sawdust was sprinkled over the mound, and the batter asked for a towel to wipe the handle of the bat. The first two batters were easy outs, but the third doubled and another double brought over the run that tied the score at 7–7. A walk and an error by the Washington shortstop, Roger Peckinpaugh (who made eight in the Series), loaded the bases. Johnson faced Kiki Cuyler, the Pirate outfielder. Cuyler lined one down the right-field line, a ground-rule double that scored two runs and gave the Pirates a 9–7 lead that didn't change in the ninth. The next batter popped up and Walter Johnson walked from the mound, not quite for the last time, but the rest would be anticlimax. In 1925, he would pitch his last game.

Death had come to Mathewson at Saranac after a five-year fight against tuberculosis. His body was taken to Lewisburg, Pennsylvania, and placed in a plot overlooking Bucknell, where more than a quarter century earlier he had pitched and played football for his college team. Among the pallbearers was John McGraw, and one of the floral tributes was signed Roger Bresnahan, his old catcher in the days when Mathewson and Bresnahan were the most famous battery in baseball —the days when the man with the megaphone came out, pointed it up at the grandstand and bellowed, "For the Giants —Mathewson pitching . . . Bresnahan catching," and all the fans, and Douglas Fairbanks and Lillian Russell too, if they were there, and the men in derbies standing on Coogan's Bluff, went wild.

It had been a bad week for pitchers and gentlemen.

After being excluded from the World Series two years in a row by the likes of Washington, the Yankees came storming back in 1926 to begin another three-year run with a team which, the following season, would reach its peak and would be acclaimed, and may still be acclaimed, as the most awesome in baseball history. Yet in 1926, the first year in the Yankees' three-pennant skein, the Series was won by the St. Louis Cardinals, a team which in this era threatened to dominate the National League almost as relentlessly as the Yankees dominated the American, and a team which in that year, 1926, included another all-time great pitcher, Grover Cleveland Alexander, and a man often spoken of as the greatest right-handed hitter in the game's history, the stormy Rogers Hornsby. Hornsby—like McGraw, like Cobb—was a man who went his own way, an individualist who felt that excellence in baseball had nothing to do with popularity, and he moved through the years chilling the league's pitchers and alienating fans, players, moguls, and even Kenesaw Mountain Landis, who awed many players but did not awe Rogers Hornsby. Aside from meeting a baseball squarely with his bat, what Hornsby loved most was betting on horses. It was his recreation, he said, and when Landis called him to the bench and pointed out that what he was doing was gambling, Hornsby said indeed it was and that he saw nothing wrong with it and remarked to Landis that if he, the judge, happened to be playing the stock market then he too was gambling. Landis, who happened to have been playing the stock market, gave Hornsby an indignant glare from beneath his white locks and Hornsby went on betting on horses and knocking the pitchers loose from their moorings. Hornsby was a second baseman, the fourteenth player elected to the Hall of Fame, and although he was not a complete performer (they said he couldn't go back for a pop fly) he made up for it with his bat. He was a traveler. He played for many clubs and managed no fewer than five. Inevitably there would be a personality clash with the club owner and often with the players themselves—it was said that playing under Hornsby was like "being in reform school"—and he would move on to another team, hired by another owner who could not resist his baseball acumen and his potent bat. With his bat he won seven batting championships, including six in a row, during which he chalked up averages of .370, .397, .401, .384, .424, and .403 in the six seasons ending with 1925. His mark of .424 is not only a National League record but the all-time major-league record. In 1926 his six-year streak was broken, but to make up for it he managed the St. Louis Cardinals to their first pennant in history and the first won by any St. Louis team since the days of von der Ahe's old Browns.

Again that year, 1926, the Series went all the way to the seventh game, and for all the heroics of Hornsby and Ruth and the Babe's young fence-busting partner Lou Gehrig, the climax of the series came down to a staring match between two men, one young, one aging. The first was Tony Lazzeri, the Yankee second baseman. The other was the veteran pitcher Grover Cleveland Alexander—Old Pete, he was called —a man who hit the bottle with frequency but one in whom epilepsy was sometimes mistaken for drunkenness. He was an epileptic for the last ten years of his career and sometimes he was seized with an epileptic fit as he stood on the mound. When this happened he was carried from the field to the dugout or locker room, where he would take a whiff from the bottle of ammonia that he always carried with him and then go back out and pitch. With all this, plus deafness in one ear, he won 373 games, including twenty-eight in his rookie year, 1911, and twenty-one when he was forty years old. Once while still with the Philadelphia Phillies, he beat the Cardinals in the first game of a doubleheader and when the Philadelphia manager expressed worry that the Phillies would miss their getaway train later in the afternoon, Alexander asked to pitch the second game as well. He shut out the Cardinals in fifty-eight minutes flat and the Phillies made their train.

That day in the 1926 Series, with the score tied 3–3 in games and the Cardinals leading after six innings, the Yankees rallied in the seventh; Alexander was called in from the bullpen with the bases loaded and asked to snuff out the rally. The batter was Lazzeri, and conceivably he could have been disheartened and even awed by the old man's very nonchalance, for as Babe Ruth himself would write later, "Just to see old Pete out there on the mound, with that cocky little undersize cap pulled down over one ear, chewing away at his tobacco and pitching baseballs as easy as pitching hay is enough to take the heart out of a fellow."

Alexander is considered by many to have been the greatest
control pitcher the game has ever known, and he showed
Lazzeri why. He struck him out with the bases loaded, the
rally was dead, and so, for that year, were the Yankees. Thousands saw and reported the strikeout pitch as a great, sharp-
breaking curve, but according to Ruth, "the ball that Tony
fanned on was not a curve at all. It wasn't even a fast ball. It
was a half-speed pitch that cut the corner of the plate within
half an inch of the spot" called for by catcher Bob O'Farrell.

There have been great teams in baseball. Connie Mack had
two, almost fifteen years apart. The Orioles of the 1890's were
remarkable for their day as were some of the Giant teams and
the Cubs of Frank Chance. The St. Louis Cardinals of the
early 1930's would become memorable and so too would some
of the latter-day Yankees teams in the DiMaggio era. But in
all the long saga of baseball there probably has never been a
team so awesome as the New York Yankees of 1927, the team
which met and crushed the Pittsburgh Pirates for the championship of the world. The Pirates may have felt beaten before the Series even began, and they could not have been
blamed. They were meeting a team whose eight regular players had a combined batting average of better than .320. There
was Babe Ruth, who had just hit his sixtieth home run that
season, and Lou Gehrig, who had hit forty-seven and who
with Ruth made up the most powerful one-two punch the
game had ever seen or likely would see again—Ruth, hitting
third and Lou Gehrig batting cleanup; Ruth with his mighty
uppercut swing that sent balls from the park in enormous arcs,
Lou with the flat-footed level swing that was as likely to send
a ball ripping against the fence as over it; Ruth with 164 runs
batted in that year, Gehrig with 175.

And yet, even with two such men, the Yankees were by no
means a two-man team. Lazzeri at second base batted .309.
Bob Meusel, the rifle-armed left-fielder, batted .337. Earle
Combs, a splendid leadoff man, batted .356.

Ruth's slugging feats are epic and so indeed are those of Lou
Gehrig. Twelve times Babe Ruth won the home-run championship. In eleven years he hit forty or more home runs during the season. Seventy times he hit two home runs in one
game. He began a home-run craze which has lasted to the
present day, when many players still swing from the heels and
some belt out thirty or forty home runs a year, catering to the
fan lust for the long ball, yet in too many cases the long ball is
the only one they hit. When they don't hit it, they all too often
pop up. Batting in the .260's and .270's, they still win accolades
as sluggers.

Babe Ruth recorded a lifetime batting average of .342. Gehrig's was .340. Each won a batting championship, Ruth in 1924
with .378, Gehrig in 1934 with .363.

In that storied year, 1927, Ruth's batting average was .356.
Gehrig hit .373.

When the Yankees of 1927 were not hitting, which was
rarely if ever, they had a superb pitching staff going for them,
with starters such as Waite Hoyt, Urban Shocker, Herb Pennock, George Pipgras, and Wilcy Moore. One hundred and ten
games the Yankees won that year and they were never out of
first place a single day. They crushed the Pirates in four
straight, and a year later did the same to the Cardinals, running their World Series streak to eight straight games.

In the first decade of their awesome dynasty, the Yankees
had won six pennants out of ten—shattering indeed for the
rest of the league, but there was worse to come. After stepping
aside for the three-year reign of Connie Mack's last great
team, the Yankees, with Joe McCarthy now managing,
breezed to the pennant in 1932 and knocked off the Chicago
Cubs four games to zero in the World Series, giving them a
consecutive game streak of twelve straight in Series play.
Again they had a three-year lapse while Washington took a
pennant and Detroit took two but then, in 1936, they began
tearing off pennants in great chunks. By now the faces were
new. After 1937 Tony Lazzeri was released, leaving the dura-

ble Lou Gehrig as the only survivor from the old Murderers Row days, but now there were new assassins and still others year after year to replace those who might fade. Gone were Combs, Meusel, Ruth, and Lazzeri, and in 1939 Gehrig himself. Overlapping them were George Selkirk, Bill Dickey, Frank Crosetti, and Lefty Gomez, and then there were Joe DiMaggio, Joe Gordon, Babe Dahlgren, Red Rolfe, Charlie Keller, Tommy Henrich. Six pennants the Yankees had won for Huggins, eight they won for McCarthy, the one in 1932, and then a streak of four from 1936 through 1939; and then finally, after an off year, another streak of three that carried them deep into the war years. And with those eight pennants, they won every World Series but one.

Babe Ruth had started it all, Babe Ruth had pointed the way, but they could do it without Ruth, and without Gehrig. Was New York getting too many pennants indeed!

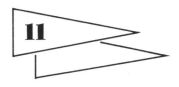

The Gas

House Gang

IS IT POSSIBLE, ASKED THE EMINENT BASEBALL AUTHORITY Lillian Russell in 1909, that baseball's main value is in providing a national safety valve?

And is it true that baseball reflects the national mood, as so many others have written? Was it significant that in the deepest pit of the Depression the most arresting baseball personalities were an Okie-esque outfielder named Pepper Martin and an Ozark hillbilly named either Jerome Herman Dean or Jay Hanna Dean? (He was never quite sure which, responding to both but responding most often to Dizzy.)

Was Babe Ruth, in the subliminal national view, truly a soaring stock market, a rumble seat, rolled stockings, a short skirt, a yellow slicker, and bootleg hooch? Was Pepper Martin truly the symbol of breadlines and soup kitchens and hardscrabble hard times, or was he merely a good ball player who exploded into brilliance in World Series play?

Dizzy Dean would have been a baseball celebrity, indeed a national celebrity, regardless of era. He was too good a pitcher and too colorful a personality for it to have been otherwise, just as Babe Ruth had no need of the 20's. It is impossible, of course, to separate him from his times, just as it is impossible to separate Dean from his, and yet surely each was too good a ball player and too colorful in his own right to have needed the atmospheric and sociological props of an era for lasting fame.

In the 1920's the public followed baseball with the high spirits of a temporarily high-spirited nation. During the Depression it turned to baseball for entertainment, for solace, just as it turned to thirty-five-cent movie houses featuring such non-Ozarkians as Shirley Temple and Marlene Dietrich, and just as, at the cost of a few cents worth of electricity, it switched on sometimes small but more often enormous and hideous console radios, listening to such nonrustics as Jack Benny, Rudy Vallee, and Fred Allen, and listening as well to Ted Husing and others who were, as they were fond of saying, now able to bring the diamond sport directly into the living room through the magic medium of radio.

Over the radio some claim to have heard Husing describe how Babe Ruth called his shot in the 1932 World Series, the Babe's last—how with two strikes on him he gestured toward the center-field stands as if promising to blast the next pitch into those very stands, which is exactly what he did. And although over the years some have said his gesture meant something else, the way it was described by Husing to those in radioland it came out as a promise specifically made and quickly executed, and the story, whether myth or fact, has endured and will endure as long as the memory of Ruth endures.

Even before 1932 radio had begun the electronic alliance with baseball which, after TV, would grow into something that threatened to become bigger than the game itself. But in 1929 it was not the tube, it was in many homes still the tiny crystal set with earphones by which a man, periodically yelling "Shhh, dammit," could follow the progress of his heroes. Others, in a hangover from the early years of the century, still gathered in the streets outside newspaper offices, watching the half-inning scores go up. Still others craned their necks in the October sunlight and followed the action through a more primitive electronic device, a depiction of the diamond with lights representing runners flickering around the bases, which were represented by four dots.

The World Series of 1929 was played as usual in October and in that same October the stock market crashed, but while the Series was in progress, as the people stood in the streets and watched the lights flicker, they were still living in the era of the prosperous 20's, even though in another few days the era would end with a sickening jolt. Those watching the fourth game of the Series had reason to wonder if the electronic gadget on the face of the building had gone crazy. Blobs of light darted from dot to dot and kept darting as roar upon incredulous roar swelled up from the floor of the canyon. But the device was not broken, nor was the operator drunk, as some had occasion to ask. It was all real and the darting lights represented the exact travels taken by members of the Philadelphia Athletics who were darting from base to base and scoring ten runs in the seventh inning to snatch away a game the Cubs, leading 8–0 when the Athletics came to bat, had good cause to feel they had won. This was the fourth game. In game number one, Connie Mack the thinker had confounded the Cubs and the public by passing up the cream of his pitching corps and starting the veteran part-timer Howard Ehmke, who responded with a 3–1 victory and a strike-out total of thirteen, then a World Series record. Crushed and demoralized after the ten-run inning, the Cubs folded, losing the series four games to one, even though they included among their ranks the memorable Hack Wilson, an outfielder built like a fire plug who the following year would hit fifty-six home runs and bat across 190, the former a National League mark and the latter a record for both leagues.

The Athletics were the team Connie Mack had been dreaming of and building for fourteen long years of often second-division and sometimes tail-end baseball, years of sifting hundreds of untried players, of occasionally paying huge sums for promising minor-leaguers, and of trying to squeeze final base hits out of stars past their prime. In 1927 Ty Cobb had found a home with Mack, lured by a huge salary after he was dropped as Detroit manager, and that season, at the age of forty-one, Cobb hit .357 and stole twenty-two bases. In one game he stole home and made an unassisted double play. In 1928, his twenty-third consecutive season as a regular, he hit .323, marking the twenty-third consecutive season in which he hit over .300. After the season of 1928 Cobb called it a career, retiring to the Coca-Cola and other interests that would make of him a multimillionaire. Tris Speaker too found a haven with Mack in his declining years, but in 1927 and 1928 the Yankees were unbeatable and Mack's younger stars had not quite hit their prime. Now in 1929 they were tops in baseball—Cochrane, Foxx, Simmons, and Grove were the superstars, but others were nearly as good—George Earnshaw and Rube Walberg, among the pitchers; Mule Haas and Bing Miller in the outfield; Max Bishop at second base; Joe Boley at shortstop; and at third base the rotund Jimmy Dykes, who would go on to a managerial career and who once in 1925, swinging each time on the first pitch, made five hits in five times at bat on five pitches. In 1929, 1930, and 1931, even while Ruth and Gehrig continued to murder the ball, the greatest team once more belonged to Connie Mack. Grove, one of the greatest of left-handers, won a career total of 300 games, including a 31–4 season in 1931, the last American League pitcher to win thirty games in a single season until Denny McLain of Detroit did it in 1968. In 1929 Al Simmons beat out the Ruth-Gehrig duo for the runs-batted-in title, and Jimmy Foxx did the same in 1932 and 1933. Simmons won the batting championship in

1930 and 1931, and Foxx won it in 1933. Foxx in 1932 came very close to Ruth's mark of sixty home runs, hitting fifty-eight, and in all won the home-run title four times. Although Ruth and Gehrig are deservedly ranked as the foremost slugging duo in baseball history, the Simmons-Foxx combination was not very far behind, and in the late 20's and early 30's all four men were playing at the same time, a day-after-day distraction from the reality of the Depression.

In the World Series of 1931 Pepper Martin hit the Philadelphia pitchers as if he owned them and ran wild on the bases, ran wild on the mighty Mickey Cochrane—and Connie Mack, who had said in 1915 that he could sense when a great team was done for, soon decided once more to break up the Philadelphia Athletics. He was influenced as well by economics, for with so many superstars on his team, the payroll had become enormous for that day, and with the Depression getting worse, the fans, for all their interest in baseball, were hardly setting attendance records. With reluctance but with a sense of inevitability, Mack sent Al Simmons to Chicago, Cochrane to Detroit, and Grove and Foxx to the Boston Red Sox, whose owner, Tom Yawkey, could afford them, just as later he could afford Joe Cronin after he had led Washington to its third pennant.

Again Mack would try to build another contender. For another two decades he tried. In 1950 he marked half a century as manager of the Athletics. Before the 1950 season began, then eighty-seven years old, he would write: "My highest ambition is to do it again in 1950 before I retire, for I believe we have a team of stars in the making; we are building up another championship team."

He was wrong. After 1950 he stepped down as manager and after 1954 the Philadelphia Athletics would no longer exist. They went west to Kansas City. Connie Mack died in 1956 at ninety-three—the game's last link to the distant days of Anson and von der Ahe and Old Hoss Radbourn, the old days of bare-handed baseball.

In 1933 Connie Mack was seventy. That same year Joe
Cronin, then twenty-six, managed the Washington Senators to their third and last pennant. At this point there were
signs for those unwitting enough to believe them that even the
Washington Senators were building a dynasty, 1924, '25, '33—
adding them up, it came to three pennants in ten seasons! But
after 1933 the Senators went quietly and they have been going quietly ever since. Entering the 1969 season they had
failed to win the pennant for thirty-six consecutive years. The
1933 team was a one-shot group, assembled in large part
through intelligent mid-winter trades engineered by the saga-
cious Clark Griffith, who spent his life in baseball and who
knew the game as well as any man who ever lived. The team
included Buddy Myer, a fine second baseman who later won
a league batting championship; the colorful and often hard-
hitting Goose Goslin; Heinie Manush, a prolific hitter tutored
by Cobb while he was managing Detroit; and two very good
pitchers in Alvin Crowder and Earl Whitehill.

When the 1933 season opened in Washington, Franklin D.
Roosevelt, on hand to throw out the first ball, had been in office
only since March 4th, a little over a month, and the cheer he
received as his limousine appeared through the gate in the
right-field corner was tremendous. Washington won the game,
and young Joe Cronin got three hits in four times at bat. After
the game he ran over to the Presidential box and Franklin
Roosevelt shook his hand. "Keep up the good work, Joe," he
said.

Joe and the Senators kept it up all season long, only to
crumble in the World Series against the first New York Giant
team ever to win a pennant under a manager other than John
McGraw, who, leaving the longevity record to Connie Mack,
had turned over the Giants to Bill Terry.

Even though the World Series of 1933 was a rather tepid
affair between teams hardly memorable, it involved no fewer
than seven players ultimately elected to the Hall of
Fame, and eight if one includes Washington owner Clark

Griffith, who made it as a pitcher. The other Washington se-
lectmen were Goslin, Manush, and outfielder Sam Rice, a part-
time player in 1933 but a splendid hitter, base runner, and defensive man in his day. The Giant Hall-of-Famers were Mel
Ott, who came to McGraw as a schoolboy and went on to place
high on the all-time home-run list with 511; Bill Terry, the
last National League .400 hitter, who hit .401 in 1930; and the
splendid pitcher Carl Hubbell, whose hurling played a large
part in the 1933 World Series victory.

Hubbell—King Carl, the Meal Ticket, famous for his screw-
ball and his low-slung pants—was a star for fifteen seasons. On
August 18, 1933, he pitched an eighteen-inning game against
the St. Louis Cardinals, going the route, shutting them out
1–0, yielding only six hits, no walks, and pitching twelve perfect innings in the process of pitching two complete ball games
in one. With that performance alone, he would have made his
mark in baseball history, but in the 1934 All-Star game, then
in its second year, he topped it for dramatic impact.

Hubbell that day faced a murderous array of American
League batsmen. In the first inning, it went as follows: Charlie Gehringer singled. Heinie Manush walked. Babe Ruth
struck out. Lou Gehrig struck out. Jimmy Foxx struck out.

And in the second inning: Al Simmons struck out. Joe Cronin struck out. Bill Dickey singled. Pitcher Lefty Gomez struck
out.

Ruth, Gehrig, Foxx, and Simmons were the most lethal hitters of their day and among the greatest of all time. Cronin
was a very good hitter in his own right. Hubbell struck out all
five in succession, and with this feat alone assured himself a
place with Mathewson, McGinnity, and Marquard among all-
time Giant and major-league pitching greats. Two years later,
in 1936, he won sixteen games in a row and continued his
streak into 1937, winning another eight straight for a total of
twenty-four.

Toward the end of the season in 1934, on Monday, September 24, Babe Ruth made his final appearance in Yankee Stadium, the House That Ruth Built. Only a meager crowd was on hand, and the Yankee management was criticized for not making it a ceremonial occasion. Ruth was then forty and he had a Charley horse.

Before the game he sat glumly in the dugout. "I know the Babe was deeply hurt," wrote Paul Gallico. "He gnawed off a corner of an oblong plug of tobacco and he said in his rare and juicy vocabulary that it was no fun playing before such a small crowd but that he would start the game anyway."

He played one inning. In his only time at bat he walked, and then retired for a pinch runner. As he limped from the field he was given a smattering of applause.

In May 1935 President Roosevelt pulled a switch in Washington, and 1,090,000 watts of electric power flooded Crosley Field in Cincinnati—and, as one national publication viewed it, "at that precise moment men who have been associated with major-league baseball all their lives winced, as if the electric charge had gone through them."

The occasion was the first night baseball game, an encounter played with apparent reluctance by members of the Cincinnati Reds against the Philadelphia Phillies.

"Birds roosting under the roof of cavernous Crosley Field flew over the field, singing as if it were daybreak," the account said, and the smell of cooking hotdogs was heavy in the night air.

"The game became a strangely colorless, synthetic affair. Like the lights, it was artificial, mechanical. Personal characteristics and facial expressions of the players became vague in the haze which hung over the field."

What had happened to the game that was played where the blue sky came down to meet the green grass? Most owners vowed to keep it that way. Never, they said, would night ball be played in *their* parks.

That night in Cincinnati the players were bitter. They were

afraid to dig in at the plate, leery of taking toeholds, fearful of being beaned. One said that major-league baseball was being turned "into a five-and-ten-cent racket."

The fans didn't like it either. They were cold and they couldn't see the players very well. The consensus was clear: night baseball would never last.

In the spring of 1936 a young outfielder of Italian descent and heavy advance billing went south with the New York Yankees. It was said that he might be the greatest right-handed hitter since Rogers Hornsby.

When the season opened he was on the injured list and it was not until early May that he took his place in the lineup. He got three hits in his first game, three in the second, two in the third, and patrolled center field as if it might belong to him for a while. His name was Joe DiMaggio and he looked like a comer.

Ever since Ruth, the New York Yankees, among other notable characteristics, have always boasted a superstar on their roster, one overlapping another, and sometimes one overlapping two. Ruth, Gehrig, and Dickey all were playing at the same time. DiMaggio and Gehrig were teammates for three seasons, and after Gehrig retired DiMaggio stood alone for a while, surrounded by teammates who were merely excellent, and then overlapped by Mickey Mantle, who, as his career faded, left the poor Yankees bereft of a superstar for the first time in almost half a century. It was a shame for the Yankees but few were the tears around the league.

Gehrig ended his brilliant career in 1939, crippled by the spinal disease that ultimately would cause his death. Along with his remarkable batting achievements, he left an endurance record that may never be approached. A New Yorker who played for Columbia University, Gehrig played his first game for the Yankees in 1923. From June 1, 1925, until his last game, on April 30, 1939, he appeared in every game the

Yankees played, recording not only a lifetime batting average of .340 and a career home-run total of 493, but an iron-man streak of 2,130 consecutive games played. Known as "Larruping Lou," he once was screentested in a leopard skin for a Tarzan role, and in 1940 he was chosen one of the "five best husbands in America," by the Divorce Reform League.

On July 4, 1939, soon after he dropped from the lineup, the Yankees held a Lou Gehrig Day at Yankee Stadium, and Gehrig, in his speech of appreciation, said he considered himself the luckiest man alive. Ruth was there, and so were some of the other old-time Yankees. Out in center field fluttered the 1927 pennant.

The Yankees that year were winning their fourth consecutive pennant, closing out a decade that had seen them win five in all. But for all their excellence, the hit show in the 30's was an off-Broadway affair with a troupe of players known as the Gas House Gang, starring a tall, loose-jointed country boy named (probably) Jerome Herman Dean and co-starring his brother Paul. The supporting cast was rowdy and superb.

Occasionally the impossible can become the possible and to watch it happen can be an experience that thrills. An underdog is essential, and America has always been said to favor underdogs. There have been notable underdogs—George Washington's ragtag army against the British, for example, and there have been others. Would Gary Cooper bring it off in *High Noon*? He did. Would Harry Truman bring it off against Tom Dewey? When he got up the morning after the election, he had. Joe Namath could not possibly smash the mighty Baltimore Colts, but he did.

When a colorful personality combines big talk with true ability, the combination can have an overwhelming effect upon the public. Cassius Clay, the fighter, was briefly such a man. Ruth was. Namath is, and so was Dizzy Dean.

When the 1934 season began Dizzy Dean was already the big noise of the Cardinal pitching staff. He had been talking

the colleges for promising material. The brand of baseball in the schools is improving in efficiency. The competition is keener and the coaching is better due to the fact that many of the mentors are former Major League players.

Every team in the Majors has one or

one of the finest examples of a college player who has

Ed. Farrell, wh
campus to the
proved a valua

made good in
recent year
from Bost
to win rec
Majors as
catchers in
his first
season. He
for B. U. an
experience
of the I
League. In
.388 for Por
eral Big Le:
competed
Mack for his
Among pres
League
have gr:
college 1
via

Gordon Cochrane, a product of Boston University, who made a sensational

Mickey Cochrane, a superb defensive catcher and a heavy hitter, managed the Detroit Tigers to the pennant in 1934 only to run afoul of the Gas House Gang in the mad, mad World Series.

Few players in history combined batting and defensive skills at such a high level as Tris Speaker.

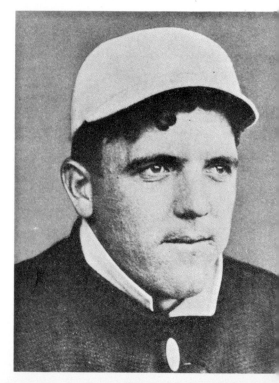

Eddie Cicotte, an excellent pitcher, was one of the White Sox who took a bribe in the 1919 World Series. Under orders in the first game to hit the first Cincinnati batter as a show of intent, Cicotte hit him squarely between the shoulder blades and the fix was on.

Carl Hubbell, who in a later era gave the New York Giants the dependability if not the glamour of Christy Mathewson.

Grover Cleveland (Pete) Alexander, control artist. Just to see him out on the mound, "pitching baseballs as easy as pitching hay, is enough to take the heart out of a fellow," wrote Babe Ruth.

TED WILLIAMS, CENTENNIAL YEAR'S ACE ROOKIE

Ted Williams, the "Splendid Splinter" of the Boston Red Sox, as a rookie in 1939. Baseball's last .400 hitter and an eminent fisherman, Williams was lured out of retirement to manage Washington in 1969.

The Babe... the one and only. "Now and again, a superman arises..."

Lou Gehrig. He and Babe Ruth were the most devastating one-two punch in baseball history.

After his fabulous career ended, Babe Ruth spent aimless days—he aged, and developed throat cancer. Toward the end of his life he paid a farewell visit to Yankee Stadium—the House That Ruth Built.

Joe DiMaggio, a man of class, a ball player of incomparable grace. Like Tris Speaker, he matched up batting and fielding skills at a superior level.

Mickey Mantle, last of the Yankee superstars.

Leroy (Satchel) Paige, who may have been the greatest pitcher of all time. In Dizzy Dean's prime, Satch Paige bested him 1–0 in seventeen innings.

Jackie Robinson, who, with Branch Rickey, opened the gates.

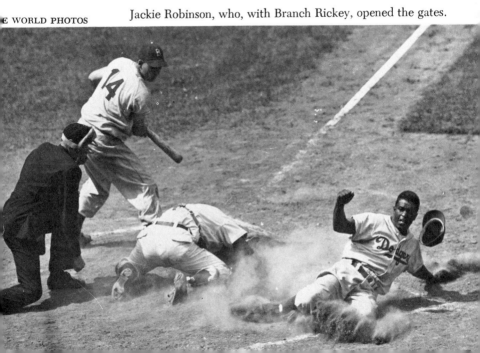

As the years passed, it was apparent that somebody in the all-time outfield of Cobb-Speaker-Ruth might have to move over to make room for Willie Mays.

Stan (The Man) Musial. His all-time-hit total is second only to Cobb's, and he topped Cobb in total bases.

heavily and winning heavily for four years, and now with him, as the season began, was his brother Paul, who would be called Daffy, for less reason than Dizzy was called Dizzy. That spring Dizzy predicted that "me 'n Paul" between them would pitch at least forty-five victories in the Cardinal cause, assuring a pennant for St. Louis and its Gas House Gang, which, aside from the Deans, included such gas-house types as Manager Frank Frisch, third baseman Pepper Martin, outfielder Joe Medwick, first baseman Rip Collins, shortstop Leo Durocher, catcher Bill Delancey, and pitcher Tex Carleton.

The drama had as its main heroes the Deans and the other gas-housers. It had a correlative hero in none other than Casey Stengel, who that year was managing the going-nowhere Brooklyn Dodgers. For large segments of the underdog-loving public, it had one who sufficed nicely as a villain—Manager Bill Terry and his New York Giants, who were champions of the world and a sure shot to repeat.

September of 1934 was a remarkable month for news. It was the month the luxury liner *Morro Castle* burned on its way up the Atlantic coast from Cuba, with the loss of 133 lives. It was the month Bruno Hauptmann was captured and accused of the kidnap-slaying of the Lindbergh baby. A nationwide strike was going on in the textile mills. Hugh Johnson's resignation was demanded as head of the NRA. Stripper Sally Rand revealed that she was planning to marry the man who served as her announcer during her fan dance at the Chicago World's Fair. Off Newport, an America's Cup race was being sailed between the *Rainbow* and the British challenger, *Endeavor*.

It was also the month that Dizzy and Daffy and the Gas House Gang had a go at the impossible.

Deep into September the Giants were considered a shoo-in. At one point they had a seven-game lead, and articles already were being written evaluating their chances in the World Series against Detroit, who seemed a good bet to beat out the Yankees for the pennant in the American League.

On September 17, the Deans won a pair at the Polo Grounds, cutting the Giants' lead to three and a half games with twelve left to play.

On September 22, fantasy:

The Cardinals played the Dodgers a doubleheader. In the first game, Dizzy pitched a three-hitter, winning 13–0. In the second game, Paul pitched a no-hitter, winning 3–0.

Said Dizzy: "The only thing that makes me mad is that I didn't know I hadn't give them any hits in the first seven innings of the first game. I should have known that. Then I'd have really breezed 'em in there and we'd both have had a no-hitter."

Said Manager Frisch: "We may catch those Giants yet."

On Monday, September 24, the Detroit Tigers clinched their first pennant since 1909, the year Ty Cobb and Honus Wagner posed for the motion-picture camera.

On Thursday, September 27, Paul Dean lost to Pittsburgh and the veteran Waite Hoyt, but the Giants, really choking now, lost to the Phillies. The following day Bill Terry told them to take the day off and relax, forget about baseball, see a movie—Adolphe Menjou in *The Human Side*, perhaps, or Grace Moore in *One Night of Love*.

While the Giants were at the movies, Dizzy Dean shut out the Reds 4–0 for his twenty-ninth victory of the season and the Cardinals' eighteenth victory in their last twenty-three games.

The two teams now were in a flat-footed tie, each with ninety-three victories and fifty-eight defeats. Each had two games to play.

Dizzy Dean was asked to take part in a calf-roping contest but demurred. "Ah just can't do it, folks. We gotta win the National League title and that's more serious than roping a calf," he said, although making it clear that he was perfectly capable of roping one if he had not been otherwise engaged.

The Cardinals' final two games were against Cincinnati,

while the Giants in their two faced, of all teams, Brooklyn. Enter Stengel. Early in the season Bill Terry had made an ill-considered remark which now came back to embarrass him. Asked what he thought of Brooklyn's chances in the 1934 pennant race, he had replied with sarcasm: "Is Brooklyn still in the league?"

Now the newspapers brought back the remark for a replay, and now all through the United States baseball fans, and even people who normally weren't fans, jammed up to their ugly console radios come evening, listening more avidly for the baseball results than they listened to Stoopnagle and Budd.

On Saturday, September 29, Paul Dean beat Cincinnati for his nineteenth victory of the season. Van Lingle Mungo, an excellent Brooklyn fireballer, beat the Giants 5–1.

The Cardinals now were a game in the lead, and the next day it was all over. Again Brooklyn beat the Giants. Dizzy Dean beat the Reds. Brooklyn was in fact still in the league. The Giants had lost the pennant, and the Gas House Gang had won it.

Dizzy's victory was number thirty and this, combined with Paul's nineteen, added up to a family total of forty-nine—four more than even Dizzy had promised.

Before the season began, a so-called Subway Series—involving New York teams from each league—had been widely predicted. Instead the World Series went to the wild West and the Series itself could hardly have been wilder. St. Louis, said the *Literary Digest*, was "the wildest club that ever reached a World Series." The less flamboyant Tigers were a good club that year, led by their scrappy, intelligent catcher, Mickey Cochrane, one of the stars traded away by Connie Mack and now winning a major-league pennant in his very first year as manager. At second base was Charlie Gehringer, a flawless fielder and excellent hitter, another of the men schooled by Ty Cobb in the Cobb method of line-drive hitting. (Yet another for whose prowess Cobb claimed at least partial credit was Harry Heilmann, who won four batting titles in the 20's with stellar averages of .394, .403, .393, and .398.) At first base for the 1934 Tigers was the mighty Hank Greenberg, one of the heavy-hitting first basemen in the American League at that time (others were Foxx, Gehrig, Hal Trosky of the Indians, and Zeke Bonura of the White Sox), and who that year, his first as a regular, had hit twenty-six home runs and batted over .330. In the outfield was the clutch-hitting Goose Goslin, acquired from Washington during the winter, and the pitchers included the curve-balling Tommy Bridges and the youthful Lynwood (Schoolboy) Rowe, who that season had pitched sixteen consecutive victories, tying the American League record held jointly by Walter Johnson, Lefty Grove, and Smoky Joe Wood.

With all the colorful performers around both leagues and with a little more money in circulation, fans had been flocking to ball games all season long, and, indeed, the *Literary Digest* said, baseball had become "the first great industry to emerge flying out of the depression." In Detroit, it said, a "mad Mardi Gras spirit has swept reason aside"—and swept from the front pages such personalities as Benito Mussolini and such events as the Spanish revolution.

The Dean brothers would not be in baseball long as major-league careers are measured. Paul never equaled his 1934 performance and although Dizzy had another great year in 1935, he would never be the same after the 1936 All-Star game when he was hit in the leg by a line drive off the bat of Cleveland outfielder Earl Averill. Pitching before he was ready to pitch, he favored the leg and adopted an unnatural pitching motion which damaged his arm and deprived him of his great fast ball. Never again would he "fog 'em through," as he once had. But in the year 1934 the world was briefly theirs.

The first two games of the Series was played in Detroit, and the Cardinals won the first game 8–3 behind Dizzy. The Tigers took the second with Rowe, 3–2. The third was won by

Paul Dean, but the Tigers came back to win the fourth, and then in the fifth Tommy Bridges bested the mighty Dizzy, 3–1.

At this point, the Gas House Gang had their backs to the wall, just as they did in the closing days of the pennant race. Trailing in games three to two, they turned once more to the brothers Dean.

In the sixth game, back again in Detroit, Paul Dean beat Schoolboy Rowe, tying the Series at three games apiece. Dizzy had something to say. In the fourth game as a pinch runner he was struck in the head with a ball thrown by Tiger shortstop Billy Rogell. After Paul's sixth-game victory, he said: "You know, that lick on my head sort of set me thinking and I just thought to myself, I know what I'm going to do. I'm going to send my little brother after them rascals and he brought 'em home with him too, didn't he?"

With such a Series and after such a season, could baseball give its patrons a fitting climax? It could. The seventh game of the 1934 World Series was one of the wildest in the game's long history. It included a riot, touched off when Ducky Medwick, running out a triple, slid into third and spiked Tiger third baseman Marvin Owen. When the inning was over and Medwick took up his outfield post—he couldn't. He was pelted with bottles, cushions, garbage, anything on which the enraged Detroit partisans could lay hands. The game was halted and after a long conference Kenesaw Mountain Landis himself decided there was nothing else for it but to remove Medwick from the ball game. This he did and the game continued. By then the Cardinals no longer needed his booming bat, for what had driven the Tiger fans to rage was not solely the unpleasant set-to at third base. They had been watching the Cardinal hitters murder Detroit pitching, and they had been watching Dizzy Dean make monkeys out of the Detroit hitters, including the mighty Greenberg.

To the *Literary Digest* man, the seventh game was a "riot of cursing fans and swirling color punctuated by flying bottles

and always the broad grin of Dizzy Dean, a confident, crow-
ing rooster on the mound. Quite a drama, the World Series
of 1934. George Arliss or Walter Hampden never would dare
walk on the stage facing such an exacting audience, surrounded by such a brilliant supporting cast. The risk of being
obscured, lost on the stage, would have terrified the doughtiest
of troupers. But the Dean boys, Dizzy and Daffy, walked
right on and dominated the dramatics."

Said Dizzy: "I let 'em get a couple of hits and then I decided to stop fooling around and throw those strikes past 'em.
Boy, was that Greenberg wild! I just had to laugh when he
missed those third swings."

Said Dizzy: "Say, but wasn't those Tigers funny! I never
saw a team get stage-fright that bad. I hope I won't be like
that when I go into vaudeville."

And said Dizzy: "We did it, didn't we? I knew we would
from the start. I felt great out there this afternoon. I had a lot
of fun."

On the Outskirts

of Town

IN 1884, IN THE OLD AMERICAN ASSOCIATION, TOLEDO HAD AN outfielder named Welday Walker and a catcher named Moses Fleetwood Walker. They were brothers. Thereafter, not until 1947 would a Negro play baseball in the major leagues.

All along they were playing, yet so far as the white world was concerned they were playing in the shadows, playing doubleheaders on the dark side of the moon, running out triples on the outskirts of town, playing on fields of their own or using the white man's field when he was away on the road.

Off to themselves they were making history but not keeping records, just pitching and batting, running and sliding and making great clouds of dust that hid them from the view of most. They were the Birmingham Black Barons and the Kan-

sas City Monarchs, the Pittsburgh Crawfords, the Baltimore
Elite Giants and the Nashville Elite Giants and the Chattanooga Black Lookouts and the New Orleans Black Pelicans,
teams like that, and for all those years they went their way,
traveling on sidetracks, staying at hotels-for-colored, riding
trains but mostly buses, gone underground just as the Negro
musicians went underground, and, like the musicians, they
were very big in Kansas City. Downstairs in the dead of
night, the jazzmen were blowing for each other, creating their
music and their legends, and so too were the ball players
making their own music, creating their own legends (Satch,
Josh, Cool Papa), except that the musicians came out of the
shadows much earlier; admired and led forth, they came
upstairs, some willingly, some with contempt, but they came
out and played at the white man's invitation on the white
man's wax and let the white man pay some of his loot to
hear them—so that the jazzmen, even the *old* old-timers, had
it on record and the world could hear what they had been
playing, know what they were capable of and could compare.
But there was no way the ball players could be seen, no
remembrance of *their* thing past except the word of people
who had watched them, or mostly heard of them, heard of
Leroy Satchel Paige and Josh Gibson and Cool Papa Bell
and Judy Sweet Juice Johnson.

What they were doing all those years was separate-but-
equal, and some were less than equal but maybe some were a
whole lot more than equal—and who would know for certain?
One of those who knew was the great Dizzy Dean, who lost a
heartbreaker to Satch; and another who knew was the mighty
Hornsby, who knew because Satch fanned him five times one
day; and Jimmy Foxx, who fanned three times; and Charlie
Gehringer, who fanned three times, and yet Charlie was the
only white man that Satch would rate even close to Josh
Gibson as a hitter. Another who knew was Joe DiMaggio,
only twenty-one then, still in California, and Satch was thirty-

six going on forty-five, when the young DiMag got a single off him in four trips, so the Yankees knew he must be ready for the big time. They had heard about Satch and they had heard about Josh because men who should know, by-God white men, said Satch was the greatest and said Josh was a better catcher than anybody and could hit with more power than Ruth, and wasn't it a shame they never made it to the Bigs?

What Bigs? they might have asked; we were the Bigs, and perhaps they were—Gibson greater than Cochrane, Dickey, Campanella? Cool Papa Bell greater than Mays? And Leroy Paige the greatest, many would say, of all. Satch didn't wanna look back. Looking back gave him the nervous stomach, but he could look back and remember beating Dizzy in Dizzy's finest hour, after his great season of 1934, beating him 1–0 in seventeen innings, Paige All-Stars vs. Diz Dean All-Stars, and afterward Dean, the southern boy, the self-styled greatest pitcher in the world, would shake his head and admit that Satch was. For years and years, maybe thirty, Satch pitched and pitched, a tall, lean, stringy black man with legs like sticks and huge feet, banging around black America and white America too, in and out of town, pitching sometimes for a team and sometimes for himself, in a solo act known as "Satchel Paige, World's Greatest Pitcher, Guaranteed to Strike Out the First Nine Men." Sometimes he didn't but most often he did, and then he would collect his guarantee and go on to the next town for the next exhibition, or to the next team, once for three years to the Pittsburgh Crawfords where his battery mate was Josh Gibson and in those three years he won, maybe, 105 games. Altogether he might have won about 2,000, including maybe 250 shutouts and forty-five no-hitters, pitching four days and five days and six days a week—so *whose* all-time records and whose all-time all-star team? Hoss Radbourn, Denton True (Cy) Young, Christy Mathewson, Walter Johnson, Ed Walsh, Robert Moses Grove,

Grover Cleveland Alexander, Rapid Robert Feller—and Leroy
Satchel Paige.

1. Pitchers like poets are born not made.
2. A player should try to get along without any stimulants
   at all
3. Water, pure cool water, is good enough for any man.
4. A man who isn't willing to work from dewy morn until
   weary eve shouldn't think about becoming a pitcher.

Thus spoke Cy Young, whose 511 major-league pitching
victories are the most ever recorded by a white man.

1. Avoid fried meats which angry up the blood.
2. If your stomach disputes you, lie down and pacify it with
   your cool thoughts.
3. Keep the juices flowing by jangling around gently as you
   move.
4. Go very light on the vices, such as carrying on in society.
   The social ramble ain't restful.
5. Avoid running at all times.
6. Don't look back. Something might be gaining on you.

Thus spake Satch.

Seldom did he look back. Time, he said, was not going to
"mess around" with Leroy, but he could look back and remember looking forward to a few things such as, for one,
pitching in the World Series some day while he still had
some of the sting left in the long right arm that once he
could crack like a buggy whip.

Before the end of the decade it would be okay for him to
pitch in the white man's game, but by then it would also be
very very late.

It was permissible by then because in 1946, playing shortstop for the Kansas City Monarchs, there was an educated,
highly articulate young man who had served as a lieutenant
during the war. For Jackie Robinson it was also late. He
was twenty-six, old for a rookie, but Branch Rickey signed

him to a Brooklyn Dodgers contract, sent him to Montreal for experience (and preparation), and in 1947 Jackie Robinson joined the Dodgers.

The war in its wake had brought revolution, a revolution in which Negro players and television would play prominent and lasting parts. Jackie Robinson and Branch Rickey opened the gates and at first there were only a trickle—Larry Doby, Roy Campanella, Satchel Paige—but soon they began to pour through and many reached stardom. Beginning with the season of 1949, in the National League, the Most Valuable Player Award would be won by Negro players in fifteen of the next twenty seasons: Jackie Robinson in 1949; Campanella in 1951, 1953, and 1955; Willie Mays, 1954 and 1965; Don Newcombe, 1956; Hank Aaron, 1957; Ernie Banks, 1958 and 1959; Frank Robinson, 1961; Maury Wills in 1962, the year he broke Cobb's record for stolen bases; Roberto Clemente, 1966; Orlando Cepeda, 1967; and Bob Gibson, 1968.

In the American League during those same twenty years there were two. Elston Howard won it in 1963. And Frank Robinson in 1966 became the only player ever to win a Most Valuable Player Award in both leagues, winning it for his slugging heroics with the Baltimore Orioles.

But it was Jackie Robinson who paved the way. In his rookie year he was subjected to some vicious bench-jockeying and other ugly incidents—which he answered with star-caliber hitting, fielding, base running, and dignity. He was chosen Rookie of the Year and went on to hang up a career batting average of .311, winning the National League batting championship in 1949 with a mark of .342. Six times he was chosen to the All-Star team and six times he appeared in the World Series. In late 1956, then nearing thirty-eight, he was traded by the Dodgers to the New York Giants—but instead of joining the Giants he retired. Robinson was the first and, until he was joined by Roy Campanella in 1969, the only member of his race selected for Baseball's Hall of Fame, where he took his place along with Eddie Collins, Johnny Evers, Frank

Frisch, Charlie Gehringer, Rogers Hornsby, and Napoleon Lajoie, the all-time-great second basemen.

Breaking the color line was doubtless the most significant
development in the decade of the 1940's, a decade which had
begun on a familiar enough note. With the young DiMaggio
leading the way, the Yankees, after their four consecutive
pennants ending in 1939, waited a year and rattled off three
more in 1941, 1942, and 1943, the one in 1943 being the eighth
and last under Manager Joe McCarthy. By then DiMaggio
was being acclaimed as the most nearly flawless ball player
the game had ever known. He had won batting championships in 1939 and 1940—and then, in 1941, he performed the
unreachable feat of hitting safely in fifty-six consecutive
games. That same year Ted Williams, Boston's youthful
"splendid splinter," became the game's last .400 hitter, recording an average of .406, and Rogers Hornsby in 1962
predicted that there would never be another. In 1941 a young
outfielder was playing his first season with the St. Louis
Cardinals, and these three—DiMaggio, Williams, and Musial
—would for years be latter-day baseball's answer to the outfield trio of Cobb, Speaker, and Ruth. Later there would be
Willie Mays, Mickey Mantle, and Henry Aaron.

By 1943 the nation was deep into the war, and baseball
was operating under a go-ahead given Commissioner Landis
by Franklin D. Roosevelt in the President's green-light letter
in which he said: "I honestly feel it would be best for the
country to keep baseball going. . . . These players are a defi-
nite recreational asset to their fellow citizens and that in my
judgment is entirely worthwhile."

The game being played on the field in 1944 was recog-
nizable but many of the players were not. Off in the service
were most of the stars and the teams were being manned by
4-F's, underage rookies, and overage veterans. So topsy-turvy
was the American League that the 1944 pennant was won by
the St. Louis Browns, their first since the league was founded

in 1903, and it would be their last, because in 1954 the Browns moved to Baltimore and became the Orioles. Although the St. Louis Cardinals have always been and still remain a consistent pennant winner, for the Browns their half century in the American League was a half century of want and depression, leavened most notably by George Sisler, two Bobos, and a midget. Sisler, a splendid first baseman chosen by many all-time teams, twice won the American League batting championship with marks over .400, equaling Cobb's .420 in 1922. The midget, Eddie Gaedel, was sent up to the plate by Bill Veeck in 1952—and Veeck's popularity with the league moguls, never remarkably high, slid lower. Eddie walked on four pitches. One Bobo was Louis Norman (Buck, Bobo) Newsom, a much-traveled eccentric who often gave the Brown's and a number of other clubs some very good pitching. The other was one Alva (Bobo) Holloman.

The great Walter Johnson went years before he pitched his first and only no-hit game in 1920. Cincinnati's Johnny Vandermeer, no Johnson, pitched two no-hit games in succession in 1938. Bobo Holloman, no Vandermeer, pitched a no-hitter for St. Louis in 1953 in his very first appearance in a major-league uniform and was little heard from thereafter.

By late 1945, with the war in Europe ended and the Pacific war ending, some of the game's greatest players were coming back and, unfortunately for the Washington Senators, one of those who returned to Detroit late in the season was Hank Greenberg. Washington, with an all-knuckle-ball starting brigade of Dutch Leonard, Mickey Haefner, Roger Wolff, and Johnny Niggeling, very narrowly missed its fourth pennant. Greenberg took it away for the Tigers with timely home runs in the last few games of the season.

By now the game had a new high commissioner. Landis had died in office in 1944, and in the spring of 1945 the owners chose a man to succeed him—a Senator from Kentucky, A. B. (Happy) Chandler, a Democrat who seemed happy at his selection and remained reasonably happy throughout his tenure, although not long after taking office he was asked to deal with two tough problems—the player raid staged by yet another outlaw league, and the case of Leo Durocher.

The outlaw league this time was based in Mexico, financed by the wealthy Pasquel brothers, who were said to have assets of $50 million, some of which they were brandishing before the established stars of the American and National Leagues. Chandler handled the threat successfully, and organized baseball continued to prosper.

Durocher had been in baseball for years—as a shortstop for the Yankees in the 20's, as a member of the Gas House Gang, and thereafter, intermittently, as a manager. At the time of his set-to with Chandler, he was managing Brooklyn. With get-tough tactics that surprised many, the new commissioner suspended Leo for the entire 1947 season for consorting with characters considered unsavory by Chandler and others.

But all this was away from the field of play.

Ever since the Japanese bombed Parl Harbor in December 1941, Americans had been fighting and working for the bright postwar era they had been assured would come. There would be postwar nylons, the War Production Board said, along with new housing, new automobiles, postwar pop-up toasters, radios that played only the very best for listening pleasure, unlimited gasoline, and perhaps before very long the miracle of television. Soon after the war many of these promises came true, even movies-as-usual, for Clark Gable was back and Greer Garson, it was said, had him. Bob Feller was back. The Cleveland Indians had him and in 1946 he struck out 348 batters to wipe out the Rube Waddell record that had stood for almost half a century. Ted Williams also was back. The Boston Red Sox once again had *him*, and in this first postwar year, with fans flocking to the ball parks, setting attendance records all through both leagues, loaded with a backlog of savings, and seeking the normalcy that baseball represented to some, it was the Red Sox who shone most brightly, finally bringing a pennant to the patient Tom Yawkey. In the 30's, Yawkey had spent a fortune trying. He had brought Joe Cronin, Lefty Grove, Rube Walberg, Jimmy Foxx, Heinie Manush, Roger Cramer, Wes Ferrell—only to see the Yankees keep winning year after year, and the Tigers win when the Yankees didn't. Finally he stopped buying players and spent his money developing a farm system which had now paid off. Williams reached his peak that year at mid-season in the All-Star game, won by the American League with the most lopsided margin on record, 12–0. Williams' personal contribution compared with Carl Hubbell's in 1934: his output for the game was four hits—two singles and two home runs. In the second half of the season he trailed off, losing both the home-run and runs-batted-in titles to Hank Greenberg, then thirty-six years old, and the batting title to Washington first baseman Mickey Vernon. In the World Series, which the Red Sox lost to the Cardinals, Williams and Stan Musial competed head on but the expected battle of base hits did not materialize. Like Ty Cobb and others, they played far below their capabilities, Williams batting .200 and Musial .222.

By now the beleaguered Yankees had been three entire seasons without a pennant to their name. With the entire league willing to make it four, the Yankees took it again in 1947 under the leadership of the managerial nomad Bucky Harris, who would be fired after the 1948 season for a third-place finish considered most un-Yankeelike, even though he had the team in neck-and-neck contention right up to the very end of the season.

The other close contenders in 1948's remarkably fierce race were Boston under old Yankee Joe McCarthy, and the Cleveland Indians, led both afield and at bat by their young shortstop and manager, Lou Boudreau. Up in the office counting the take and giving away orchids was Bill Veeck, who had taken over the Indians in mid-1946. About two years later, in June 1948, Veeck had persuaded Satchel Paige to drop whatever he was doing and come to pitch for the Cleveland Indians. Satch somewhere along the line had dubbed his medium-fast ball Little Tom and his really *fast* fast ball Long Tom. By now Long Tom was long gone, but Satch brought what he had and hung up a 6–1 record, pitching mostly in relief. He sat out most of September because by then he wasn't pitching as well as he had pitched in July and August. A man could get tired.

In September the Indians hardly needed him. They kept getting masterful jobs from their starters—Bob Feller, Bob Lemon, Gene Bearden, and occasionally Steve Gromek. Lemon already had won twenty, Feller was yielding earned runs at the rate of one per game, and Bearden was winning in the clutch.

As late as September 25 there was a three-way tie for the league lead, brought about when the Red Sox lost a 9–6 slugfest to the Yankees, who by then were featuring DiMaggio, Keller, and Lindell in the outfield; Tommy Henrich at first; Bobby Brown, Phil Rizzuto, and George Stirnweiss at the other infield posts; and young Yogi Berra behind the plate.

While Dewey and Truman campaigned, with *The Babe Ruth Story* playing at first-run movie houses, and while Stan Musial got five hits in a game for the fourth time that season, the three teams made their stretch run for the pennant. At Cleveland they were playing to packed houses almost nightly. After the war, night baseball had come to stay. Perhaps the official blessing had come that very year, 1948, after the Tigers drew 54,000 on a cool night in June, for it was after that game that American League president Will Harridge announced that he had now come to accept night baseball. He said that he had always thought of baseball as a "game of sunshine" but now found that he loved "the picture under the lights. I love the tempo of competition in the glare of the mazdas. The game is speeded up. The flight of the ball is faster. The movement of the fielders appears to be accelerated. The pitching looks so much speedier."

The click-click of the turnstile was also accelerated, and Bill Veeck kept counting. On September 22, 77,000 had been at Cleveland's vast Municipal Park to watch Feller throw a three-hitter at the Red Sox. In a weekend game at Detroit, Feller again was handed the job of keeping the Indians in the race. His opponent was the great left-hander Hal Newhouser, who had won twenty-nine games in 1944, twenty-five in 1945, twenty-six in 1946, and now was going for number twenty. Instead, Feller won his eighteenth and Joe Gordon hit his thirty-first home run.

The night of Tuesday, September 28, was something special even for Cleveland. That night, Veeck announced, 20,-000 orchids would be passed out at the ball park, one to each of the first 20,000 ladies who passed through the gates. They had been flown in direct from Hawaii in a temperature-controlled plane, accompanied by their keeper, one Marne Obernauer, a Honolulu florist who before the game conveyed an enormous amount of information about orchids to the Cleveland fans. The flowers, he related, were "Princess Aloha orchids, measuring about two and a half inches in diameter."

This was dutifully reported by the Cleveland papers.

"I brought a native Hawaiian girl along with me," he said, further, "and she will wear a grass skirt and pass them out at the ball park."

This too was recorded, along with the following: "We will then go back to Hawaii right after the game."

By now, Mr. Obernauer was unstoppable; "This is practically unheard of! We have shipped orchids all over the world but never twenty thousand of them at one time! We feel quite pleased too. A survey not long ago showed that only two women in ten ever receive orchids. This will be something to remember!"

With the orchids, it all came to pass just as Obernauer and Veeck had planned it, but there was more. In addition to being Princess Aloha Orchid Night, it was also Joe Earley

Night—Joe Earley, a young ex-serviceman, having been selected as Joe Average Fan. From a grateful ball club, Joe received a model-T Ford as well as a new Ford convertible along with assorted livestock. A fan selected at random and dragged out of the grandstand was given three stepladders. When Gene Bearden finally got around to it, he shut out the White Sox 11–0. There were only about 60,000 fans on hand but it was, after all, only a week night.

On September 29 a couple of rookies, Bob Porterfield and Hank Bauer, pitched and batted the Yankees to victory, keeping their faint pennant hopes alive, but by the weekend they were dead. On Saturday, October 2, Bearden clinched at least a tie for the Indians by shutting out the Tigers, 8–0, before a mere 56,000. The next day, with attendance back up to a respectable 74,000, Feller had a chance to nail it down but Newhouser beat him, 7–1, while the Red Sox were winning, and the season ended in a tie. The next day Cleveland and Boston met in the only playoff in all the long history of the American League. Again Bearden came through in the clutch, winning 8–3, with Boudreau contributing two home runs and four hits in all. In his second full season Bill Veeck had brought a pennant to Cleveland—and set a new all-time major-league attendance record of 2,621,229, which added up to a lot of money even after deducting the cost of 20,000 orchids and three stepladders.

In the Series the Indians met the Boston Braves, who had won their first pennant since the "miracle club" climbed from the cellar to win it all in 1914. The Indians took the Series, four games to two, and the starting pitchers for the most part pitched so well that relief was rarely needed. For a time it appeared that Satchel Paige might have to forget about pitching in a World Series, probably forever.

But in the fifth game the Braves belabored Bob Feller, knocking him out of the box in the seventh inning. A relief pitcher was brought in and then a second, but neither of them had it that day. Turning now to his fourth pitcher of the inning, Lou Boudreau once more made a sign to the bullpen, and Satchel Paige started the long, slow walk, jangling a little as he came. Paige faced two men. The first was Warren Spahn, one of the game's all-time-great left-handed pitchers. Spahn flied out. The next hitter was Tommy Holmes, who held and still holds the National League record for hitting safely in consecutive games, thirty-seven. Holmes grounded out. The inning was over.

Satchel Paige walked from the mound to the dugout and was removed for a pinch hitter. He had finally done it—two-thirds of an inning, the World Series record of Satchel Paige, who had already done most of it way out on the outskirts of town.

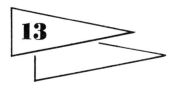

The New York Game

THE 1940'S ENDED WITH ANOTHER PENNANT FOR THE NEW YORK Yankees, and yet it was more a beginning than an ending—the beginning of many things, most of them distasteful to that portion of the baseball public that happened to reside and root beyond the west wall of Manhattan Island. For one, it was the beginning of the Casey Stengel era. The 1949 pennant was Stengel's first, and for the New York Yankees he would win nine more. Soon it would be the Mickey Mantle and the Whitey Ford era. It became the era of Yogi Berra, Elston Howard, Willie Mays, Don Newcombe, Mel Allen, Red Barber, Jackie Robinson, Roy Campanella, Duke Snider, Sal Maglie, Leo Durocher, Bobby Thomson, Sandy Koufax—and Stengelese. New York, or so it seemed to outsiders, had the game of baseball all to itself, had it all locked up behind the high walls of the city. The "New York Game," it had been called in the mid-1850's, to distinguish between the game played in New England and other sections of the provinces, and the game played in the metropolis by such groups as the old Knickerbocker Club and the Gotham Club, who played the game for themselves, occasionally taking the ferry over to Hoboken and the Elysian Fields. Now in the 1950's it was once more the New York Game, a game apart. Outsiders might watch on television. They might go out and watch when the New York teams took their show on the road. On a visit to New York they might look in on Yankee Stadium as they looked in upon other aspects of the mystique and glamor that belonged to the metropolis, but baseball, like the theater, belonged to New York.

For New Yorkers, there was little worth noticing beyond the compound, for they had it all right there. They had for their very own the amusing antics of Casey Stengel, a very knowledgeable baseball man and an able manager but one whom New Yorkers also found colorful, at first for the "platooning" of players that he began so successfully in the 1949 campaign and continued as needed. As if this were not enough, the rest of the country was asked to chuckle with New York at Casey's mannerisms, his whimsey, his speech, his circumlocutory explanations and anecdotes. Stengel was a man for whom a pronoun seldom had an antecedent and New York found this delightful, a little bit of Americana right there in little old New York, and doubtless Stengel *was* delightful to New Yorkers—he practically *never* lost the pennant. The fans in the provinces might try to grin at all this colorful Stengelese only to feel the grin grow stiff. What's to grin? Yankee pennants in 1949, 1950, 1951, 1952, 1953—*five pennants in a row?* Indeed, and 'World Series victories each year. Listen to Stengel dodge from pronoun to pronoun, leaving nary a clue, never a trail. Ha ha. Regard and sympathize with our boy Mantle, so brittle in the knees that he's hard-pressed to hit over .335. If some sounded bitter, they were.

It was New York's show and it was peopled with colorful characters of local choosing, not only the guys on stage but the in-crowd in the front rows of the audience. Hark to our announcer Mel Allen delivering himself of alliterative catch phrases known in New York to mean home runs, all too often New York *Yankee* home runs: White Owl wallop, Ballantine blast. Regard our Berra and his break-you-up malapropisms: "Bill Dickey is learning me his experience." Regard Berra in a prolonged hot streak at bat, refusing day after day to change his underdrawers until his bat went cool. Laugh with us at the colorful characters here in New York. To the rest of America it might have been far funnier if Berra, for example, had been willing to leave a few runners stranded occasionally instead of driving them across the plate in great clutches. Or if Mantle the switch-hitter had switched now and then to futility. And what could be done with Henrich, Rizzuto, Raschi, Ford, MacDougald, and others to enrich baseball's folklore? Very little. Just sit there and watch them, with no show of eccentricity whatever, play flawless baseball year after pennant-winning year.

How did the Yankees keep doing it? What of Connie Mack's feeling that each great club contained the seeds of its own collapse? The answer perhaps is that the Yankees were not merely a great club but a series of great clubs, piled one upon another.

1b: From Gehrig to Dahlgren to Collins to Skowron.

2b: From Lazzeri to Gordon to Stirnweiss to Martin to Coleman to Richardson.

ss: From Durocher to Koenig to Crosetti to Rizzuto to Kubek.

3b: From Dugan to Rolfe to Brown to Johnson to Carey to MacDougald to Boyer.

c: From Bengough to Dickey to Rosar to Berra to Howard. And the outfielders: Meusel, Combs, Ruth, Chapman, Powell, Selkirk, DiMaggio, Keller, Henrich, Lindell, Cerv, Mantle, Bauer, Woodling, Maris.

And the pitchers: Shocker, Shawkey, Hoyt, Pipgras, Pennock, Ruffing, Gomez, Allen, Murphy, Pearson; and Bonham, Byrne, Shea, Reynolds, Raschi, Lopat, Page, Ford, Turley, Larsen, Bouton, Stottlemyre.

Seldom did they have to make trades, and when they did look elsewhere for a player it was most often toward the end of yet another pennant-winning season when, for insurance, they said, they reached into the National League for a fading star who almost invariably had a little bit of stardom left for the benefit of the Yankees. Johnny Hopp, for example; and Johnny Sain, a marvelous pitcher for the Boston Braves; and Johnny Mize, the huge buster of fences who had been busting them for years with the Giants and Cardinals. But trade within their own league—hardly ever, and never to their own detriment. They let Joe Gordon go to the Indians but they got in return Allie Reynolds, who gave them long pitching mileage, and they got Roger Maris and saw him break Babe Ruth's home-run record. Bob Turley and Don Larson came in a trade, and Turley was the league's top pitcher for a season or two; Larsen performed the supreme feat of retiring twenty-seven men in a row in the 1956 World Series. But mostly during all those years they didn't need to trade. Year after year they had all the players they needed and more, and the best reason available is the cold, relentless efficiency of their minor-league farm system. For many years the Yankees had clubs in the high minors, most notably at Kansas City and Newark, capable of beating some of the teams in the American League. When they needed a player all they had to do was blow the bugle. Newark or Kansas City or some other city would respond, and all down the line other players in the Yankee chain would move up a notch.

For the fans in the provinces it was merely to watch and hate, or grudgingly admire. If a provincial fan refused to chuckle at all that color, if he took no pleasure in watching the performance of a flawless machine, if he insisted upon hating the Yankees and looking toward home for his pleasure and his hope—then he had very little to cheer about. Usually it was some quite modest accomplishment—his team might finish second one year, or simply finish in the first division, in fourth place, say, twenty-nine and a half games behind the league-leading Yankees. Or somebody on the home team might have been the league batting champion—curiously, in that interminable streak from 1949 through 1964, the Yankees were careless enough to lose the batting championship in every year but one: Mantle won it in 1956. Thus the home-town fan could muse with pleasure over the doings of such non-Yankees as Mickey Vernon, George Kell, Billy Goodman, Ferris Fain, Bobby Avila, Al Kaline, Harvey Kuenn, Pete Runnels, and Norman Cash, all of whom won the batting title in this era, some twice. Or, for those in Boston, there was always Ted Williams, who, even though his career was interrupted twice by war service, remained over the years one of the greatest batsmen the game has ever known. In 1957 he won the title with a mark of .388, and won it again the following year—seventeen years after his .406 mark in 1941. Batting titles seventeen years apart were an achievement beyond the reach even of the great Cobb.

In the provinces there were also home-run hitters to admire but the championships were fewer because in those sixteen long seasons of Yankee domination Mantle himself won the home-run title four times and Maris hit his sixty-one. Nonetheless, west of the Hudson there were such sluggers to watch as Larry Doby, Al Rosen, Luke Easter, Al Kaline, Harmon Killebrew, Roy Sievers, and Rocky Colavito, and such fine all-round ball players as Nelson Fox, such pitchers as Herb Score, Mike Garcia, Early Wynn, Billy Pierce—and for base stealing, Luis Aparicio. At least they weren't Yankees. For National League fans there was always the great Stan Musial, who was elected to the Hall of Fame in 1969 for a long career in which he established countless records, including a total-hits mark

second only to Ty Cobb's. Seven times he led the National
League in hitting and three times was chosen Most Valuable
Player. There were also Frank Robinson, Ernie Banks, Hank
Aaron, Ralph Kiner, Richie Ashburn, Ken Boyer, Warren
Spahn, Lou Burdette. For the later hapless but then delirious
fans of Milwaukee there were two consecutive pennants in
1957 and 1958, and the heady experience of beating the Yan-
kees in the 1957 World Series.

But meanwhile in New York, in addition to the notables who
performed for the Yankees, there was a huge brigade of all-
stars performing daily for the Dodgers and Giants—Ralph
Branca, Sal Maglie, Preacher Roe, Carl Erskine, Johnny Antonelli, Don Newcombe, Willie Mays, Joe Black, Peewee
Reese, Carl Furillo, Duke Snider, Roy Campanella, Jim Gilliam, Bobby Thomson, Sandy Koufax, Johnny Podres.

For the deprived fan, of course, there was always television,
which let him see what was going on behind the wall down
there on the playing fields of New York, let him share their all-
New York World Series or the pennant playoffs which for a
time occurred with such surprising frequency in the National
League. And even though all too often New York teams were
involved on both sides, it was hard not to get excited over the
home run Bobby Thomson hit in 1951 to give the Giants a
tingling playoff victory over the Dodgers for the pennant. In
any year it was impossible not to get excited over the way Willie Mays turned his back on the ball and caught up with it out
by the flagpole as his cap fell off. For a fan in the provinces,
watching Mays on the screen year after year, it was hard to
deny the conclusion that somebody in that all-time outfield of
DiMaggio-Williams-Musial—and even the one of Ruth-
Speaker-Cobb—might have to move over and make room for
Willie, who not only could do everything asked of a ball
player but overtook and passed every all-time home-run hitter
except Babe Ruth. To watch Mays, a fan could forget for a
while that he wasn't playing for the home team, just as one
could admire the way Roy Campanella handled pitchers and

belted home runs, and enjoy the spectacle as the Dodgers knocked off the Yankees in the 1955 World Series, Brooklyn's first world championship and the first time the Yankees had lost a Series since 1942. Yankee fan or no, it was easy to thrill to the perfect game Don Larsen pitched in the 1956 World Series, and to smile as Berra, after the last out, leaped into Larsen's arms. And in 1961, even though many had mixed feelings, it was undeniably exciting to watch and see if Roger Maris would indeed hit that sixtieth and then that sixty-first home run. For the fact was that the Yankees and the other New York teams were doing mighty things year after year, and that was the hell of it.

So how did Cleveland get in there again? They did, in 1954, one of the two years out of sixteen the Yankees blew the pennant—but there was another New York team waiting to knock off the Indians four straight in the World Series, a team of Giants managed by Durocher and led by Mays.

And Chicago? In 1959 the White Sox won their first pennant since the year of the Black Sox, a lapse of exactly forty years—and then lost the Series to Los Angeles. To look at the record, one might say that here, at last, was a World Series without a New York representative, and it would be technically accurate but not quite true in spirit, for the Los Angeles Dodgers were after all the Brooklyn Dodgers playing 3,000 miles from home. And indeed in all the years from the Cleveland-Boston Braves World Series of 1948 until the St. Louis Cardinals-Boston Red Sox Series of 1967, there was never a World Series that did not involve either a New York team or a New York transplant.

For a long while, for half a century, the universe was fixed and permanent. There were eight planets, forty-eight states, five continents, five oceans, and sixteen major-league baseball clubs, located as follows: Boston(2), Brooklyn, Cincinnati, Chicago(2), Cleveland, Detroit, New York(2), Philadelphia (2), Pittsburgh, St. Louis (2), and Washington.

That's how it was until the Boston Braves, willing to gamble that the world could not possibly be as flat as it seemed in Boston, set out for Milwaukee, Wisconsin. That was the beginning. Then the St. Louis Browns headed east for Baltimore, on the way almost passing the Philadelphia Athletics, who were headed in the opposite direction, bound for Kansas City. Mostly the flow was westward—the Dodgers to Los Angeles, the Giants to San Francisco, the Washington Senators to Minnesota—but later southward, as the whilom Boston Braves, after their hop to Milwaukee, skipped to Atlanta.

If the years after 1900 were baseball's golden age, then the 1950's were perhaps the Age of Loot.

If baseball was a sport, then why was it acting like a business?

Baseball of course is a business as well as a sport, and any businessman who is losing money, or sees the prospect of making more, is entitled to move. But this wasn't just an ordinary business, this was the national pastime, the National Game, and its patrons were not ordinary patrons, they were *fans*—"All the time his vital organs are summoned into strenuous sympathy with his frame of mind and he draws deep breaths of pure air. He may be weary when the game is over but for it he will eat and sleep better, his step will be more determined, his eyes will cease resembling those of a dead fish"—fans who believed that a home team was their birthright and had been encouraged so to believe by the very men who owned the club, some of whom, right up to the very eve of departure, vowed they would never forsake the old town, *never*.

One by one the clubs moved away, because there was nothing that said they couldn't, and baseball went on; but now as the decade neared an end, with the dominance of television steadily greater, with the big show closing in some cities and opening in others, with the power centers unmistakably in New York and Los Angeles, baseball more than ever was reminiscent of the entertainment biz—because, as almost anyone knows, all entertainers spend their lives flying back and forth between New York and "the coast" and there is nothing very much in between except maybe a thick layer of clouds. Even on a clear day it is impossible to look down and make out the tumbledown, derelict small-town ball parks that once were said to link the nation and were cited as the sort of grass-roots strength that a national theater might do well to emulate.

For a baseball fan groping around for something familiar, there were, of course, still the New York Yankees, if that helped. After the White Sox beat them out for the pennant in 1959, they won another in 1960 for Casey Stengel, who thereupon was fired for old age—it could hardly have been for incompetence. Ten pennants out of twelve was an honorable performance. Casey then went on to pursue his destiny with the fun-loving Mets, who, the worse they became, the more campily they were loved by New Yorkers trying to fill the void left by the flight of the Giants and Dodgers. Meanwhile, if there were any who felt Stengel's departure might signal ill times for the Yankees they were mistaken, because the Yankees reeled off another three pennants for Ralph Houk and one for Yogi Berra, making a streak of five under three different managers—and twenty-nine pennants in forty-four years.

By now there were Al Downing, Jim Bouton, and Mel Stottlemyre. Still around were Bobby Richardson, Clete Boyer, Elston Howard, Roger Maris, and Mickey Mantle. There were the bright rookies Joe Pepitone and Tom Tresh. When would it ever end?

And then—thud. For the rest of the league, it had a beautiful sound.

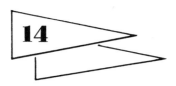

The White Ceiling
and the Beige Rug

THERE HAD PERHAPS BEEN SIGNS AND PORTENTS. IN THE 1960 World Series the Yankees scored more runs than any team in Series history and yet were beaten by the Pittsburgh Pirates, who were scoring when it counted.

After a couple of winning Series efforts against Cincinnati and (barely) San Francisco, the Yankees found real trouble, for in the National League now there were two of the greatest pitchers the modern game has produced—Sandy Koufax and Bob Gibson. In the 1963 World Series Koufax and his running mate Don Drysdale teamed up to silence the Yankee bats, and when it was all over the Los Angeles Dodgers had done the unheard of—they had taken four straight from the Yankees, who never before had been blanked in a World Series. The following year they lost their second Series in a row, and their tormentors this time were Bob Gibson and the St. Louis Cardinals.

In the view of some there had been another portent, perhaps an evil eye. Not long before the 1964 World Series began, the New York Yankees were bought by the Columbia Broadcasting System, a purchase that evoked screams of outrage all around the country, although few from the American League club owners who passed on it. Some critics expressed their indignation in diatribes warning of the dangers of monopoly and conflict of interest, others in savage satires asking how long it would be before CBS took the Yankees off the air. If their ratings slipped, would they pass into limbo along with Milton Berle, *Howdy Doody,* and boxing?

Whatever psychological effect CBS ownership may have had, the Yankees after 1964 have never been the same. That fall they fired Yogi Berra, who in his first year as manager had won the pennant only to lose the Series, replacing him in a sort of managerial musical-chairs game with the manager who *had* won the World Series, Johnny Keane. Under Keane, in 1965, the Yankees stupefied the world of baseball—and delighted large parts of it—by falling into sixth place and the following year all the way into the American League cellar.

Their collapse, when it finally came, was not gradual. It was instant and total, which, as virtually nobody commented, seemed eminently unfair to the poor Columbia Broadcasting System. To buy the most powerful dynasty in baseball and to find it in the cellar!

A number of reasons have been advanced for the club's demise. One, which says not a great deal, is that the rest of the league finally caught up with it. Another is the death of several excellent Yankee scouts who had been in the organization for years and had consistently turned up prize talent. Another is the Yankees' refusal to participate in the mad scramble for bonus players, an expensive war in which many clubs vied

with huge chunks of money for the services of promising young-
sters. But if in the years of their greatness the foundation for
that greatness was their superb farm system, then it seems reasonable to conclude that they collapsed when their farm system
stopped producing. And, ironically, the reason it stopped producing is because the minor leagues were killed by television
—the very monster that made CBS wealthy enough to buy
the New York Yankees. For it was undeniably television that
killed minor-league baseball. In terms of television, even fans
in remote villages are still part of Chicagoland or Greater Minneapolis, or the Baltimore Orioles Baseball Network. Flick a
switch and see a big-league ball game. Who needs to go out to
the edge of town and watch a couple of Class D teams in action? Civic pride and grass roots were all well and good but
the fan in the small town was part of a bigger network now,
he was linked up all over the country by television, and the
small minor-league ball park was as obsolete as the bandstand
on the village green.

Meanwhile, as the Yankees collapsed, life for the rest of the
league grew brighter. While the Yankees slid in and out of the
cellar, the pennant was being passed happily about from city to
unaccustomed city. In four years it was won by four different
teams—Minnesota, Baltimore, Boston, and Detroit.

For the Minnesota Twins, it was their first pennant, yet they
were the old Senators and there were some who said it was not
so much Minnesota's first pennant as Washington's *fourth* pennant, and whose all-time home-run champion *was* Harmon
Killebrew, anyway? With all the franchise shifting, things got
confused, just as the Twins were terribly confused in the World
Series by the marvelous pitching of Sandy Koufax, who with
each successive season was assuring himself a spot among baseball's all-time elite. That very season, 1965, soaring far beyond
the marks of Rube Waddell and Bob Feller, he set an all-time
major-league record for strikeouts, 382.

In 1966, led by the Robinsons, Frank and Brooks, the Baltimore Orioles won their first pennant since the rowdy days of Keeler, McGraw, and Jennings. The Orioles of 1966 were no rowdies. Their clean-cut young pitchers mowed the Dodgers down in the World Series, 4–0, and the Dodgers by now were ending a dynasty of their own. Koufax would retire with chronic arm trouble and all their best hitters were gone.

In the American League in 1967 there was a splendid three-way race for the pennant, not decided until the final day of the season—and the Yankees had no part in it. They were down near the cellar again. Boston won it by beating the Twins but then lost in the World Series to the Cardinals, who, since 1920, have been second only to the Yankees in performance, upholding the honor of the midlands with twelve pennants and seven world championships.

In 1968 Detroit pitcher Mickey Lolich outshone his more illustrious teammate Dennis McLain and ultimately even the great Bob Gibson, pitching the Tigers to victory over the Cardinals in one of the most thrilling World Series of all time.

While all this was going on, Johnny Keane, after his sixth-place finish in 1965, was fired in early 1966 and Ralph Houk became the Yankee manager for the second time. After lowly finishes in both 1966 and 1967 there were indications in 1968 that Houk had pulled the club together. They finished fifth, and late in the season still were in contention for third—a meager performance for the Yankees of old but a giant step upward for the Yankees of CBS.

What effect has the collapse of the Yankees had on baseball? Lovers of the game muttered and groaned when the Yankees for so many years dominated the league so heartlessly, claiming that Yankee invincibility was injurious. Yet it is since the Yankees' collapse that baseball's hold upon the public has seemed to loosen, regardless of all the attendance figures and television-rating percentages that organized baseball may cite to the contrary. A number of factors unrelated to the Yankees may explain baseball's apparent loss of popularity, but it also may very well be, as the *Reach Guide* warned so long ago, that baseball *needs* a powerful team in New York. It may be, as a psychologist might attest, that the public badly needs a giant to kill, a villain to hate. There is simply no pleasure in beating the stuffing out of a weakling, and there has been no sense of accomplishment in trampling such an impotent team as the Yankees of 1965, 1966, and 1967. It is as though the old man has left home and, bullying bastard though he may have been, it is strange without him. If the Yankees once more become a power it may be all for the best. Perhaps the public wants, and baseball badly needs, this assurance of sempiternal excellence, this year-in, year-out devil figure or father figure, or whatever the Yankees in their years of dominance may have represented to those who watch ball games.

With the season of 1968 the book was closed on one hundred years of professional baseball in the United States. It also marked the end of a pennant-race format that had prevailed since 1903.

As an anniversary present to the American public, the men who control the game offered something new for 1969. Two new cities were added to the American League and to the National League, making twelve teams in each. Each league in turn was divided into two divisions, east and west. This was the setup:

AMERICAN LEAGUE

Western Division	*Eastern Division*
MINNESOTA	DETROIT
OAKLAND	BOSTON
CHICAGO	BALTIMORE
CALIFORNIA	CLEVELAND
KANSAS CITY	NEW YORK
SEATTLE	WASHINGTON

NATIONAL LEAGUE

Western Division	*Eastern Division*
SAN FRANCISCO	ST. LOUIS
ATLANTA	CHICAGO
CINCINNATI	PITTSBURGH
LOS ANGELES	PHILADELPHIA
HOUSTON	MONTREAL
SAN DIEGO	NEW YORK

At the end of the season the two divisional leaders in each league will meet in a best three-out-of-five playoff for the right to enter the World Series. Regardless of which division leader has the better season-long record, the playoff winner will go to the Series.

What is it exactly? Four major leagues of six teams each? Or two leagues of twelve teams each?

In baseball history there are pertinent footnotes. Time and again over the years, baseball has proved that it could never sustain more than two major leagues. And in the 1890's, when the National League had its deadly monopoly, it soon became evident that a twelve-team league was not only unwieldy but unattractive to the fans.

The new setup is neither one thing nor the other, and yet it is something of both. It is baseball's answer to the problems created by the expansion of the major leagues into all sections of the country and even into Canada, into cities which wanted a team, but nothing less than a major-league team.

As baseball entered its hundred and first season, it faced other problems, one being the boring performance of American League hitters. Another was the slow, dragged-out pace of the games. The players were threatening to strike, demanding a larger share of television money for their pension fund, already liberal by many standards. There was also the problem of schedule making and of travel, with all the new franchises and the vast distances from city to city. Baseball had grown up with the railroads; for long years the lives of the two were intertwined. The smoking car, the diner, the sleeper, the sway and unending click-click as the train sped through the night, the crossing gates, the small-town depots, the country roads with their buggies and then their automobiles, the semaphore arms, the three verticle lights of a block signal—once all these were as familiar to ball players as the feel of the earth beneath their spikes. But now travel means jet planes, air terminals, and abrupt overnight time-zone transitions from one coast to the other.

The steadily increasing competition of professional football was another problem, and there were confusing questions. Was baseball's season too long? Would twenty-four major-league teams be too many? Would greed kill baseball as it had nearly killed it in the 1890's? By now the United States is a different country, of course. Its population is roughly double the population of 1900. Nearly everybody is greedy and nearly everybody expects to be rich. To get rich in America is a birthright —as much of a birthright as baseball.

And there was always the problem of TV, the friendly, greenback-laden giant whose grip on the soft pliant throat of the club owners and even of the players felt so very good, felt better each year.

What might the future hold if, for example, the government decided to heed the piteous cries of some city like Milwaukee and forced the owners to stop moving around? And if in such a city or cities attendance truly had sunk to abysmal levels? And yet there was enough television revenue to keep the club going, because even though it was too much trouble to go out to the game, people still watched it on TV? Then might baseball become a game played in an empty ball park—an outdoor studio?

If television guaranteed a profit, if the club owners had to stay put, and if the fans stayed away from the park, what then? Are fans in the stands necessary? Will the players need the sound of a crowd? Will the guy watching at home on the tube really care? When a home run is hit, how important is it to him that live human beings in the bleachers should scatter or clutch for the ball as it comes to rest? And the sound—how important, really? Is sound necessary for the man at home? Must the crowd sing for him, sing with him, sing his song of despair, bellow and roar his triumph? Would a soundtrack serve as well, with piped-in applause, screams, groans, hushes, and an occasional hoarse cry of "Kill the umpire"?

Corporate baseball, high-rise baseball, electronic baseball, picture-tube baseball. Where did *my* team go—where are all the players? Whatever happened to Ty Cobb and the universe that was fixed and permanent? Where are all the minor leagues and what are all those little figures in uniform running around a screen at eleven o'clock at night? They're playing it right in the *living* room, for God's sake, where the white ceiling stares down upon the beige rug.

Yet it is probable that the fan watching on television may still feel linked to the past, that as he sits in his living room or his den or his favorite bar, watching the little figures run around on the screen, he is somehow also watching a game played in the sunlight, back in an earlier day in a younger America when men in derbies stood on the roof of the grandstand and lined Coogan's Bluff to watch the young Christy Mathewson take off his cardigan sweater and begin to warm up; when Ty Cobb with savagery in his eye sliced a double down the left-field line and stretched it into a triple, kicking the ball out of the third baseman's hand; when Honus Wagner pounded far to his left, stretched out a huge paw, and nailed the runner at first with an arm of steel; when Walter Johnson, with his easy pitching motion and his smoking fast ball, went along year after year, winning and losing 1–0 games; when the young Babe Ruth minced his way about the base paths after yet another towering home run; and for the fan himself there was the day when he was ten or eleven and hit a high outside fast one up against the schoolhouse wall.

And it is probable too that even as he watches alone in his living room the fan can feel tension and involvement, for baseball at its best seems to satisfy a deep craving for spectacle, drama, and conflict, a craving that has been characteristic of the human race ever since the dawn of history. Baseball, true, has been given sociological and chauvinistic props. Often it has been given massive propaganda aid. Yet by its very nature as a physical contest—the marrow of its rule and rudiment—it has always been a game that can produce thrills in the beholder. Within the space of two or three hours it can provide listless moments but it also can provide an infinite variety of dramatic episodes, as well as an array of physical feats and contests so varied as to offer a virtual olympiad in miniature. The game may at times seem merely a set-piece, a tableau of men frozen—yet at any given instant the tableau can explode. With one pitch, one swing of a bat, as many as thirteen men can be set in swift motion, each darting his way through an intricate pattern of movement, a pattern with the precision and often the grace of choreography. To those who watch and know, each movement is meaningful and contributory, each can affect the outcome of the drama that is unfolding, for baseball, even though it is a spectacle, is a spectacle presented within the context of drama, with rules and structure that can produce the utmost in suspense.

On the afternoon of the 1951 pennant playoff, as the drama neared an end, the Brooklyn Dodgers had the game and the pennant won; the odds in their favor were astronomical. Only by a feat of epic proportion could the Brooklyns be denied. Suspense has been defined as hoping something will come to pass and fearing it will not. Giant fans hoped and feared, and their fear was far stronger than their hope, yet in all the huge crowd at the Polo Grounds that autumn afternoon few were leaving because the fans knew the improbable might happen, that by the rules of baseball it *could* happen, even though the odds said it surely would not. And then with one swing of

Bobby Thomson's home-run bat the tableau exploded, and the improbable became the real.

With its drama, its pageantry, its color, its star performers, its heroes, baseball at its best seems truly atavistic in its appeal, but to be at its best the emphasis must be on the field of play—on the game, not the business. The fans must be able to believe that baseball is something more than a barnstorming tour, a traveling circus, or a TV spectacular. A cuckolded fan is a fan no longer. Each time a club owner pledges to stay put forever and then sneaks out of town on the midnight train, baseball is the loser. Baseball is a business. It is also entertainment. But to the fans who have paid its way over the years it is something much more than both.

Already baseball has had a good long run, longer than Alexander Cartwright might have guessed the day they all took the ferry over to Hoboken; longer surely than Harry Wright could have expected when he and his full-of-ginger Red Stockings stormed out of the West to beat the New York Mutuals at the old Union Grounds in Brooklyn. With few lapses it has been a thriving business for a hundred years. But what if the ratings fall?

Baseball has come to depend upon television, yet television is by no means dependent upon baseball. If the ratings drop, if the sponsors no longer pick up the tab, televison in the end may prove faithless to the game it wanted so badly for its own. It may decide the public has had enough baseball for one lifetime—that like *The Milton Berle Show, Ben Casey, The Fugitive,* and *Howdy Doody,* baseball has had its run, a good long run, but that like *Howdy Doody* all programs must end some day. With baseball gone from the screen would there be any turning back? Then may come the ultimate test of baseball's hundred-year mystique.

Appendix

The .400 Hitters

Rogers Hornsby	.424	1924	Ted Williams	.406	1941
Napoleon Lajoie	.422	1901	Harry Heilmann	.403	1923
Ty Cobb	.420	1911	Rogers Hornsby	.403	1925
George Sisler	.420	1922	Ty Cobb	.401	1922
Ty Cobb	.410	1912	Rogers Hornsby	.401	1922
Joe Jackson	.408	1911	Bill Terry	.401	1930
George Sisler	.407	1920			

According to Rogers Hornsby, there will never be another.

All-Time Leaders

TOTAL HITS

Ty Cobb	4,191
Stan Musial	3,630
Cap Anson	3,516
Tris Speaker	3,515
Honus Wagner	3,430
Eddie Collins	3,313
Nap Lajoie	3,251
Paul Waner	3,152

LIFETIME BATTING AVERAGE

Ty Cobb	.367
Rogers Hornsby	.358
Joe Jackson	.356
Lefty O'Doul	.349
Willie Keeler	.345
Tris Speaker	.344
Ted Williams	.344
Babe Ruth	.342
Harry Heilmann	.342
Bill Terry	.341
George Sisler	.340
Lou Gehrig	.340

HOME RUNS (through 1967)

Babe Ruth	714
Willie Mays	587
Mickey Mantle	536
Jimmy Foxx	534
Ted Williams	521
Eddie Mathews	512

Mel Ott	511
Hank Aaron	510
Lou Gehrig	493
Stan Musial	475

FIFTY OR MORE HOMERS IN SEASON

Roger Maris	1961	61
Babe Ruth	1927	60
Babe Ruth	1921	59
Hank Greenberg	1938	58
Jimmy Foxx	1932	58
Hack Wilson	1930	56
Babe Ruth	1920	54
Babe Ruth	1928	54
Mickey Mantle	1961	54
Ralph Kiner	1949	54
Mickey Mantle	1956	52
Willie Mays	1965	52
Ralph Kiner	1947	51
Willie Mays	1955	51
Johnny Mize	1947	51
Jimmy Foxx	1938	50

PITCHING—TOTAL VICTORIES

Cy Young	507
Walter Johnson	414
Grover Alexander	373
Christy Mathewson	373
Warren Spahn	363

Records of Five Leading Pitchers

CY YOUNG	
1890	9–7
1891	28–20
1892	36–11
1893	34–17
1894	25–21
1895	33–10
1896	29–14
1897	21–18
1898	24–14
1899	26–14
1900	20–16
1901	31–10
1902	32–11
1903	28–9
1904	26–16
1905	16–18
1906	13–21
1907	22–15
1908	21–11
1909	19–15
1910	7–10
1911	3–4
1912	4–5
Total	507–307

CHRISTY MATHEWSON	
1900	0–2
1901	20–16
1902	13–18
1903	30–13
1904	33–12
1905	32–8
1906	22–12
1907	24–12
1908	37–11
1909	25–6
1910	27–9
1911	26–13

1912	23–12
1913	25–11
1914	24–13
1915	8–14
1916	1–0
Total	373–186

WALTER JOHNSON	
1907	5–9
1908	14–14
1909	13–25
1910	25–17
1911	23–15
1912	32–12
1913	36–7
1914	28–18
1915	27–13
1916	25–20
1917	23–16
1918	23–13
1919	20–14
1920	8–10
1921	17–14
1922	15–16
1923	17–12
1924	23–7
1925	20–7
1926	15–16
1927	5–6
Total	414–281

GROVER ALEXANDER	
1911	28–13
1912	19–17
1913	22–8
1914	27–15
1915	31–10
1916	33–12
1917	30–13

1918	2–1
1919	16–11
1920	27–14
1921	15–13
1922	16–13
1923	22–12
1924	12–5
1925	15–11
1926	12–10
1927	21–10
1928	16–9
1929	9–8
1930	0–3
Total	373–208

WARREN SPAHN	
1946	8–5
1947	21–10
1948	15–12
1949	21–14
1950	21–17
1951	22–14
1952	14–19
1953	23–7
1954	21–12
1955	17–14
1956	20–11
1957	21–11
1958	22–11
1959	21–15
1960	21–10
1961	21–13
1962	18–14
1963	23–7
1964	6–13
1965	4–12
1966	3–4
Total	361–245

Babe Ruth's Historic Day—The Sixtieth Home Run

September 30, 1927 (Final game of the season)

WASHINGTON	AB	R	H	PO	A	E
Rice, rf	3	0	1	2	0	0
Harris, 2b	3	0	0	3	4	0
Ganzel, cf	4	0	1	1	0	0
Coslin, lf	4	1	1	5	0	0
Judge, 1b	4	0	0	8	0	0
Ruel, c	2	1	1	2	0	0
Bluege, 3b	3	0	1	1	4	0
Gillis, ss	4	0	0	2	1	0
Zachary, p	2	0	0	0	1	0
°Johnson	1	0	0	0	0	0
Totals	30	2	5	24	10	0

° Batted for Zachary in the ninth

NEW YORK	AB	R	H	PO	A	E
Combs, cf	4	0	0	3	0	0
Koenig, ss	4	1	1	3	5	0
Ruth, rf	3	3	3	4	0	0
Gehrig, 1b	4	0	2	10	0	1
Meusel, lf	3	0	1	3	0	0
Lazzeri, 2b	3	0	0	2	2	0
Dugan, 3b	3	0	1	1	1	0
Bengough, c	3	0	1	1	2	0
Pipgras, p	3	0	0	0	2	0
Pennock, p	1	0	0	0	1	0
Totals	31	4	9	27	13	1

WASHINGTON	0	0	0	2	0	0	0	0	0—2
NEW YORK	0	0	0	1	0	1	0	2	X—4

Two-base hit—Rice. Three-base hit—Koenig. Home run—Ruth. Stolen bases—Ruth, Bluege, Rice. Sacrifice—Meusel. Double plays—Harris to Bluege; Gillis to Harris to Judge. Left on bases—New York 4, Wash. 7. First base on balls—off Pipgras, 4; off Pennock, 1; off Zachary, 1. Struck out—by Zachary, 1. Hits off Pipgras—4 in 6 innings; off Pennock—1 in 3 innings. Hit by pitched ball—by Pipgras (Rice). Winning pitcher—Pennock. Umpires—Dineen, Connolly, Owens.

Bibliography

Allen, Lee, *100 Years of Baseball*. New York: Bartholomew House, 1950.

Anson, Adrian C., *A Ball Player's Career*. Chicago: Era, 1900.

Asinof, Eliot, *Eight Men Out*. New York: Holt, Rinehart & Winston, 1963.

Carlson, S. W., *Lou Gehrig, Baseball's Iron Man*. Minneapolis: S. W. Carlson, 1940.

Chadwick, Henry, *The Art of Pitching and Fielding*. Chicago: A. G. Spalding, 1885.

Church, Seymour R., *Baseball, the History, Statistics and Romance of the American National Game from Its Inception to the Present Time*. San Francisco, 1902.

Cobb, Ty, *My Life in Baseball*. Garden City, N.Y.: Doubleday, 1961.

Danzig, Allison, and Reichler Joe, *The History of Baseball*. New York: Prentice-Hall, 1959.

Dime Baseball Player. New York: Beadle & Adams, 1858.

Ellard, Harry, *Baseball in Cincinnati*. Cincinnati, 1907.

Hornsby, Rogers, *My War with Baseball*. New York: Coward-McCann, 1962.

Lieb, F. G., *The Baltimore Orioles*. New York: G. P. Putnam's, 1955.

Lieb, Fred, *Comedians and Pranksters of Baseball*. St. Louis: C. C. Spink, 1958.

Mack, Connie, *My Sixty-Six Years in the Big Leagues*. Philadelphia: Winston, 1950.

A Manual of Cricket and Baseball. Boston: Mayhew & Baker, 1858.

Menke, F. G. *Encyclopedia of Sports*. New York: A. S. Barnes, 1968.

Morse, Jacob C., *Morse's Annual Baseball Book*. Boston: J. C. Morse, 1889.

Palmer, H. C., *Stories of the Baseball Field*. New York: Rand McNally, 1890.

Ruth, Babe, *Babe Ruth's Own Book of Baseball*. New York: G. P. Putnam's, 1928.

Seymour, Harold, *Baseball*. New York: Oxford University Press, 1960.

Stengel, Casey, *Casey at the Bat*. New York: Random House, 1962.

Tracy, D. F., *The Psychologist at Bat*. New York: Sterling, 1951.

Turkin, Hy, and Thompson, S. C., *The Official Encyclopedia of Baseball*. New York: A. S. Barnes, 1968.

Veeck, Bill, with Linn, Ed, *The Hustler's Handbook*. New York: G. P. Putnam's, 1965.

Veeck, Bill, with Linn, Ed, *Veeck as in Wreck*. New York: G. P. Putnam's, 1962.

Ward, John M., *How to Become a Baseball Player*. Philadelphia: Athletic Publishing Co., 1888.

Other sources included the *Reach Guide;* the *Spalding Guide;* the *Encyclopaedia Britannica;* the files of various newspapers, most notably the *New York Times*, the *Washington Post*, and the *Cleveland Plain Dealer;* and the following magazines: *St. Nicholas, Sports Illustrated, Literary Digest, Harper's Weekly, Collier's, McClure's, Top Notch, Baseball Magazine, American Mercury, Everybody's Magazine, Outing, The New Republic, Saturday Review,* and *Current Literature*.

Index

Aaron, Hank, 80, 219, 220, 234
Adams, Babe, 156
Ahe, Chris von der, 57, 64, 65–69, 72, 78, 92–93, 168, 194, 203
A. J. Reach & Co., 25
Alexander, Grover Cleveland, 105, 159, 167, 193, 194–95, 218
Alger, Horatio, 106, 116
Allen, Fred, 200
Allen, Lee, 23, 37, 54, 55
Allen, Mel, 229, 231, 232
Allison, Doug, 17, 40
All-Star game of 1934, 205; of 1936, 212; of 1946, 223
Altrock, Nick, 142
Amateur Athletic Union, 25
American Association, 57, 62, 64–65, 67, 72, 78, 84, 85–86, 215
American League, 57, 59–60, 62, 79, 91, 94–95, 103, 105, 106, 115, 128, 131, 137, 141, 142, 145, 146, 148, 149, 162, 165, 166, 176, 190, 192, 202, 205, 209, 212, 219, 220–21, 222, 223, 224, 226, 232, 240, 242, 243, 244
Anson, Adrian Constantine (Cap), 41, 57, 62–63, 67, 72, 94, 203
Antonelli, Johnny, 234
Aparicio, Luis, 233
Arliss, George, 214
Art of Pitching and Fielding, The, 70
Ashburn, Richie, 234
Asinof, Eliot, 169
Attell, Abe, 172, 173, 177, 178
Austen, Jane, 32, 33
Averill, Earl, 212
Avila, Bobby, 233

Babe Ruth Story, The, 224
Baker, Frank (Home Run), 105, 143, 147, 148, 161

Baltimore Colts, 208
Baltimore Elite Giants, 216
Baltimore Orioles, 63, 64, 69, 87–91, 105, 106, 127, 146, 148, 164, 165, 195, 219, 221, 241, 242
Baltimore Sun, 134
Banks, Ernie, 219, 234
Barber, Red, 229
Barry, Jack, 133, 229
Barzun, Jacques, 22
Baseball, amateur status of prior to 1869, 35–38; Cartwright theory of origin of, 27–30; checks-and-balances ratio between batting and pitching, 70–71, 141–46, Doubleday theory of origin of, 23–27; as early American game, 31–34; effect of Civil War on, 23; effect of crookedness in on fans, 113–14; effect of television on, 236–37, 241, 245–48; effect of Yankees' collapse on, 242–43; English origin of, 32–33; establishment of professional, 38–39, 52–53; gambling in early days of, 18, 37–38, 44, 51–52, 53, 55–56; as an industry, 19–21, 38; lexicon of, 110; mystique of, 99–121; nationalistic character of, 21–30, 49–51, 107–10, 111–13, 119–21; night games, 206–7, 224–25; pitching rules in early days of, 71–72; players' revolt of 1890, 81–85; problem of early retirement of players, 54–55; psychology of players, 83–84; status of players, 79–81; resistance to change of, 20; rules in early days of, 31–32, 33–35, 36–37, 45, 71–72; thinking man's, 87–89; treatment of umpires in 1800's, 17, 23, 75–78
Baseball Brotherhood, 57

Baseball Correspondence School, 116
Baseball Hall of Fame, 27, 28, 115, 132, 179, 193, 204, 219, 233
Baseball in Cincinnati, 39
Baseball Magazine, 21, 41, 46, 50–51, 52, 55, 57, 74, 107, 108–9, 114, 120, 148, 152, 176
Bauer, Hank, 226, 232
Bearden, Gene, 224, 226
Beethoven, Ludwig van, 35
Bell, Cool Papa, 216, 217
Bender, Chief, 105, 137, 160–61
Bengough, Benny, 231
Benny, Jack, 200
Berle, Milton, 240, 248
Berra, Yogi, 34, 145, 224, 229, 231, 235, 237, 240
Birmingham Black Barons, 215
Bishop, Max, 202
Black, Joe, 234
Black Sox scandal, 103, 105, 168–79, 184, 235
Boley, Joe, 202
Bonham, Ernie, 232
Bonura, Zeke, 212
Boston Braves, 163–64, 165, 183, 187, 226, 27, 232, 235, 236; *see also* Milwaukee Braves
Boston Red Sox, 79, 105, 106, 124, 131, 136, 161–63, 166, 167, 168, 183, 188, 203, 220, 222, 223, 224, 225, 226, 235, 241, 242
Bostons, 53, 63, 89, 90, 91
Boudreau, Lou, 223, 226, 227
Bouton, Jim, 232, 237
Boyer, Clete, 237
Boyer, Ken, 231, 234
Boy's Own Book, The, 32, 33
Brainard, Asa, 17, 40, 45
Branca, Ralph, 234
Brandt, William E., 33
Bresnahan, Roger, 111, 151, 192
Bridges, Tommy, 212, 213
Bridwell, Al, 154
Brooklyn Atlantics, 46

Brooklyn Dodgers, 88, 130, 166, 209, 210, 211, 219, 222, 234, 235, 236, 237, 247; *see also* Los Angeles Dodgers
Brooklyn Eckfords, 53, 73
Brown, Bobby, 224, 231
Brown, Mordecai (Three Finger), 105, 140, 144, 145, 165
Bruce, H. Addington, 121
Brush, John T., 82, 151, 154
Bulkeley, Morgan, G., 25, 56
Burdette, Lou, 234
Burns, Sleepy Bill, 172, 178
Byrne, Tommy, 232

California Angels, 17
Campanella, Roy, 217, 219, 229, 234–35
Carey, Andy, 231
Carleton, Tex, 209
Carrigan, Bill, 166
Cartwright, Alexander, 28–30, 34, 35, 41, 45, 248
Cash, Norman, 233
Cepeda, Orlando, 219
Cerv, Bob, 232
Chadwick, Henry, 18, 25, 41, 70, 71, 153
Champion, Aaron, 46
Chance, Frank, 105, 123, 137, 139–40, 151, 154, 155, 160, 165, 166, 195
Chandler, A. B. (Happy), 221–22
Chapman, Ben, 231
Chase, Hal, 166
Chatham Stars, 120
Chattanooga Black Lookouts, 216
Chesbro, Jack, 105
Chicago Cubs, 54, 105, 106, 124, 137, 139–41, 142, 151, 153–54, 160, 165, 195, 196, 201, 203
Chicago Herald Examiner, 176
Chicago White Sox, 54, 66, 105, 133, 141, 142, 143, 159, 167, 168–69, 212, 226, 235, 237; *see also* Black Sox scandal

Chicago White Stockings, 25, 41, 53, 62, 67
Church, Seymour, 30, 52
Cicotte, Eddie, 159, 168, 170–71, 173–74, 175, 176
Cincinnati Buckeyes, 44, 45
Cincinatti Reds, 167, 168, 169, 170, 172, 173–75, 206–7, 210, 211, 221, 239
Cincinnati Red Stockings, 15–19, 20, 25, 35, 38–47, 50, 52, 87, 132, 248
Civil War, 23, 24, 36, 147, 149
Claudy, Carl H., 150
Clay, Cassius, 208
Clemente, Roberto, 219
Cleveland Indians, 105, 106, 133, 134, 177, 212, 222, 223–24, 225, 226, 232, 235
Cobb, Ty, 29, 34, 89, 103, 104, 105, 124, 137, 139, 144–51, 154, 156, 159, 166, 167, 169, 178–79, 188, 189, 191, 202, 204, 210, 211, 219, 220, 221, 223, 233, 234, 246
Cochrane, Mickey, 132, 157, 164, 202, 203, 211, 217
Colavito, Rocky, 233
Coleman, Jerry, 231
Collier's, 112
Collins, Eddie, 68–69, 101, 105, 133, 161, 171, 174, 176, 219
Collins, Joe, 231
Collins, Rip, 209
Columbia Broadcasting System, 240, 241, 242
Columbia University, 207
Columbus Dispatch, 135
Combs, Earle, 195, 197, 231
Comiskey, Charles, 66, 67, 168, 169–70, 171, 175, 176, 177
Coolidge, Calvin, 185, 187
Coombs, Jack, 105, 133, 160
Cooper, Gary, 208
Cooper, James Fenimore, 27
Cooper, Morton, 39
Cooper, Walker, 39

Cooperstown, and question of baseball's origin, 24, 26–28
Cramer, Roger, 223
Crawford, Sam, 105, 146
Cronin, Joe, 203, 204, 205, 223
Crosby, Ernest Howard, 120
Crosetti, Frank, 197, 231
Crosley Field, 206
Crowder, Alvin, 204
Cummings, William Arthur (Candy), 72
Current Literature, 153
Cuyler, Kiki, 192

Dahlgren, Babe, 197, 231
Day, Associate Justice, 163
Dean, Jerome Herman (Dizzy), 39, 199–200, 208–9, 210, 211, 212–14, 216, 217
Dean, Paul (Daffy), 39, 208, 209, 210, 211, 212–14
Delancey, Bill, 209
Delehanty, Ed, 57
Dempsey, Jack, 187
Devlin, Arthur, 125
Devore, Josh, 127–28
Detroit Tigers, 89, 104, 106, 124, 137, 146, 147, 154, 156–57, 202, 203, 204, 209, 210, 211–14, 221, 223, 224, 226, 241, 242
Dewey, Thomas, 208, 224
Dickey, Bill, 197, 205, 207, 217, 231
Dietrich, Marlene, 200
DiMaggio, Joe, 101, 149 ,162, 195, 197, 207, 216–17, 220, 224, 232, 234
Dime Baseball Player, 71
Doby, Larry, 219, 233
Donlin, Michael, 110–11, 125, 151
Downing, Al, 237
Doyle, Larry, 125
Doubleday, Abner, 24, 25–27, 28, 32, 33, 34, 41
Drysdale, Don, 79, 239
Dugan, Joe, 231

Durocher, Leo, 16, 34, 209, 222, 229, 231, 235
Duryea's Zouaves, 23
Dykes, Jimmy, 202

Earley, Joe, 226
Earnshaw, George, 202
Easter, Luke, 233
Ebbets Field, 130
Edison, Thomas, 189
Ehmke, Howard, 201
Eight Men Out, 169
Eisenhower, Dwight D., 50
Elberfeld, Kid, 75
Ellard, George B., 46
Ellard, Harry, 39, 46
Encyclopedia Britannica, 26
England, 25, 32, 33
Erskine, Carl, 234
Evans, Billy, 128, 154
Evers, Johnny, 140, 151, 154, 166, 219
Everybody's Magazine, 121

Faber, Urban, 171
Fain, Ferris, 233
Fairbanks, Douglas, 152, 192
Federal League, 165–66
Feeder (ball game), 33
Feller, Robert, 218, 222, 224, 225, 226, 241
Felsch, Happy, 171, 174, 176
Ferrell, Rick, 39
Ferrell, Wes, 39, 223
Fitzgerald, John F., 162, 163
Flick, Elmer, 142
Forbes Field, 156
Ford, Whitey, 229, 231, 232
Forest Cities Club of Cleveland, 53
Forest Cities Club of Rockford, Ill., 35, 53
Fort Wayne Kekiongas, 41, 53
Fox, Nelson, 233
Foxx, Jimmy, 132, 164, 202, 203, 205, 212, 216, 223
Freedman, Andrew, 151

Frisch, Frank, 209, 210, 219–20
Fullerton, Hugh, 172, 175–76
Furillo, Carl, 234

Gable, Clark, 222
Gaedel, Eddie, 221
Gallico, Paul, 206
Gandil, Chick, 159, 169–70, 171, 173, 174, 176, 178
Garcia, Mike, 233
Garson, Greer, 222
Gas House Gang, 208–14 *passim*, 222
Gehrig, Lou, 194, 195, 196, 197, 202, 203, 205, 207–8, 212, 231
Gehringer, Charlie, 126, 205, 211, 220
Genins, Frank, 68
Gibson, Bob, 219, 239, 240
Gibson, Josh, 216, 217
Gilliam, Jim, 234
Gleason, Kid, 169, 172, 173
Gomez, Lefty, 197, 205, 232
Goodman, Billy, 233
Gordon, Joe, 197, 225, 231, 232
Goslin, Goose, 204, 205, 212
Gotham Club, 230
Gould, Charlie, 40
Gould, Jay, 53
Grant, Ulysses S., 22, 42, 53
Graves, Abner, 25
Graves, Louis, 119, 120, 121
Greenburg, Hank, 157, 212, 213, 214, 221, 223
Griffith, Clark, 166, 204–5
Gromek, Steve, 224
Grove, Robert (Lefty), 132, 162, 164, 202–3, 212, 217, 223

Haas, Mule, 133, 202
Haefner, Mickey, 221
Hampden, Walter, 214
Hanna, W. B., 119
Harper's Weekly, 111–12, 119
Harridge, Will, 224
Harris, Bucky, 190, 223
Harvard University, 33

Hauptmann, Bruno, 209
Hayes, Rutherford B., 56
Heilmann, Harry, 212
Henderson, Robert W., 26
Henrich, Tommy, 197, 213, 224, 231, 232
Henry VIII, 186
Heydler, John, 89
High Noon, 208
Hirohito, Emperor, 50
Hoffman, Malvina, 49, 130
Hofman, Danny, 136
Holloman, Alva (Bobo), 221
Holmes, Oliver Wendell, 32, 33
Holmes, Tommy, 227
Hopp, Johnny, 232
Hornsby, Rogers, 54, 128, 179, 193, 207, 216, 220
Horst, Harry von der, 64, 69
Houk, Ralph, 237, 242
Howard, Elston, 219, 229, 231, 237
Howard, Frank, 80
Hoyt, Waite, 196, 232
Hubell, Carl, 125, 205, 223
Huggins, Miller, 184, 186, 189–90
Hulbert, William A., 56
Hurley, Richard, 40
Husing, Ted, 200

Jackson, Joseph Jefferson (Shoeless Joe), 105, 133–34, 159, 169, 171, 174, 175, 176–77, 178–79
Jackson, Travis, 125
Jennings, Hugh, 57, 75, 89, 123, 137, 146, 242
Johnson, Andrew, 22
Johnson, Byron Bancroft (Ban), 94–95, 114, 176, 190
Johnson, Hugh, 209
Johnson, Judy Sweet Juice, 216
Johnson, Walter, 103, 105, 114, 115, 116, 124, 130, 145–46, 149, 159, 162, 166–67, 169, 190–92, 212, 217, 221, 231, 246
Johnstone, James, 76–77

Kaline, Al, 233
Kansas City Monarchs, 215–16, 218
Katzenjammer Kids, The, 66
Keane, Johnny, 240, 242
Keeler, Wee Willie, 57, 87, 88, 89
Kell, George, 233
Keller, Charlie, 197, 224, 232, 242
Kennedy, John F., 162
Kerr, Dickie, 171, 173
Killebrew, Harmon, 233, 241
Kilroy, Matthew Aloysius (Matches), 69–70, 72
Kiner, Ralph, 234
Kling, Johnny, 140
Knickerbocker Club, 28, 29–30, 35, 230
Koenig, Mark, 231
Koufax, Sandy, 70, 229, 234, 239, 241, 242
Kubek, Tony, 231
Kuenn, Harvey, 233

Lajoie, Napoleon (Nap), 101, 103, 104, 105, 123, 144, 145, 148–49, 167, 220,
Landis, Kenesaw Mountain, 177–78, 186, 193, 213, 220
Lardner, Ring, 191
Larson, Don, 232, 235
Last of the Mohicans, The, 27
Latham, Arlie, 66–67
Lazzeri, Tony, 194–95, 196–97, 231
Leatherstocking Tales, 27
Lemon, Bob, 224
Leonard, Andrew, 40
Leonard, Dutch, 221
Lindbergh, Charles, 184, 185, 187, 209
Lindell, Johnny, 224, 232
Lindstrom, Fred, 125
Literary Digest, 127, 136, 150, 165, 188, 211, 212, 213–14
Little Pretty Pocket-Book, A, 32, 33
Lolich, Mickey, 242

Lopat, Eddie, 232
Los Angeles Dodgers, 79, 235, 236, 239, 242; *see also* Brooklyn Dodgers
Louisville, 63, 106, 134, 155
Lovitt, James, 143
Lowe, Bobby, 57

MacDougald, Gil, 231, 232
Mack, Connie, 105, 123, 125, 131–34, 135, 136–37, 140, 146, 148, 159, 160–61, 163, 164–65, 169, 195, 201, 202–3, 204, 211, 231
Magill (umpire), 76
Maglie, Sal, 299, 234
Mantle, Mickey, 79, 145, 207, 220, 229, 230, 231, 232, 233, 237
Manual of Cricket and Baseball, A, 31–32, 34, 36–37
Manush, Heinie, 204, 205, 223
Maris, Roger, 232, 233, 235, 237
Marquard, Rube, 105, 125, 127, 205
Martin, Billy, 231
Martin, Pepper, 199–200, 203, 209
Marx, Karl, 84
Mathewson, Christy, 49, 92, 103, 105, 107, 114, 115–16, 123, 125, 129–31, 137, 140, 141, 144, 145, 151, 159, 167, 172, 191, 192, 193, 205, 217, 246
Matson, Baseball Joe, 116–17
Mays, Willie, 34, 49, 79, 217, 219, 229, 234, 235
McCarthy, Joe, 196, 220, 223
McGillicuddy, Cornelius, *see* Mack, Connie
McGinnity, Joe (Iron-Man), 125, 137, 145, 205
McGraw, John, 16, 57, 75, 88–89, 92, 105, 116, 123, 125–29, 131, 132, 136–37, 139, 140, 151, 159, 160–61, 162, 188, 190, 192, 193, 204, 205, 242
McLain, Dennis, 80, 202, 242

McMullin, Fred, 171, 174
McVey, Carl, 40
Medwick, Joe (Ducky), 209, 213
Menjou, Adolphe, 210
Merkle, Fred, 151, 154
Merriwell, Frank, 116
Meusel, Bob, 195, 197, 231
Mexico, 222
Millar, Henry, 18
Miller, Bing, 133, 202
Mills, A. G., 25
Milwaukee Braves, 234; *see also* Boston Braves
Minnesota Twins, 241, 242
Mize, John, 232
Moore, Grace, 210
Moore, Marianne, 130
Moore, Wilcy, 196
Morrissey, John, 18, 19
Mullane, T. J., 73
Mungo, Van Lingle, 211
Murphy, Johnny, 232
Musial, Stan, 220, 223, 224, 233–34
Mussolini, Benito, 212
Myer, Buddy, 204

Namath, Joe, 208
National Association of Baseball Players, 35–36, 52–53
National Baseball Library, 27
National Baseball Museum, 27
National League, 25, 56, 57, 59–60, 62, 63–64, 67, 72, 76, 78, 80, 84, 85–86, 87, 89–90, 91–95, 104, 106, 115, 124, 131, 134, 137, 141, 155, 162, 165–67, 183, 192, 193, 202, 205, 210, 219, 227, 232, 233, 234, 239, 243, 244
National Recovery Act, 209
Newcombe, Don, 219, 229, 234
Newhouser, Hal, 225, 226
New Orleans Black Pelicans, 216
Newsom, Louis Norman (Bobo, Buck), 221

New York, baseball in in 1890's, 91–92; in early 1900's, 151–54; in 1920's, 187–88; in 1950's, 230–37 *passim*

New York Giants, 67, 82, 88, 91–92, 94, 106, 110–11, 115–16, 124–31, 136–37, 140–41, 151–52, 153–54, 160–61, 162–63, 166, 167, 168, 188, 190, 192, 204, 205, 209–10, 211, 219, 232, 234, 235, 236, 237, 247; *see also* San Francisco Giants

New York Gothams, 35

New York Herald, 153

New York Highlanders, 91, 105, 106, 124

New York Metropolitans, 54, 72–73, 237

New York Mutuals, 15–19, 35, 41, 45, 53, 63, 248

New York Public Library, 26

New York World, 175

New York Yankees, 44, 79, 81, 91, 105, 124, 141, 157, 161, 168, 183, 186, 187, 188, 189, 190, 194–97, 202, 207, 208, 209, 220, 223, 224, 226, 229–33, 234–35, 237, 239–41, 242–43

Niggeling, Johnny, 221

Nimick, W. A., 93

Northanger Abbey, 33

Obernauer, Marne, 225

O'Farrell, Bob, 195

Old-cat (ball game), 33, 34

100 Years of Baseball, 55

O'Neill, Tip, 66

One-knocker (ball game), 34

O'Rourke, Jim, 46

Ott, Melvin, 125, 205

Outlook, 121, 163, 168

Overall, Orvall, 57, 140–41

Owen, Marvin, 213

Page, Joe, 232

Paige, Leroy Satchel, 216–18, 219, 224, 226–27

Palmer, H. C., 83

Pasquel brothers, 222

Patten, Gilbert, 117

Pearson, Monte, 232

Peckinpaugh, Roger, 192

Pennock, Herb, 196, 232

Pepitone, Joe, 237

Philadelphia Athletics, 53, 63, 104, 106, 124, 132–34, 136–37, 143, 160–61, 164–65, 167, 169, 201, 202–3, 236

Philadelphia Olympics, 35

Philadelphia Phillies, 73, 106, 166, 167, 194, 206–7, 210

Pierce, Billy, 233

Pipgras, George, 196, 232

Pittsburgh Crawfords, 216, 217

Pittsburgh Pirates, 93, 106, 110–11, 124, 131, 140, 145, 154, 155, 156–57, 190–92, 196, 239

Plank, Eddie, 105, 133, 160

Players League, 55–56, 62, 84–85

Podres, Johnny, 234

Polo Grounds, 49, 92, 108, 110, 116, 124, 130, 152, 153, 210, 247

Porterfield, Bob, 226

Powell, Joe, 231

Providence, 63, 72–73

Radbourn, Charles (Old Hoss), 57, 72, 73, 125, 137, 203, 217

Rand, Sally, 209

Raschi, Vic, 231, 232

Reach, Alfred J., 25

Reach Baseball Guide, 24, 25, 77, 84, 90, 91, 93, 141–42, 243

Reese, Peewee, 234

Reulbach, Ed, 140, 141, 145

Reynolds, Allie, 232

Rice, Grantland, 74–75

Rice, Sam, 205

Richardson, Bobby, 231, 237

Rickey, Branch, 218, 219

Risberg, Swede, 171, 174

Rizzuto, Phil, 224, 231

Robinson, Brooks, 69, 242

Robinson, Frank, 69, 80, 219, 234, 242
Robinson, Jackie, 218–20, 229
Robinson, Wilbert, 88
Rockefeller, John D., 177
Roe, Preacher, 234
Rogell, Billy, 213
Rolfe, Red, 197, 231
Roosevelt, Franklin D., 204, 220
Roosevelt, Theodore, 75, 106
Rosar, Buddy, 231
Rosen, Al, 233
Rothstein, Arnold, 172–73, 175, 177–78
Rounders (ball game), 33
Rowe, Lynwood (Schoolboy), 162, 212, 213
Ruffin, Chief, 44
Ruffing, Red, 232
Rugby, 33
Runnels, Pete, 233
Ruppert, Jacob, 186, 190
Russell, Lillian, 152, 192, 199
Ruth, George Herman (Babe), 49, 50, 105, 114, 157, 166, 167, 168, 183–87, 188–90, 194, 195–96, 197, 199, 200, 202, 203, 205, 206, 207, 208, 217, 220, 231, 232, 234, 246

Sain, Johnny, 232
St. Joseph, University of, 120
St. Louis Browns, 63, 65–69 *passim*, 72, 74, 92, 93, 106, 135, 149, 168, 194, 220–21, 236
St. Louis Cardinals, 106, 192–95, 196, 205, 208–9, 210–14, 220, 221, 223, 232, 235, 236, 240, 242
San Francisco Atlantics, 44–45
San Francisco Giants, 79, 236, 239; *see also* New York Giants
Sangree, Allen, 57–60, 62, 78, 121
Sawyer, Rev. Roland D., 120
Schalk, Ray, 169, 171, 172, 173, 175
Schreckengost, Ossie, 135

Score, Herb, 233
Selkirk, George, 197, 232
Seymour, Harold, 66, 93
Shawkey, Bob, 232
Shea, Francis (Spec), 232
Shibe Park, 148
Shocker, Urban, 196, 232
Short, Robert, 20
Sievers, Roy, 233
Simmons, Al, 132, 133, 164, 202–3, 205
Sinclair, Harry, 173
Sisler, George, 221
Skowron, Bill, 231
Snider, Duke, 229, 234
Snodgrass, Fred, 163
Sousa, John Philip, 55
South Atlantic League, 147
Spahn, Warren, 227, 234
Spalding, A. G., 25, 26, 35, 41, 94
Spalding commission, 24–26, 32, 34, 50
Spanish-American War, 86, 92
Speaker, Tris, 101, 104–5, 149, 161–62, 166, 202, 220, 234
Sporting Life, 92
Sporting News, 93
Stallings, George, 159, 164
Standard Oil Company, 177
Standish, Burt L. (Gilbert Patten), 117
Stengel, Casey, 132, 209, 211, 229, 230, 237
Stirnweiss, George, 224, 231
Stories of the Baseball Field, 83
Stottlemyre, Mel, 232, 237
"Subway Series," 211
Sullivan, Sport, 170, 172, 174, 175, 178
Sweasy, Charlie, 40

Taft, William Howard, 50
Tarkington, Booth, 106
Teapot Dome scandal, 173
Temple Cup series, 89–90
Temple, Shirley, 200
Tenney, Fred, 125

Terry, Bill, 125, 204, 205, 209, 210, 211
Thomson, Bobby, 229, 234, 248
Tinker, Joe, 140, 165–66
Top-Notch Magazine, 117
Town ball (ball game), 33
Tracy, Dr. David F., 74
Tresh, Tom, 237
Trosky, Hal, 212
Troy Haymakers, 44, 45, 53
Truman, Harry, 208, 224
Tunney, Gene, 187
Twain, Mark, 27
Two-knocker (ball game), 34

Union Association, 57
Union Grounds, 16, 248
Union League, 78
Unitas, John, 69

Vallee, Rudy, 200
Vandermeer, Johnny, 221
Veeck, Bill, 65, 74, 221, 223–24, 225, 226
Vernon, Mickey, 223, 233
Virginia League, 129

Waddell, George Edward (Rube), 103, 105, 133, 134–36, 137, 139, 144, 222, 241
Wagner, Honus, 103, 104, 105, 111, 123, 144, 145, 154–56, 159, 167, 210, 246
Walberg, Rube, 202, 223
Walker, Charles, 17
Walker, Jimmy, 187
Walker, Moses Fleetwood, 215
Walker, Welday, 215
Walsh, Ed, 105, 141, 142, 144, 217
Waner, Lloyd, 39
Waner, Paul, 39
Washington, George, 208
Washington Senators, 20, 106, 115, 132, 162, 166, 190–92, 203, 204, 212, 221, 223, 236, 241
Waterman, Fred, 40, 43

Weaver, Buck, 171, 174, 178
Western League, 94
West Point, 24
White, Doc, 142
Whitehill, Earl, 204
Whitman, Walt, 101, 119–20
Williams, Claude, 159, 168, 171, 173, 174, 175
Williams, Ken, 188
Williams, Ted, 162, 175, 176, 220, 223, 233, 234
Wills, Maury, 29, 150, 219
Wilson, Hack, 201–2
Wolff, Roger, 221
Wood, Smoky Joe, 105, 159, 162, 212
Woodling, Gene, 232
World Series of 1884, 72–73; of 1885, 67; of 1903, 131; of 1905, 136–37, 142, 191; of 1906, 142; of 1907, 151; of 1909, 156–57; of 1910, 160; of 1911, 143, 160–61; of 1912, 162–63; of 1914, 164, 165; of 1915, 166; of 1916, 166; of 1917, 168; of 1918, 167; of 1919, 167, 168–75 *passim,* 178; of 1923, 188; of 1924, 190; of 1925, 190–92; of 1926, 192–95; of 1928, 196; of 1929, 201; of 1931, 203; of 1932, 196, 200; of 1933, 204; of 1934, 209, 212–14; of 1946, 223; of 1948, 226–27; of 1949, 1950, 1951, 1952, and 1953, 230; of 1955, 235; of 1956, 232, 235; of 1957, 234; of 1959, 235; of 1960, 239; of 1963, 239; of 1964, 239–40; of 1966, 242; of 1967, 235, 242; of 1968, 242
World War I, 164, 165, 167–68
World War II, 50, 220–21
Wright, George, 25, 39, 40, 45, 46
Wright, Harry, 16, 17, 19, 20, 25, 39, 40–41, 43, 44, 45, 50, 52, 87, 132, 186, 248
Wynn, Early, 233

Yankee Stadium, 184, 187, 206, 208, 230

Yastrzemski, Carl, 79, 80, 142

Yawkey, Tom, 188, 223

Young, Nicholas E., 25

Young, Denton True (Cy), 104, 123, 144, 149, 217, 218

Zachary, Tom, 184

Zettlein, George, 46